PROGRAMMER'S GUIDE
TO ONLINE RESOURCES

PROGRAMMER'S GUIDE
TO ONLINE RESOURCES

Bob Kochem

John Wiley & Sons, Inc.

New York • Chichester • Brisbane • Toronto • Singapore

Publisher: Katherine Schowalter
Editor: Tim Ryan
Managing Editor: Bob Aronds
Text Design & Composition: Benchmark Productions, Inc.

Designations used by companies to distinguish their products are often claimed as trademarks. In all instances where John Wiley & Sons, Inc. is aware of a claim, the product names appear in initial capital or all capital letters. Readers, however, should contact the appropriate companies for more complete information regarding trademarks and registration.

This text is printed on acid-free paper.

This publication is designed to provide accurate and authoritative information in regard to the subject matter covered. It is sold with the understanding that the publisher is not engaged in rendering legal, accounting, or other professional service. If legal advice or other expert assistance is required, the services of a competent professional person should be sought.

Library of Congress Cataloging-in-Publication Data:

Kochem, Bob.
  Programmer's guide to online resources / Bob Kochem.
        p.   cm.
     Includes index.
     ISBN 0-471-12852-X (pbk.: alk.paper)
     1. Computer software—Development. 2. Computer network resources.
  I. Title.
  QA76.76.D47K63 1996
  025.06'0051–dc20   95-38014
                                                                          CIP

Printed in the United States of America

10 9 8 7 6 5 4 3 2 1

ACKNOWLEDGMENTS

I would like to acknowledge the support given by some of the maintainers and authors of several popular online lists. Some parts of this book were prepared by extracting and/or modifying material from their publications. I would also like to fulfill here requests made about properly identifying the lists.

List of Active Newsgroups

David C. Lawrence (**tale@uunet.uu.net**) maintains this list. Its author is Gene Spafford (**spaf@cs.purdue.edu**).

You may obtain a current copy of the list by anonymous FTP from **rtfm.mit.edu/pub/usenet-by-group/news.announce.newgroups/ List_of_Active_Newsgroups**. (It is a multi-part file.)

List of Periodic Informational Postings

This list is generated by custom software scripts software and maintained by a team at MIT. The most recent version of the postings making up the List of Periodic Informational Postings can be found in the newsgroups **news.lists** and **news.answers**. You can also obtain them by anonymous FTP from **rtfm.mit.edu/pub/usenet/news.answers/periodic-postings**.

DEDICATION

DEDICATION

This book is dedicated to Liz, my mom, who always told me I could do anything that I set out to do.

CONTENTS

PREFACE

The rapid growth of the Internet and other online communication services has made available a large body of new reference materials and other resources of value to software developers. This book will provide a roadmap for programmers to benefit from those resources.

Growth has been so rapid that it is hard to keep track of what "the net" is and double hard to follow what is on it. Every day we hear more about "The Information Superhighway," "The World Wide Web," and the explosion of services like America Online, CompuServe, Prodigy, and Genie. As these services grow in capability, companies and individuals contribute to the warehouse of software, development tools, and information.

This book will start by describing and showing how to use the many categories of online services available, such as bulletin-board-systems, commercial services (CompuServe, America Online, etc.), and the Internet. Having provided these tools, a comprehensive catalogue of the many services available will then be described. This will contain such things as

- ➤ Sources of code and tools

- ➤ Vendor support sites

- ➤ Fellow-Programmer "support groups"

- ➤ Magazine archives

Besides providing hard information on specific resources, this book will also illustrate the techniques for searching so you'll be able to pursue areas not covered and stay in step with resources as they continue to evolve.

Readership

Material will be presented that is of benefit to programmers in many different situations. Whether you work at a small, medium, or large size company, operate as a consultant, or are just learning the ropes in software development, you will find here access to a wider range of tools, code, and vendor support than any one organization could maintain in-house. Information will be organized by platforms, operating systems, and languages. A major amount of attention will be paid to the PC/compatible, DOS/Windows environment, but there is a lot of information on Apple/Mac systems, different flavors of UNIX, and various other interests. C++ wizards, UNIX hackers, Assembler bit-bangers, and numerous other programming disciplines will all find itemized areas here.

Prerequisites

This book will not be a detailed instruction manual for online services like CompuServe or for the Internet. There are plenty of good books already on those subjects. This book will give some general background in those areas, but the focus will be on locating resources of specific interest to programmers. It is expected that the reader should be somewhat fluent in accessing dial-in services, and doing things like uploading and downloading files.

How the Book is Organized

The overall organization of the book is to first provide information on what the different types of online resources are and how to use them, and then to provide a catalogue of resources that are out there.

Chapter 1 provides some very basic information on what "online resources" means: basically BBSs, Online Data Services (CompuServe, America Online, etc.), and then the Internet. Each of these has some architectural aspects that define the types of resources they can provide, and how you go about accessing them.

Chapter 2 goes into detail on the Online Data Services themselves. Some basic information is provided on each of the major providers—what features are available, how to get an account, some pricing considerations, and so forth. More importantly, there is a discussion for each Service of the features provided specifically of interest to software developers.

Chapter 3 addresses the Internet. Since the Internet is not truly one entity but instead a network of networks, some information will be provided on the Internet's organization, and what functions are available on it that a software developer would need to get around. There will also be some discussion of how to select a means of access to the Internet. There are many options, and some may be more appropriate for you than others depending upon your goals, where and how you work, and your budget.

Many major vendors of software tools, languages, operating systems, and the like are now providing one or more means of electronic access to their customers. This can include libraries of free code, product updates, knowledge bases of programming techniques, or question/answer centers. Chapter 4 will review some of the major players and describes the many services they each provide.

Chapter 5 addresses the User Groups formed by many users of particular computing platforms.

Chapter 6 describes the wide range of magazines and other periodicals which are increasingly offering archives of articles, code examples, and mail contact to the editorial staff.

The remaining chapters of the book provide detailed listings of the many resources available. Much of this is sorted by platform/ operating system/language, but there are numerous generic topics such as "graphics."

Some appendices are provided with a variety of useful tables and lists such as a list of must-have Internet sites and resource lists. If you don't have the patience to read this whole book, you can still maximize your bang-for-the buck by familiarizing yourself with the materials listed in the appendices.

CHAPTER ONE

OVERVIEW OF DIFFERENT TYPES OF RESOURCES

Online resources provide a wide range of services. This book addresses three major types: bulletin board systems (BBSs), online data services (like CompuServe and America Online), and the Internet. Most material in this book focuses on the last two, which look more and more alike as time goes on. However, the unique architectural features of each define the types of services they provide and how you go about getting these services. This chapter provides some background information on each.

Bulletin Board Systems

A bulletin board system typically consists of a single large personal computer or server. This computer has a device that supports multiple dial-in telephone lines, from ten to several hundred. It runs a software package that lets users dial in, establish an account, and accomplish a number of tasks, such as using e-mail and uploading or downloading files from library areas. (See Figure 1.1.)

It's possible to have a BBS with a low-power PC, a small hard-disk drive, and a single telephone line, but it would have limited usefulness. The operators of BBSs generally acquire as much computer hard-disk size and as many telephone lines as they can afford—this means they can offer

Figure 1.1
Typical BBS
configuration.

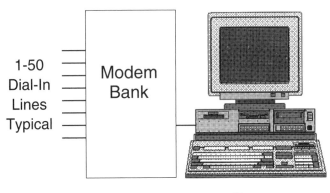

more users more features and more speed. Today BBSs typically have at least hundreds of megabytes and, more likely, gigabytes of storage.

BBS software comes from a handful of suppliers. (TBBS, PC Board, Major BBS, and Wildcat are frequently used BBS software packages.) Each supplier's products have their own unique interface. However, after you learn to operate one or two of them, you can easily handle any of them. The user interfaces are typically "terminal-like." (See Figure 1.2.) Although they don't offer the ease of a graphical interface, their functionality is generally so simple that anyone capable of writing a computer program can easily master them. Also, many BBSs tend to stay up to date, supporting the latest high-speed modems, so screen update isn't a problem.

BBSs usually have these main features:

➤ A library of files that can be uploaded or downloaded. The files may be general in nature or fit a special purpose.

➤ A system for sending mail from one user to another.

➤ An organized way to post notes on one or more discussion topics or to special interest groups (SIGs).

➤ "Real-time" electronic discussions or "chat" between two or more users.

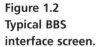

**Figure 1.2
Typical BBS
interface screen.**

> ➤ Increasingly, some form of Internet access. This is typically either an e-mail link or the ability to subscribe to electronic maillists.

Individuals or organizations may set up BBSs. Many suppliers of software tools provide BBSs for dial-in access to product updates, problem reporting, or general product support. Very often, a BBS is one of several forms of support a vendor offers and serves as an alternative for customers who don't have access to other channels such as CompuServe or the Internet.

Actually, individuals and small companies have set up the largest number of BBSs. A large percentage focus on a specific interest group or recreational activity, such as gardening or beer-making. However, significant numbers are general in nature, somewhat like small versions of CompuServe. These BBSs often have large numbers of files archived in libraries, and some have areas for programmers' tools and utilities.

A couple of final comments on BBSs:

> ➤ They may be free or may charge a membership fee.

> ➤ They usually don't have 800-number telephone service, so users tend to be local.

A lot of BBSs are out there—thousands—and the number grows weekly. Magazines are even published just for BBS operators. Appendix 2 includes a list of U.S. BBSs.

Online Data Services

These are large companies like CompuServe, GEnie, America Online, and Prodigy. Structurally they are large-scale BBSs with greatly enhanced telephone access. Their computers tend to be mini-computers or mainframes, often with some sort of built-in redundancy. America Online's computer system (see Figure 1.3) in Vienna, Virginia, consists of nine Stratus Inc. fault-tolerant computers. A fault-tolerant computer keeps running without loss of computation or loss of data even when certain elements fail.

Online services also deal with telephone access on a larger scale. The services contract with a national or worldwide telephone system carrier, rather than having individual users dial directly into their services, which would involve a toll call. America Online uses Sprintnet. When you dial AOL in Pittsburgh, you're really dialing a number AOL has bought from Sprintnet in Pittsburgh. Sprintnet routes the call through its system from Pittsburgh to their Virginia office and then into AOL headquarters.

Online services charge money and in turn provide an enormous range of services and access to a large subscriber base.

Online services increasingly offer some connectivity to the Internet, which will be described in Chapter 3.

Figure 1.3 America Online system.

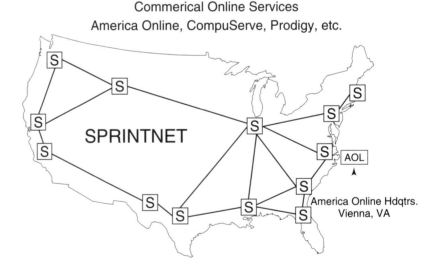

Commerical Online Services
America Online, CompuServe, Prodigy, etc.

SPRINTNET

AOL

America Online Hdqtrs.
Vienna, VA

The Internet

Unlike BBSs and online data services, which are typically isolated computer systems, the Internet is a network of thousands of computers. Before exploring the Internet, it's useful to know some terminology and history.

Computer Networks

The average home or small-business computer user is familiar with a PC operating by itself. Connection to "networks" may often only mean using a communication tool such as PROCOMM to dial into a BBS or commercial online service.

However, many medium- to large-size companies have many computers that are often "networked" together. (See Figure 1.4.) This means that cables run between the computers, and files and electronic mail messages can be moved between different machines or to commonly shared devices such as printers or mass-storage systems.

Typically "local area networks" (LANs) consist of a variety of "Ethernet" or "Token-Ring" hardware and software that perform this networking. To connect between multiple LANs at remote sites (say sales offices for one company, spread around the country or the world), other hardware and software are used with cabling from the telephone carriers (including microwave technology) to form "wide area networks" (WANs).

Figure 1.4 Diagram of a simple network.

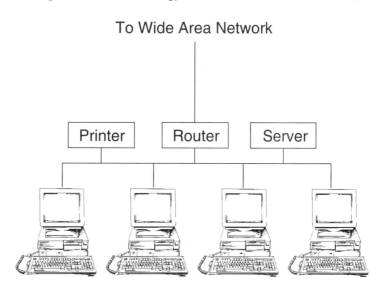

To Wide Area Network

Printer Router Server

The Internet Is a Network of Networks

The Internet grew out of an early attempt to set up a wide area network. Established in the late 1960s to link numerous remote sites involved in government-sponsored research, the ARPANET was very successful and started growing. Its use spread to applications that did not require government security restrictions. (See Figure 1.5.)

A technical strength of the Internet is that it uses one communication protocol, TCP/IP, as a standard for communication between all sites. This means that a wide variety of computer architectures and media can work together, because they all share the same "language."

Numerous networks like the ARPANET were formed and interconnected. (Incidentally, the ARPANET itself was dismantled in the early 1990s.)

Collectively, this "network of networks" is called the Internet. As of fall 1995, the Internet consisted of over 10,000 networks. One network on the Internet could consist of a single computer or thousands of computers on one company's network. (Digital Equipment Corporation has some 40,000 nodes on its one network.) Imagine that many mini-computers or mainframes might have hundreds or even thousands of user accounts; the total number of Internet user accounts can be seen to be in the millions.

Who and What Are on the Internet?

The Internet is often drawn schematically as a cloud with individual networks connecting to the cloud. (See Figure 1.6.) Anyone on a network connected to the cloud can utilize various services to communicate with other networks. It's not important (for this book) what goes on inside

Figure 1.5
The Internet is a network of networks.

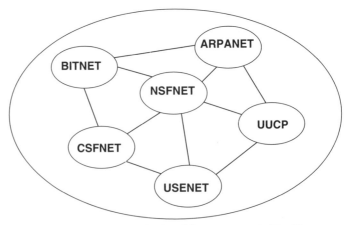

Diverse Network Architectures & Media
One Protocol: TCP/IP

Figure 1.6
Who and what
are on the
Internet.

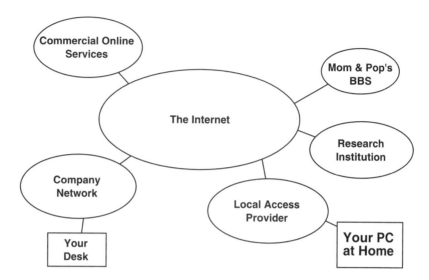

the cloud—it's just important that any points connected to it can communicate.

Here are some comments about specific types of networks connected to the Internet:

➤ Online services—Major services like CompuServe and Prodigy all have an interconnection point to the Internet. Initially these only provided a subset of the wide range of Internet services available, such as e-mail. Online services are racing to provide as many of the available Internet services as possible.

➤ Individual companies—If you work for a company of, say, 500 or more employees, your company's internal network may be connected to the Internet. (It costs from $5000 per year up to perhaps $100,000 per year, depending on the rate of traffic supported and the range of services subscribed to.) This means you may be able to access some Internet services from a PC or Mac on your desk.

➤ Educational or research institutes—A large number of these are on the Internet; in fact, as stated above, they were the "core" of the start of the Internet. Still a large part of the Internet member community, these organizations, in addition to their private materials, have many tools of interest to the networking community. For example, NASA offers a large amount of public information and pictures of space activities. CERN (European Center for Particle Physics) in Switzerland is the founding organization of the World Wide Web—the current standard tool for wide area document searching.

➤ Local access providers—Increasingly, companies are being set up whose main service is to provide individuals inexpensive access to the Internet. These companies have a mini-computer and a number of dial-in lines. Individuals can call and register for relatively low-priced accounts (for example, $5 per month plus $2 per hour of connect time). When you dial in with a PC using a terminal-emulator communication program, such as PRO-COMM, you have access to the full range of Internet services, and you're also allocated a reasonable amount of storage (1 to 2 megabytes) on their system for moving files.

➤ Local BBSs—The small-time BBSs, including vendor support sites, are increasingly buying Internet connections. This means that once you have an Internet account, you can log onto their BBS without dialing over long-distance land-lines. Virtually no telephone charge is involved. (However, some may charge a membership fee.)

Software publishers—You can distribute a lot of software much less expensively this way. A pointer to a list of Internet-accessible BBSs is included at the end of this book.

Everybody's Starting to Look Alike!

Online data services and the Internet are looking more and more alike. Online services quickly realized that ease-of-use was a crucial factor in gaining widespread acceptance (or, more to the point, getting more customers). Consequently all major providers attempted early on to develop graphical interface programs for customers' home platforms (typically PCs or Macs). Online data services have moved every year to include more and more Internet connectivity; initially they offered just e-mail, but now newsgroups and access to the World Wide Web are becoming available. These Internet add-ons have typically tried to keep the look and feel of other features available on the service.

Coming from the other direction, Internet access providers initially provided only a dial-in command-line interface. However, the dynamics of "ease-of-use equals more customers" has driven them to provide graphical interfaces also. In many instances, the complex web of Internet functions is so simplified that customers access remote files, mail, and other services in the same manner that online data service customers access their own functions.

However, we are still a long way from the point where we can't tell by looking at the screen if we are on an Internet access provider or an online data service provider. And we are a long way from the point where we can navigate the Internet with the same ease as we navigate our own systems' directory structure.

CHAPTER TWO

WHAT'S ON ONLINE SERVICES

Overview of Commercial Online Resources

The last decade has seen the development of a number of services geared towards bringing electronic information to the home and business environments. The ongoing boom of purchases of computers for home use has resulted in dynamic growth and competition since 1990 in particular. Despite statistical gamesmanship in calculating subscribers, clearly several major players have users numbering in the millions.

Over the past couple years, a certain sameness has crept into these services. While each service started with a fairly specific customer target, growth and price competition drove them to cover more and more of the same subjects. Efforts to employ user-friendly graphical interfaces also narrowed distinctions between services. (I don't mean to imply that the GUIs themselves are identical.)

Still, each service has certain strengths and weaknesses, and as a result some have much more content of interest to the programming community. This chapter addresses these following major online data services:

- ➤ Existing major providers—CompuServe, America Online

- ➤ New services on the horizon—the Microsoft Network and the Interchange

- ➤ Services originated by magazine publishers—BIX and ZIFFNET.

By the way, you'll frequently see CompuServe referred to as "CIS," an acronym for its formal name, "CompuServe Information Service." I trust that the term "AOL" is clear. Typing these full names gets tedious!

What's Not Here?

➤ DELPHI—More an Internet access provider than a generic online data service, DELPHI will be covered in the next chapter.

➤ Prodigy and GEnie—These fine systems for many customers have not historically been geared towards customers in the programming community. Prodigy, for example, does not accept code uploads from subscribers, thus does not offer the tool-sharing ability of CompuServe and America Online.

This chapter provides some top-level general information about online data services. It's not a detailed how-to manual for any service. Each service already provides plenty of information when you join, as well as online help and an online service staff. Also, a number of good books have been written for each of the major services.

Magazines periodically provide reviews that help the newcomer decide which service to join. This chapter tries to highlight the services on each that could influence your decision on which to join, from a programmer's viewpoint.

Before starting, here are some general considerations;

Access

All major services provide dial-in numbers in hundreds of metropolitan areas. They also provide some kind of free method, such as an 800 number, to help you determine the access numbers in your area. Besides selecting an access number at enrollment time, the 800 number can help if you travel and need to find numbers at your destination. After you enroll, you'll usually find an online list of access numbers. Access is via a standard modem. Most systems support 9600 bit/second (b/s) lines, and some support higher speeds. The speeds offered may vary depending upon your area. This becomes more important as graphical interfaces develop and can also be significant if you upload or download a lot of files.

Charges

Be very careful about charges! Even a casual user can incur a monthly bill of $20 to $40. If you transfer a lot of files or spend a lot of time searching for materials, it's easy to spend $50 to $100 monthly. And people maintaining a small business can easily spend over $100 per month. Price structure can make it difficult to manage your expenses. There can be a flat monthly fee. Per-minute charges can be applied that vary depending upon which features you access, the time of day that you're using the system, and the modem speed you use. You may incur communications surcharges depending upon how you dialed into the system. And apart from the cost of the service, you have to pay your own telephone line/service charges.

Here are a few, perhaps obvious, cost-control tips:

➤ Try to compose messages offline and upload them. If you're reading something, download it and read it offline when practical.

➤ Carefully understand the costs associated with modem speeds. Rates for using 9600 b/s access can be twice that of 2400 b/s. If so, use 2400 b/s for general activities; the gating items are your hunt-'n'-peck typing speed and your reading speed. Use 9600 b/s for downloads—even though it costs twice as much per second, you'll download your file four times as fast and save money!

➤ Watch your downloading, especially when you're new to a service. This can run up a lot of expense.

➤ Above all, learn your service's rate structure, and pay attention when it changes. Also, some services offer different plans depending upon which features you use and how much you use the service per month. Study your usage habits and determine the best rate for you. This is a lot like selecting the most cost-effective telephone carrier and rate plan for your personal use.

Features

Like any user, you should become familiar with functions of primary interest to you:

➤ communications—electronic mail and faxing

➤ help-desk and new-member services

➤ ability to locate other members, especially by interest

To realize the special needs of a programmer, consider this example.

I recently wanted to do something in Visual BASIC and didn't know how to do it. I asked the Microsoft staff if I was overlooking something and they said, "No, you understand VB properly. It just doesn't easily do what you want." I discussed the matter with several other programmers and found that a number of them wanted to do the same thing. No one knew of an existing third-party tool that would do it. We also determined that it wouldn't be too hard to develop a utility that would do 90 percent of what we wanted to. I ended up writing such a utility in two evenings. I submitted it to a few people who made slight improvements. I posted the program and several hundred programmers used it. (While useful, this utility was not sophisticated enough to charge money for. This was strictly a good citizenship exercise.)

This anecdote represents the type of programmer support network you can develop online. What are the means for doing this?

Information is usually organized in "forums." These consist of two primary resources: file libraries and bulletin boards. Libraries can contain software or informational files. The variety here, and benefit, is limitless. Useful tools, complete applications, and source code abound. On the bulletin boards you exchange messages with other members. You might ask for a solution to a problem (to avoid reinventing a wheel), obtain advice or direction in looking for a product, or even run a trial balloon for a new product idea past target customers or fellow developers. (Obviously you need to use some discretion here to avoid "giving away the farm.")

The forums on any one service may number in the thousands. The service itself might establish some, in response to member requests. Vendors establish a large number of forums to provide service and promote their product. (Sometimes the forum is actually a link to the vendors on-site support system.) Questions posed in the bulletin boards here may be answered by both fellow members and the company's service staff (or just company members who also happen to be subscribers). This can be an amazing source of information, like walking around the halls of the vendor's building and directly asking the staff questions. Extending this analogy further, it's like having access to a "virtual company" of fellow product users in the same building and being able to ask about their experiences.

It's probably useful to take off the rose-colored glasses and admit that here, as elsewhere, shortcomings exist. You're still dealing with people, and we all make mistakes. I've seen service representatives of vendors, as well as other members, give multiple, conflicting, answers to questions.

You ultimately depend on your own good judgment, just as you do in any other situation.

Software quality is also a consideration. Material a vendor posts in its forum is likely to be reliable. At the other extreme, the quality of a lot of freeware and shareware is quite variable. It can hit the highs of usefulness and quality, even exceeding mainstream commercial products, but it can also be buggy and without service backup. One very comforting fact is that online services are nearly fanatical about checking files for viruses before posting them. Also, it is not unheard of for services to do some initial testing on a program or utility to make sure it has no blatant errors.

Last comment: The phrase "computing" is used a lot on online data services. When looking for material, it's important to distinguish between "applications" and "development." Because services try to attract a broad range of customers, they pay significant attention to how average users can employ commercial applications such as word processing, databases, spreadsheets, and so on. These terms can also mean "how to buy or maintain computer hardware." In general "applications" may be of less interest to programmers, except of course those applications specifically intended for software development. The real "meat" for programmers is in the areas specifically about how to develop software—and there are a lot of them. Keep this point in mind when you scan titles on the services.

CompuServe

CompuServe is one of the oldest and largest online data services. More importantly, programmers have always made up a significant part of the target membership. CompuServe offers a large number of subject areas related to programming, and vendors are strongly present.

Access

Basic access is via telephone dial-in to numbers in all major cities. Graphical interface front-end software packages are available to install on your system for PCs under DOS or Windows and also for Macs. (When I bought a PC from Gateway, it came with Windows installed and with the Windows version of CIS GUI. See Figure 2.1.)

A few products are actually competing for the DOS and Windows markets. CIS also supports having just a plain terminal-emulator dial-in interface. In some instances this is actually easier to use than the graphical interface. Downloading information for offline reading can often be easier using the log file or capture mechanism on a terminal emulator.

Figure 2.1 CompuServe main screen.

A unique feature of the CompuServe system is that, in addition to telephone lines, it accepts remote login via a function called "TELNET" over the Internet. In some cases this results in a much higher apparent bit rate of access than can be obtained over a telephone line. However, a large surcharge is applied to TELNET access during peak usage times, so use it judiciously.

How to Join

Make a voice call to the company's support line at 1-800-848-8199 in Columbus, Ohio.

Structure

Other than general functions like e-mail and help, you access most functions as forums, which consist of a library area and a messaging area. Libraries are each subdivided into five to 20 interest areas, usually including a general or catch-all area.

Finding Files or Subjects

From the basic members service area you can search all forums on the system, or search all downloadable files on the system. Additionally, file finder sections specifically for PCs (use the command GO IBMFF) and Macs (GO MACFF) let you search by keyword, author, filename, and a few other options. Often finding a file that matches a keyword, and learning what forum it is stored in, is a good way to locate forums that cover related areas of interest.

Features

Following are some relevant features.

Links to Other Networks

ZIFFNET is discussed later in this chapter.

ASPFORUM

The Association of Shareware Professionals maintains this forum. Even non-shareware, commercial programmers can find many useful contacts here. Small companies find it useful to participate in relevant business discussions.

Highlights

CompuServe has over 1000 forums and several hundred are relevant to programmers in some way. (See Figure 2.2. This screen was obtained using a terminal-emulator connection to CIS.)

Rather than review every one, we'll highlight here some of the "big-ticket" items.

PC Software Forums

It's hard to cover this topic without sounding like an advertisement for IBM, Intel, and Microsoft. This isn't too surprising, since from day one the "center of gravity" of CompuServe's programming-related materials has been IBM/Intel-architecture machines and the Microsoft operating systems, applications, and development tools that run on them.

**Figure 2.2
A forum on
CompuServe.**

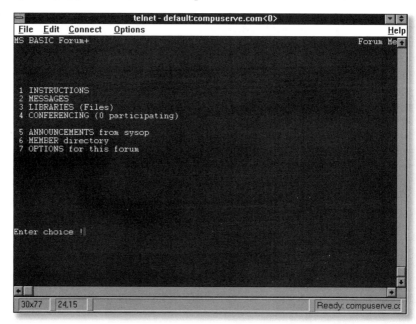

It's perhaps best to give details for one forum and then simply refer to many related forums that operate much the same way.

Over 50 forums on CompuServe are specifically related to Microsoft. One that I have used extensively is the Microsoft BASIC Programming Forum (GO MSBASIC).

Here's a list of its libraries:

MS BASIC Forum+Libraries Menu

MS Info and Index

Setup Wizard/Kit

Data Access Objects

The Data Control

Programming Issues

ODBC Connectivity

SQL Queries

ProEdition Controls

Calling APIs/DLLs

VBWIN-ODBC/Database

MSCOMM control

MCI/MAPI controls

DOS Visual BASIC

DOS and Mac BASIC

Non-Tech Info

CDK

Third-Party Products

Crystal (Peer Help)

As you can see, this forum covers a wide variety of topics on the BASIC programming language, including DOS BASIC and GW-BASIC, Visual BASIC for DOS, and Visual BASIC for Windows. Postings here consist of informational files, source code, patches, application-level code for general utilities, and trial versions of third-party products.

My earlier example of developing a utility was conducted in this forum, using both the accompanying message board area and the libraries listed. (The utility was posted in the Programming Issues library.)

MSBASIC is just one forum covering development under one family of languages.

The remaining 50+ Microsoft forums cover just about any aspect of any language or operating system you could want to know about. Some of the key ones are :

MS 32bit Languages Forum	MSLNG32
MS CE Systems Forum	MSCESYSTEM
MS Central Europe Services	MSEURO
MS DEV Network Forum	MSDNLIB
MS DOS 6.2 DLOAD (Microsoft)	MSDOS62
MS DOS 6.2 DOWNLOAD (PCWORLD)	PCWDOS62
MS DOS 6.2 STEPUP (GERMAN)	DMSDOS
MS DOS Forum	MSDOS
MS Foundation Classes Forum	MSMFC
MS Fox Users Forum	FOXUSER
MS Knowledge Base	MSKB
MS Language Forum	MSLANG
MS Networks Forum	MSNETWORKS
MS SQL Server Forum	MSSQL
MS Software Library	MSL
MS TechNet Forum	TNFORUM
MS TechNet Services	TECHNET
MS WIN32 Forum	MSWIN32
MS WINFUN Forum	WINFUN
MS Win Multimedia Forum	WINMM
MS WinNT SNA Forum	MSSNA
MS Windows Extensions Forum	WINEXT

MS Windows Forum	MSWIN
MS Windows News Forum	WINNEWS
MS Windows Objects Forum	WINOBJECTS
MS Windows SDK Forum	WINSDK
MS Windows Shareware Forum	WINSHARE
WinNT Forum	WINNT
WindowShare France Forum	WSHARE
Windows 3rd Party A Forum	WINAPA
Windows 3rd Party App. D Forum	WINAPD
Windows 3rd Party App. F Forum	WINAPF
Windows 3rd Party App. G Forum	WINAPG
Windows 3rd Party B Forum	WINAPB
Windows 3rd Party C Forum	WINAPC
Windows 3rd Party E Forum	WINAPE
Windows Components A Forum	COMPA
Windows Components B Forum	COMPB
Windows Connectivity Forum	WINCON
Windows Networking A Forum	WINETA
Windows Sources Forum	WINSOURCES
Windows Utility Forum	WINUTIL

I want to particularly highlight the MS Knowledge Base Forum, an incredibly large library of code examples, answers to "frequently asked questions," tips, and otherwise undocumented features. It goes way beyond the documentation supplied by most Microsoft program development documentation. The Knowledge Base is made available as a Windows Help file as part of some development packages, such as the Professional Edition of Visual BASIC, but many development tool packages do not include it. This is definitely worth accessing. (The section in Chapter 4 on Microsoft's overall online presence provides more information about the Knowledge Base.)

While Microsoft offers the largest number of forums here, many other vendors are also represented. IBM maintains a big presence with a large number of forums on a variety of software products for both their PC platform and other platforms. Borland and Computer Associates also each provide forums for development using their products.

Apple Software Forums

While CIS is somewhat PC-centric, it also has always strongly and actively supported the Apple product line. Several forums are of interest to programmers:

Apple Feedback(FREE)	APLFBK
Apple II Prog. Forum	APPROG
Apple II Users Forum	APPUSER
Apple II Vendor Forum	APIIVEN
Apple News Clips($)	APPLENEWS
Apple Support Forum	APLSUP
Apple Tech Info Library	APLTIL
Apple What's New Library	APLNEW
Mac A Vendor Forum	MACAVEN
Mac Applications Forum	MACAP
Mac B Vendor Forum	MACBVEN
Mac C Vendor Forum	MACCVEN
Mac D Vendor Forum	MACDVEN
Mac Developers Forum	MACDEV
Mac Hypertext Forum	MACHYPER
Macintosh File Finder	MACFF
Macintosh Forums	MACINTOSH
Macintosh Hardware Forum	MACHW
Macintosh Multimedia Forum	MACMULTI
Macintosh O/S Forum	MACSYS
IBM PowerPC Forum	POWERPC

Related Forums

Besides direct software development, CIS offers a lot of information on related topics:

➤ PC vendors—Gateway, Dell, Compaq, IBM, and many others

➤ Other systems—Amiga, Apple, Commodore, Digital Equipment Corp., HP, IBM, NeXT

➤ Components—Intel, Standard Microsystems Inc.

➤ Networking—Novell, Banyan

➤ Magazines—*PC Magazine*, *PC World*, Ziff-Davis magazines, *Dr. Dobb's Journal, Computer Life*

Forums also exist on programming topics that are not vendor- or platform-specific, for example:

```
AI EXPERT Forum               AIEXPERT

Animation Vendor A Forum      ANVENA

Client/Server Computing Forum MSNETWORKS

Comics/Animation Forum        COMIC

Computer Animation Forum      COMANIM

Desktop Publishing Forum      DTPFORUM

Game Developers Forum         GAMDEV

Graphics Developers Forum     GRAPHDEV

Imaging Vendor A Forum        IMAGAVEN

Multimedia Forum              MULTIMEDIA

Pen Technology Forum          PENFORUM

Software Development Forum     SDFORUM
```

ASPFORUM

This forum is related to shareware development but has much of interest to individuals doing software development in small businesses.

The Association of Shareware Professionals (ASP) promotes shareware as an industry. To this end, it establishes standards for shareware's format, quality, distribution practices, and so on, and provides general support for shareware authors. "General support" includes such things as identifying resources and publishing lists of favorable distribution channels.

ASP maintains the ASPFORUM on CompuServe to serve its goals. In a very active message area, authors can solve problems and share experiences. ASPFORUM also has a number of library areas:

ASP/Shareware Forum+Libraries Menu

General Info [ASP]

Product Supp [ASP]

ASP Official Files

Shareware! [ASP]

Author/Vendor [ASP]

PC Authors [ASP]

Mac Authors [A]

Finding Shareware

ASP maintains a catalog of its member authors' software that meets its standards. The entire catalog is available in Shareware! [ASP] (listed above). There are also short- and long-version index files of the software. The ASP catalog is also available on CD-ROM.

Business Forums

If you're in a small to mid-size company, you're probably at least partially interested in your company's business side in addition to its software development side.

Besides Fortune 500–style business resources, like the Dow-Jones News Service, CompuServe has many resources of interest to smaller businesses, such as:

```
Entrep. Small Business Square      ENTMAGAZINE

Entrepreneur Magazine (FREE)       ENT

The Entrepreneur's Forum           SMALLBIZ
```

CompuServe Wrap-up

This section presents only some aspects of CompuServe that can assist software developers. It really only scratches the surface. Later chapters of this book provide information organized by areas of programming interest.

America Online

America Online has been one of the primary contenders for the "largest service" designation. While its original target audience was a bit more diverse than CIS's business/professional target, it still has a major amount of material of interest to software developers.

Access

Access is by direct telephone line with entry points in all major metropolitan areas. There are wide selections of both 2400, 9600, and 14,400 b/s lines. AOL is noted for providing good graphical interface for many platforms. The process of joining, in fact, requires that you first obtain and install the graphical interface front end on your system, and then it leads you through the process of identifying a local dial-in number and registering. The graphical interface is a real plus for both new and seasoned computer users. In my case, which may apply to some programmers, I would prefer at times that AOL also support a terminal interface (or TELNET) to let me capture material.

How to Join

First you must obtain a diskette with the graphical interface program for your system. This is pretty easy—besides having a toll-free number to order the free diskette, the Windows version of the program is widely distributed in magazines. You may also receive it in a mail advertisement. The toll-free number is 1-800-827-3338.

Structure

Most online material is organized using forums. Forums consist of a message area, multiple library areas, and conference areas that simulate group discussions. Occasionally, industry leaders or celebrities are featured in selected conference areas. Besides the forum areas, there are auxiliary functions such as mail, member support, and an Internet connection (more about that later).

Finding Files or Subjects

In addition to the easy-to-use graphical interface, a few other features help you locate topics or files. You can locate topics using predefined keywords, as well as a simple mechanism to search the keywords lists. There are several levels of "file finders," including a top-level file finder, a file finder for each major forum, and, somewhat redundantly, a focused file finder for each subarea within the forums.

Features

AOL has (at least) a few unique features of interest to programmers:

Programmer's University

You can take a series of online courses at Programmer's University. Courses are offered in several areas related to Assembler, BASIC, Visual BASIC, C/C++, OOP, and Pascal for PC and Mac platforms. Course work combines offline reading and exercises with online instruction, and includes an opportunity to communicate real-time with your instructor. No tuition is charged although you pay for connect time.

Vendor Support Catalog

This amounts to an online directory of several hundred major hardware- and software-related vendors. Each entry lists a number of means to contact the vendor, including land-mail, telephone, and Internet address.

Industry Connection

Numerous vendors maintain online support areas.

User Groups

You can link to several computer user groups directly over the system. Groups include Apple Users Group, Berkeley Mac Users Group, Boston Computer Society, ClarisWorks Users Group, and the National Home and School Users Group.

Highlights

The computing area and its numerous forums and features are where the real "meat" is on AOL for programmers. Computing is accessed via an icon at the Welcome screen. (See Figure 2.3.)

Figure 2.4 shows that the Industry Connection is essentially a series of support forums for several hundred vendors of PC and Mac hardware and software products.

Each entry typically includes

➤ Contact information

➤ Descriptions of products and some form of online catalog, with pricing and ordering information

**Figure 2.3
America Online
Welcome screen.**

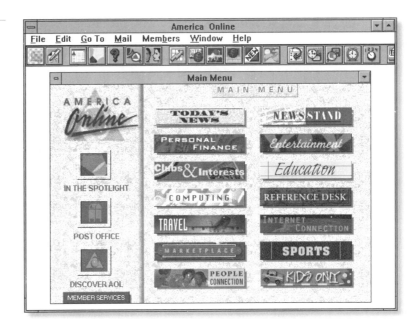

> ➤ A software library, which may include related utilities, code
> updates, and so on

> ➤ A message board for support questions

**Figure 2.4
America Online's
computing
forums.**

The Software Library icon represents a mechanism for searching all files in the computing area. This represents the merged database of individual libraries in all forums.

There are so many forums that it is impractical to list and describe them all. I list here just some sample highlights of the computing area:

Development

DOS

Games

Graphics and Animation (and Virtual Reality)

Hardware

Multimedia

Music/Sound

OS/2

Personal Digital Assistants

User Groups

Windows

Apple Computing Forums

Note that each forum includes a very active messaging area, its own libraries, and a shortcut link to specific vendors. Typically there is also an upload area for members to offer useful information, utilities, code, or applications. The next sections highlight some specific forums.

Development Forum

This area is specifically for software developers. Programmer's University is located here. The Development Forum also includes a reference guide with brief introductory technical articles on selected subjects, a game designers area, the Microsoft Knowledge Base, and a section on development of software for personal digital assistants (PDAs).

Games Forum

This also includes a game designer's section with a message area and an upload area.

Hardware Forum

The major feature here, the PC Vendors Database, provides information from several thousand hardware and software vendors. There is some overlap between the "vendor databases" and "industry contacts" across the entire computing area. A number of computing newsletters are located here (see Chapter 6, "Publications"), as well as a hardware-specific technical reference guide.

Multimedia Forum

Libraries located here include CD-ROM Utilities, Image Converters, Multimedia Text & Utilities, Sound Utilities, and Windows Drivers.

OS/2 Forum

This area includes over 20 libraries on a wide range of topics: Systems Tools, Text/Information, Development, Drivers, File/Disk Utilities, and Graphics/Images to name a few.

Windows and DOS Forums

Mostly application oriented, these forums do contain many useful utilities.

User Groups

This gives direct access to a number of national computer users groups, including those groups mentioned previously.

The Apple Computing Forum

This area contains a number of subareas for all aspects of Apple-related development and products. Subareas include Mac Computing, Mac Software, Mac System 7, Apple II, and PowerMac. (Note: At the time I wrote this, the PowerMac area didn't show up in the Apple Forum for some reason. It exists and is accessible via the keywords POWERPC or POWERMAC.) Within each of these subareas are a number of special-interest groups with diverse programming topics such as game development and PDA programming.

Services Originated by Magazine Publishers

Several services perform a subset of the functions of major online services and serve a more focused customer base. The contents of two of these in particular, BIX and ZIFFNET, are highly interesting to programmers. BIX, established by *BYTE* magazine, caters almost exclusively to programmers. ZIFFNET, run by Ziff-Davis Publications, is more diversified across the general computing industry but still has a very high content of interesting material.

BIX

BYTE was one of the first magazines to address personal computer hardware and software, in those days before "PC" started meaning "IBM/Intel architecture." The magazine's content has always been highly technical, and programmers make up a significant part of its readership. The Byte Information Exchange (BIX), that BBS *BYTE* started (they've since sold it) reflects this strong focus on computer programming.

At a top level, BIX offers many of the same types of services as the "big guys"—electronic mail, libraries, message boards, Internet connection, and so on. While its more focused clientele means less depth in non-programming areas, it offers far more depth on programming topics. There's no effort to provide a user interface that's simple enough to attract general customers who aren't computer knowledgeable. BIX's primary interface is a terminal-emulation line, with a series of nested menus. An option to drop the menus lets power-users familiar with the system use a command-line interface. A Windows-based interface is available, but it's not the primary method customers use to access the system. This system is oriented towards people already familiar with computing and programming—and that's fine with me!

Besides electronic mail and Internet connectivity, the primary features on BIX are its messaging boards (conferencing) and libraries. Both cover such wide areas that it would be impractical to describe every one. So, again, I'll give some samples —hop on the service and scan for more details!.

There are (at present) 13 primary conference areas (called "exchanges"):

1	amiga.exchange	Amiga Exchange: Everything for Amiga users
2	bix	BIX conferences and special subsystems
3	byte	On line with *BYTE* magazine, your authority
4	e.and.l	Entertainment and Leisure Exchange

5	ibm.exchange	Complete information about IBM computers and workalikes
6	mac.exchange	Everything you want to know about the Macintosh
7	other	Computers, news, technology, society, and anything else
8	professionals	Professional and User Groups Exchange
9	programmers	Programmers Exchange
10	tojerry.ex	Chaos Manor, mathematics, space, technology, and more
11	wix	The Information Exchange for Windows
12	writers.ex	Writers Exchange
13	vendor.support	Conferences run entirely by vendors, not BIX

Each conference area consists of about one to three dozen focus areas. A good example is the 36-area professionals conference:

1	professionals	Professional and User Groups Exchange
2	animation	Animation techniques and forms
3	apple	Apple II family conference
5	atari.st	Atari ST machines
6	cd.rom	Optical storage for micros
7	commodore	Commodore computers other than the Amiga
10	cpus	Microprocessor chips
12	digital	DEC computers conference
14	graphic.disp	Graphic displays
20	lans	The conference on local area networks (LANs)
21	listings	Listings from *BYTE* and the public domain
23	multimedia	Computer-generated sights and sounds
24	networks	Information networks

25	next	The NeXT computer conference
26	other.brands	The conference on brands of computers not covered elsewhere
29	pen.computing	Pen-based computing
31	protocols	Computer communications protocols
32	sun	Sun workstations; SPARC
36	zenith	Heath/Zenith computers

Again, each of these are message boards, mechanisms to post statements and queries, and receive replies. In the library areas a large amount of files and code are uploaded.

There are over 150 library areas on BIX. For this section, suffice it to say that (at least) the following are covered:

➤ Languages—C++, Pascal, FORTRAN, Assembler, BASIC, Ada, LISP

➤ Machines—Amiga, Atari, IBM PC-Compatibles, HP, SPARC Workstations

➤ Operating systems/environments—DOS, OS/2, System 7, Windows, UNIX

Two more items to note about the BIX conferences and libraries:

➤ A large number of vendors provide support areas in the Vendors Conference.

➤ Back issues of *BYTE* magazine articles and code are available in several conference and library areas.

BIX Wrap-up

Before leaving BIX I do want to note one thing: While the variety of conferences and libraries is wide, not all areas exhibit the same high traffic. I noted a few Commodore conferences still on the system that didn't appear to have had any postings in over a year. Still, overall this valuable BBS is definitely focused on programming.

ZIFFNET   Established by Ziff-Davis Magazines, ZIFFNET is run by their Ziff-Davis Interactive Subsidiary. Ziff-Davis publications include *PC Magazine*,

PC/Computing, PC Week OnLine, Computer Shopper, Windows Sources, Computer Gaming World, MacUser, MacWEEK, and many other publications.

Access

Although it is possible to access ZIFFNET directly via dial-in, it is usually accessed from the CompuServe Network (GO ZIFFNET). There is a flat monthly surcharge above the CompuServe membership fees for joining ZIFFNET. A particularly interesting ZIFFNET feature is that it's one of the few organizations to specifically offer a toll-free number (1-800-426-3425) for shareware authors to upload submissions.

Features

ZIFFNET features include

➤ Magazine forums—ZIFFNET provides individual forums for a large number of their many magazines. Each forum contains a messaging center and libraries. You can use the messaging centers to communicate with the editorial staff. The libraries include software published in articles. *PC Magazine* Programming Forum is particularly notable for focusing specifically on programming issues. The libraries cover such areas as Utilities Code, Power Programming, Languages, Environments, Toolkits, Corporate Development, and a C++ Study Group.

➤ Databases—ZIFFNET offers several major searchable databases (at an extra charge for each):

Computer Database Plus catalogs information from over 200 publications. It covers news, product descriptions, and reviews.

Magazine Database Plus lets you search for and retrieve full-text articles from Ziff-Davis publications, going back in many cases as far as 1986. Graphics are generally not supported.

Business Database Plus is a focused, searchable database on topics in Ziff-Davis's business-oriented magazines.

➤ Online News—Online retrieval of current news from such publications as *PC Week News, MacWeek News,* and *NewsBytes.*

➤ Software libraries—Ziff-Davis provides an extensive series of software libraries from two areas:

➤ Shareware—Ziff-Davis distributes online the *Public Brand Software* catalog of shareware.

➤ Magazine software—A central point of access is provided to utilities, patches, and other tools posted in Ziff-Davis magazines.

➤ Books—Not surprisingly, ZIFFNET provides a means to order from the catalog of Ziff-Davis hard copy publications. Beyond that, many books are also available in purely electronic format for downloading. You can also access a subset of books from Project Gutenberg, an effort to electronically encode classic and contemporary books.

Coming Soon—Microsoft Network, AT&T Interchange

Expect two other providers to become big players in the field of commercial online data services soon. (They may have been launched as this book goes to publication.)

Microsoft has introduced its Microsoft Network as an integral part of Windows 95. While many of its components are still developing, preliminary information indicates it will cover many of the same services as CompuServe and America Online, with a target of doing more of it and doing it better. Given Microsoft's widespread online product support, programmers can expect to find some combination of all capabilities found on CompuServe, America Online, and Microsoft's existing Internet FTP and WWW sites.

Programmers' support on Microsoft Network (I'll call it "MSN") is not guaranteed to become the one-stop shopping area, replacing all other services. Although it might be possible for Microsoft to make available on MSN all files currently available elsewhere, a host of user groups and bulletin boards are already in place and not likely to relocate to the MSN. For example, even if (hypothetically) Microsoft staffers no longer participated in CompuServe's MSBASIC forum, will all the regular participants there switch to MSN? A smaller-scale precedent may be seen in the case where Apple maintains its own Eworld network, but the independent MAUG (Micronetworked Apple Users Network) is still going strong on CompuServe.

The other big player coming on board is AT&T, which is hanging out the shingle for its Interchange Online Network. Again, information is limited at this time, but it is reasonable to expect significant areas of interest to programmers. It has been stated that Ziff-Davis is creating an area called Interchange Computing, so we can expect some of the software libraries and online databases presently available through CompuServe.

CHAPTER THREE

THE INTERNET

Overview

Thrills! Excitement! Snappy Dialogue and Easy Money!

On the Internet?—I don't think so.

There has been a lot of hype about the Internet. Ever since a certain administration got its hands on the nation's steering wheel, "The Net," under a host of fanciful descriptive names, has been promoted as the next great exciting cultural revolution. It is indeed true that a lot more people are obtaining access to the Internet. It is equally true that the amount of junk and wasted bandwidth has increased. And a lot of newcomers find themselves blinded by the light—the Internet can be one darn confusing place to find your way around.

But at its heart it remains a basic, perhaps not glamorous, tool for distributing information.

Fortunately, at least for the purposes of this book, that's just what we want.

This chapter first identifies some basics: what the Internet is and how to use it. Then it discusses some specific areas on the Internet that you, as a programmer, may wish to use.

Types of Services—How Do I Get Connected?

The first step is obviously to get access to the Internet if you don't already have it.

There are three main ways to get connected. Each is different in terms of ease-of-use, cost, and initial setup. It is very important that the different connection methods end up performing the basic Internet functions in different ways.

➤ Using a direct gateway—This method ranges from being incredibly simple to extremely difficult. If you work for a large enough company you may already have access to the Internet through the company's own Internet gateway. However, if you're an individual or work for a small company, setting up your own gateway can be an expensive and complicated proposition.

➤ Subscribing to a service provider—Many individuals and smaller companies use this "John Q. Public" approach. Service providers set up an Internet gateway. Then they open accounts for anybody to use on a dial-in basis. You dial into the service just like you dial into CompuServe. The interface may range from UNIX command lines to graphical interfaces rivaling those of CompuServe and America Online.

➤ Using an online data service—The major online data services such as CIS, AOL, and Prodigy all provide some degree of Internet connectivity. Initially this was just e-mail, but every year they all come closer to providing full Internet functionality. Still, depending upon the specific service, there may be limitations, and the cost may exceed that of other approaches depending upon your situation.

These Internet functions are described in more detail in the next section (yes, older programmers, this is an illegal forward reference), but for now they'll be identified as

e-mail—sending messages to people

newsgroups—group mailings, sort of like BBS posting areas

TELNET—ability to log onto someone else's host

FTP—ability to transfer files between different systems

GOPHER, WAIS, World Wide Web—tools for locating information

Using a Direct Gateway

The most comprehensive method of accessing the Internet is to obtain a direct connection to it. This is done by obtaining a gateway (actually an IP router) and a high-speed connection to the Internet wiring itself. You won't find an orange cable running down your street labeled "Internet" that you can splice into. You work with the Internet Network Information Center (NIC) to set up a connection. The actual connecting wires (or fiber or microwave link) may be run to your company's site through a communications provider such as the telephone company.

This can be an expensive proposition. The equipment required is both expensive and complicated to set up. You pay ongoing monthly connection costs and need to maintain the system.

While possible, it's unlikely that an individual or small company would actually want to do this.

Fortunately though, if you work for a large enough company or are associated with a university or research institution, you may find this already in place.

Many high-tech companies (of, say, 500 or more technical employees) maintain one or more connections to the Internet. Very often anyone in the company who has access to the company's internal LAN or WAN has access to at least some Internet functionality. Typically you at least have access to e-mail. Very often newsgroups, TELNET, and FTP are also available.

The exact mechanism for you to interface with the Internet depends on how your company operates its internal network. For example, for a long time it was common to find only a terminal-line interface provided for each desk. This meant that you accessed Internet functionality using a command-line interface, which may be unique to your company's LAN implementation.

It is becoming very common to have a PC (or Mac or some form of workstation) on each employee's desk, with a direct LAN connection (i.e., Ethernet or Token-Ring).

It's also common for all endstations to at least be able to send mail off site through the company's e-mail system. Typically this is done by modifying the address. (I'm used to using Lotus Notes for internal mail; mail sent to the Internet is identified by adding the suffix @SMTP.)

You can have additional software installed on your machine that lets you communicate through your company's gateway with the Internet and access a wide range of functions. Two systems I've used are NetManage's Chameleon (see Figure 3.1) and Network Telesystems' TCP-PRO (see Figure 3.2). Products available for a number of operating systems provide an easy interface to these Internet functions. These packages are described in a bit more detail later.

One more thing—even if you only have e-mail access to the Internet, you can use numerous clever mechanisms to activate other functions, such as FTP, just by sending mail. A later section covers these.

Subscribing to a Service Provider

There has been a mini-boom in the last several years of Internet access providers. These are companies that do all the work described in the preceding section to set up an Internet gateway. Then, they rent monthly accounts to anyone. Accounts are accessed via dial-in lines. The sophistication of these systems runs from providing local telephone access of a command-line interface on a terminal-emulation session, to a nation-wide-access dial-in system with a graphical interface.

There are many ways to find these providers. They advertise, both locally in newspapers and nationally in relevant magazines such as *Internet World*. Also, lists of dial-in access providers are maintained on the Internet. (We'll skip over the chicken-and-egg situation of needing to get

Figure 3.1 Chameleon FTP screen.

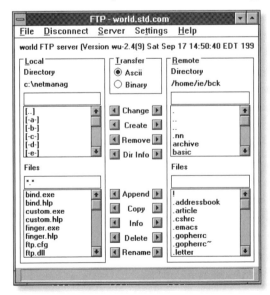

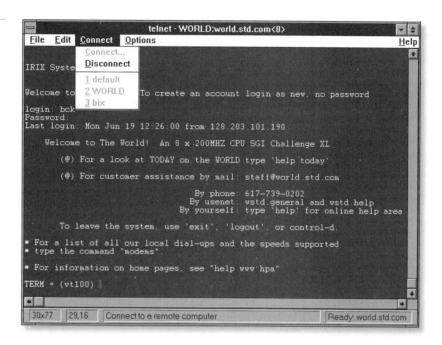

Figure 3.2
TCP-PRO TELNET
screen.

on the Internet first to find the list.) One list, PDIAL, is described in the appendices.

A few have achieved some national fame for the depth of their services, or the depth of their membership. Two are The WELL in the San Francisco area and PANIX in New York City.

Two new features have appeared on many of these providers:

➤ You can create your own World Wide Web home page.

➤ They can create a network address for you that looks like your own commercial business address. Instead of being **username@provider_name.com** you can now be **username@your_businessname.com**. For example, I can change my name from bck@world.std.com to bobk@minuteman.com. This is a real plus for establishing a company presence.

Basic-service Providers

In this no-frills system you get an account on the provider's system. When you use a terminal emulator to dial in, you are presented with a command-line interface. You are allocated a certain amount of storage space on the system for composing and/or moving files.

Fees are rather reasonable—there may be no sign-up fee, and monthly costs may be as low as $5 basic fee plus $2 per hour. I've heard some systems are as inexpensive as $20 per year.

Very often these systems are UNIX systems. A UNIX command line may appear a bit cryptic to someone familiar with DOS, and downright puzzling to business persons trying to get their first exposure to the Internet. However, if you have the skills to do any level of programming you will have no difficulty learning to use at least the basics of a UNIX command-line system. Most systems have a HELP command and a UNIX command summary. There are also many good books around on UNIX. A very rudimentary UNIX command summary is provided in Table 3.1, UNIX Command Summary.

If I had to give one piece of advice to UNIX neophytes, it is: Watch out for case sensitivity! UNIX paths and filenames are case sensitive—this can cause a lot of grief until you get used to it.

Advanced-service Providers

Many providers try to appeal to a wider customer base. One way they do this is to offer a graphical interface that eliminates the complexities of both command-line interfaces and the Internet functions themselves. Also, instead of just providing a regional telephone number, some services work with major telephone carriers to provide access lines in major urban centers.

The next level up of service providers (over the UNIX command-line method) consists of providers who offer SLIP and PPP protocols over their dial-in lines. This lets you create what amounts to a direct Internet connection to your own machine. A primary use of this is to allow installation of the Mosaic Web browser on your system. Mosaic, described later, is an advanced graphical interface for scanning the World Wide Web. It offers text, graphics, and audio access to Web sites.

I should point out that some Mosaic browsers are available as freeware—they're not proprietary programs of service providers. The providers' main job is the SLIP or PPP connectivity. They may or may not also make it easy for you to locate and install Mosaic.

At the top level of functionality, some service providers do offer a proprietary graphical interface to overall Internet functions. Some are also expanding their telephone access and advertising nationally. These companies are beginning to merge into the same market service level as the online data service companies like CompuServe.

Two such top-level services are The Pipeline and NETCOM On-Line Communications Services. Figure 3.3 shows a screen from The Pipeline.

One other service to mention is DELPHI Internet Services. At one point, DELPHI provided services similar to the online data services. However, its focus became Internet connectivity. It has been somewhat late, though, in developing a graphical interface. At time of writing, the release of DELPHI's graphical interface is imminent. It thus rests in a position somewhere between the large online data services and the small but upcoming graphically oriented Internet access providers.

A Low-cost Alternative—Free-nets

Free-nets are free-access computer systems. They give the general public limited access to the Internet as well as access to local bulletin boards and discussion groups. Run through a library or educational institution, they are often sponsored by local government. After you've located a Free-net, if you have a computer and a modem you can log on, often for no charge.

Free-net systems may have a few drawbacks. They don't generally have full Internet access and are usually limited to text-only environments. Also, their overall size may be limited, and, if demand is high, you may find it difficult to avoid a busy signal when dialing in.

Many Free-nets are also accessible via TELNET from other systems, so once you log onto one Free-net node, you can hop to others.

The National Public Telecomputing Network (NPTN) serves as an umbrella organization for Free-nets. You can contact them by sending mail to **info@nptn.org**. They publish a weekly updated list of worldwide Free-nets. You can find it posted in the Newsgroups **alt.freenet** and **alt.online-service.freenet**.

**Figure 3.3
The Pipeline's
main screen.**

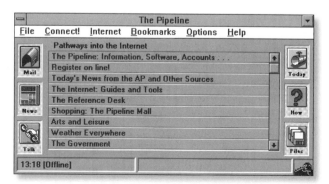

Table 3.1
UNIX Command
Summary

Command	Summary
Append to a file	Command: cat file1 > file 2
Change Directory	Command: cd directory [example cd /pub] [cd without argument returns to home or top directory]
Copy a file	Command: cp file1 file2
Current Directory	Command: pwd ["present working directory"]
Compress File	Command: compress file1 [compresses to file1.z]
Decompress File	Command: uncompress file1.z
Disk Space Left	Command: du
List Files	Command: ls -argument (include the "-") arguments -s = filesize -F = file type -cl = by date -a = invisible files
Make New Directory	Command: mkdir new-directory-name
Move a File	Command: mv filename directory
Remove Directory	Command: rmdir directory-name
Remove File	Command: rm filename
Rename File	Use "Move File" to do this
View Contents of a file	Command: more filename

Above all else, remember that file and directory are case sensitive!!!

Using an Online Data Service

All major online data services now provide at least an e-mail connection to the Internet. Most also offer some mix of additional features such as newsgroups, FTP, GOPHER, or Web access. And most are rushing to add as many features as they can. (Even if you only have an e-mail connection, you can activate other functions such as FTP just by sending mail messages. I'll describe these later.)

One advantage of using an online data service for Internet access is that the service will try to provide a "look and feel" for accessing Internet functions that is consistent with the rest of the service. This may end up just being a Windows representation of something that is still a text menu, but some people will still find it more familiar than the UNIX command-line interface of some low-end Internet access providers. Figures 3.4 and 3.5 show examples of the graphical interfaces for America Online's GOPHER browser and Prodigy's Web browser, respectively.

On the downside, features may still be limited, and costs may be higher. Besides not having all the Internet features, there may be quirks. For example, at one time some services could only support mail messages shorter than 56 Kbytes, whereas much larger messages could be supported via an Internet access account.

Some other considerations:

➤ Internet access providers at present may be found to support higher modem speeds than some online data services.

➤ An online data service's basic rate structure may be higher than that of an Internet access provider. There may also be additional surcharges for using Internet functionality.

As a rule of thumb, an online data service provider may be appropriate for fairly limited access, say a few hours a month. If you use the Internet more frequently, or need specific features, another means of accessing the Internet may be more effective.

**Figure 3.4
America Online
GOPHER browser.**

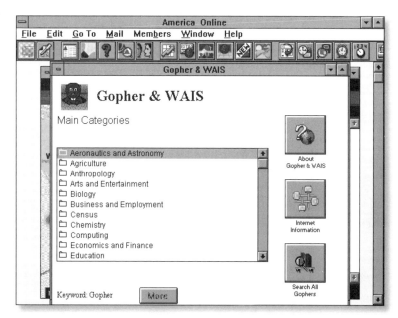

**Figure 3.5
Prodigy WEB
browser.**

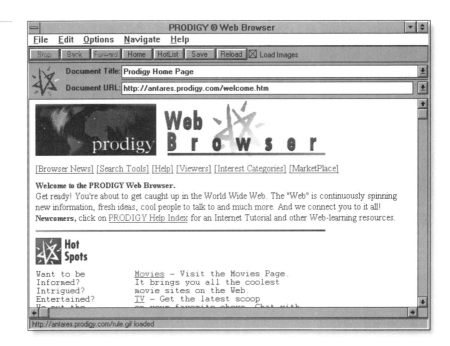

Internet Basics

This section describes Internet's basic capabilities and tools.

We're going to apply a principle used in elementary schools. Even though everybody uses calculators nowadays, schools still insist on teaching basic math. Similarly, someday we'll access the Internet with simple point-'n'-click tools. Because it's not that way yet we're going to describe the "basic math" techniques that you need to maneuver around.

Much of this description assumes that your interface to the Internet is via a UNIX command line. This is something of a "lowest common denominator," and if you have access to a more graphical interface you can easily apply the concepts presented here. In a few cases examples are also given from other types of interfaces.

Nomenclature

Before proceeding, it's necessary to describe the Internet's nomenclature for user accounts and sites. You'll see many strange names in the general shape **username@organization**, as in Figure 3.6.

Figure 3.6
Internet
nomenclature.

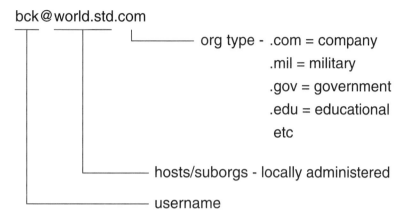

The organization consists of several names separated by periods, such as "**oak.oakland.edu**" or "**world.std.com**." The rightmost name is one of several broad-brush categories.

com = commercial

edu = educational

mil = military

gov = government

net = network support company

org = other organizations

The rest of the organization usually consists of a topmost name (**oakland**) assigned by a central naming committee. The organization then assigns its own suborganization name (**oak**) and user-account names. This system greatly simplifies the naming process.

**Host Hopping
—TELNET
and FTP**

The Internet consists of a network of computers (or more properly a network of networks of computers). The most fundamental level of operation is to access one computer, or host, from another computer, and to move files between them.

TELNET—Connecting to a Member Host

Assume that you have a terminal session running on a host. You can establish a session on another host, almost anywhere on the Internet, by typing TELNET and the other host's name, for example:

```
>telnet oak.oakland.edu.
```

At this point you're prompted for a username and a password. Many systems accept a generic username such as **anonymous** or **guest** and then accept any password. Obviously, many do require a valid username/password—without one you can't get on. Very often responding with **new** or **newuser** as a username initiates an enrollment procedure.

After you enter an acceptable username/password, you receive that system's prompt, and you have a session running on that system as if you had logged on locally.

You have full access to all system commands and services, within any limits the system's security imposes.

You can view directory structures and files, and perhaps even utilize the local mail facility. Generally you can type `help` to find out what's available.

You cannot transfer files to and from the site. For that, you need the next service, FTP.

File Transfer Protocol—FTP

At your local host prompt, you can type FTP followed by the name of a valid host to establish a connection, much like TELNET, to a remote host. Like TELNET, you're prompted for a username/password, an **anonymous** often gets you on the system.

After you're on the remote system, you get a prompt symbol like this:

```
FTP>
```

You can do some directory browsing, but more importantly you can transfer files to/from your home/host using the commands "get" or "put." You can usually enter the command "help" for a listing of FTP commands available on that system. (An abbreviated command summary is given in Table 3.2, FTP Command Summary.)

Unlike TELNET, you cannot do some functions directly like type a file or send mail. (In UNIX, the rough equivalent of the DOS "type" command is "more.") An indirect way to read a remote file is

```
FTP> get filename |more  (Note: There can be no space between "|"
                          and "more.")
```

Table 3.2	`ascii`	set ASCII transfer type
FTP Command	`binary`	set binary transfer type
Summary	`bye`	terminate FTP session and exit
	`cd`	change remote working directory
	`cdup`	change remote working directory to parent directory
	`close`	terminate FTP session
	`cr`	toggle carriage return stripping on ASCII gets
	`delete`	delete remote file
	`dir`	list contents of remote directory
	`get`	receive file
	`ls`	list contents of remote directory
	`mkdir`	make directory on the remote machine
	`open`	connect to remote TFTP
	`"put"`	send one file
	`mdelete`	delete multiple files
	`mdir`	list contents of multiple remote directories
	`mget`	get multiple files
	`rmdir`	remove directory on the remote machine
	`send`	send one file
	`system`	show remote system type

I cannot overemphasize that FTP is the primary mechanism for moving files around the Internet. You can move some files using e-mail, but there are limitations on file types and/or file size; for example, binary files are hard to move reliably using mail—FTP guarantees movement.

FTP via e-mail

Even if you don't have full Internet access, you may still be able to access much FTP functionality by sending e-mail to sites. There are two approaches: info servers and FTP mail servers.

Info servers—Some FTP sites respond to e-mail requests as well as direct FTP connections. In general you mail a message to the FTP handler address, and it executes the message contents as if it came from an FTP connection. In the event of a get instruction, it then e-mails the requested file back to you.

I said "in general" for several reasons. First, not all FTP sites (anonymous or otherwise) support this feature. Second, those that do support FTP via mail do not all use the same command set. To find out how to use a particular site's FTP mail functions, you (usually) can send it a message with the single word "help" (lowercase) in the body, and it mails you back a file with instructions. While just the word "help" often works, sometimes other commands are supported. For example, mail a message to the info server at **info-server@nnsc.nsf.net**. The *Subject:* field can be anything, but the body has to be

```
request: info
topic: help
```

and you will receive a set of instructions.

A list of info servers is available via anonymous FTP at host **pit-manager.mit.edu/pub/usenet/news.answers**. Not surprisingly, it's also available by e-mail server. Send a message to **mail-server@pit-manager.mit.edu** with the command "help" in the *Subject:* field. (Note that this differs from other systems where you "put" "help" in the body.)

FTP mail servers —An info server can only send files from its own system. A limited number of FTP via e-mail systems let you access files on any anonymous FTP host. An FTP mail server accepts a command string in a message from you. It then does its own anonymous FTP logon to the requested host, executes the command string, and mails you the results.

Send a message with the one-line body "help" to **ftp@pa.dec.com** or **ftpmail@decwrl.dec.com** to receive instructions for using those FTP mail servers. (Note that Digital Equipment Corporation ["DEC"] sponsors both.)

Important Information about Transferring Files !!!

You need to know about, or be warned about, two very basic things regarding file transfer. These result from two basic facts:

➤ Binary files may need different handling than text files.

➤ Some parts of the Internet have limits on file size.

FTP actually handles binary and text files differently. ("Binary" can mean graphics files, executable files, or any file that's been compressed, for example, with PKZIP.) On many systems when you do a "get" or "put," the resident FTP program automatically detects the file's type and handles it appropriately. However, some systems require you to manually set a toggle to indicate if you're moving a binary or text file. If you get corrupted files, try setting the file type manually. (Enter the FTP command "binary" or "ASCII.")

Also, many mail programs can't handle binary files at all. (Tools for fixing this are described later.)

Even though the receiving and transmitting hosts may handle large files perfectly, the path across the Internet can be quirky, and you may run across a link that rejects or corrupts files exceeding some size limitation. Some equipment rejects files greater than 56 Kbytes in size.

The tool pair UUENCODE/UUDECODE translates binary files into text files for transmission and back into binary at reception. Also, these tools can take a large file and break it into numerous small ones, below a size you specify, and then reassemble the files at reception. Versions of these tools are available to run on all platforms. The appendices tell how to access them from archive sites.

Broadcast Services—Newsgroups, Maillists, List Servers, EZINES

A number of useful functions are really just extensions of broadcast mail functions.

Newsgroups

These postings of series of messages on specific subjects are broadcast across the whole Internet. You call up a newsreader program on your Internet host to browse the different newsgroups and read the entries in each. Because many Internet hosts are UNIX-based, newsreaders tend to be rather difficult to use, with cryptic commands. Windows-based newsreaders on some systems tend to be a little more user friendly. (See Figure 3.7.)

There are an incredible number of newsgroups—thousands, with more being created daily. They range from new-service postings and financial news, to computer-professional information, to recreational and alternative lifestyles.

Figure 3.7
TCP-PRO
Windows
newsreader.

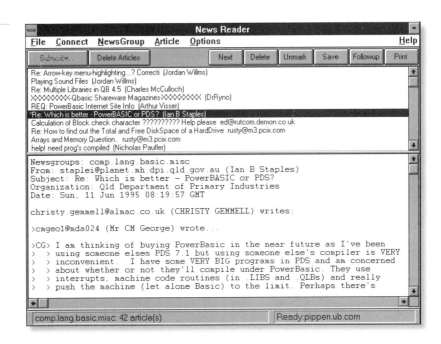

Some sample names:

alt.beer—discussions about beer

rec.humor—jokes!

comp.msdos.announce—announcements about MS-DOS services and programs available

news.newsgroups.announce—news about new newsgroups

alt.answers—miscellaneous info about how to use the Internet

A list of active newsgroups is published monthly and archived in several places. The appendices show how to access the archive list at a server at MIT.

The first word of the newsgroup name (**alt**, **comp**, and so on) is a broad-brush category. The presently defined list is

alt—alternative systems

biz—business related

comp—computer-related

k12—education (kindergarten through grade 12)

misc—miscellaneous

rec—recreation

sci—science

soc—social topics

talk—controversial subjects

When you use a newsreader, you see that postings in any specific news-group generally consist of a numbered series of titles, with the phrase "RE:" indicating postings that are replies to earlier postings. Unfortunately, there is a high content of REs and a lot of junk. The news-reader usually has functions for saving the contents of one or more post-ings to a file, creating replies, and posting new messages.

```
****** 101 unread articles in alt.lang.basic — read now? [ynq]

Reading overview file.

7095 Re: Getting ERRORLEVEL from a SHELLed Program?
7096 Re: QBASIC and ASM. How to?
7097 Re: Getting ERRORLEVEL from a SHELLed Program?
7098 Putting data in keyboard
7099 Re: Getting ERRORLEVEL from a SHELLed Program?
7100 Re: QBASIC and ASM. How to?
7101 Re: Registration keys, registering...passwords..DEMO
7102 Re: Yet another password prog.
7103 Re: error trapping
7104 QuickBASIC to C converter
7105 The C Hoax
7106 Re: QBASIC Questions
7107 Help on VB
7108 Re: [q!]print stars...
7109 Trapping file sharing errors w/o ON ERROR?
7110 Re: How do I use the PIPE: device in QBASIC Interpreter?
7111 Re: Password program...
7112 Debugging Assembler Routines in PowerBASIC
7113 Visual BASIC decompiler needed

What next? [npq]
```

A typical individual news posting looks something like this:

```
*****************************************************************
alt.movies.humorous #7093 (98 more)
From: fields.bill@souse.com (Uncle Claude)
Subject: Unhealthy Beverages?
Date: Wed Mar 22 20:49:00 EST 1995
Distribution: world
Organization: Bogle Pictures
X-Newsreader: PCBoard Version 15.21
X-Mailer: PCBoard/UUOUT Version 1.10
Lines: 2

Does anyone know how to get the grapefruit juice out of my
grapefruit juice?
End of article 7093 (of 7191) — what next? [npq]
*****************************************************************
```

Maillists and List Servers

Maillists are a variant on newsgroups. These are mailings to your specific mailbox on selected topics. There are thousands of maillists, and you have to subscribe to those you want. You generally send a generic message with "subscribe listname" or just "subscribe" in either the body or the *Subject:* field to the maintainer of the maillist, and a program automatically enrolls you. (You may have to experiment.) Similarly, the maillist has an address where you mail messages you want to post, and are automatically re-mailed to all maillist members. Some maillists are moderated—the maintainer censors messages deemed inappropriate. This can mean illegal, immoral, or just a waste of bandwidth. Bookstores generally carry several books that list maillists and provide enrollment instructions. The appendices include a pointer to a maintained list of maillists.

List servers are very closely related to maillists. You subscribe by sending an enrollment message to an administrative address. You then receive via mail copies of anything posted to the list server. Messages are posted by sending to a publication address, which differs from the enrollment address. You can execute various other administrative commands by sending predefined messages to the administrative address. There are many list server lists.

For example, to obtain a list of list service discussion groups, send a message to **listserv@bitnic.bitnet**. Include the single entry "list global" (without the quotation marks) in the body of the message. Leave the *Subject:* field blank. You'll be mailed a long file. To obtain instructions on other commands available, send a message to the same address with the body including just "INFO REFCARD."

Electronic Magazines (EZINES)

An increasing number of periodicals are being distributed, usually for free, on the Internet. Not repostings of commercial efforts, these are individual special-interest efforts, many on professional topics. I don't believe there's any advertising in them. Enrollment is much like that for maillists. Lists can be found in bookstores. The appendices provide a pointer to a list of EZINES.

Finding People

Unfortunately, there's no equivalent of a telephone system white pages for locating individuals on the Internet. Several methods are under development, and some can even be used on a trial basis.

Finger

If you TELNET to any one host, you can identify user accounts on that host by entering >**finger username**. This comes (I guess) from the depression-era expression "to finger (point out) someone." You see a list of user accounts with **username** as part of the string.

WHOIS

WHOIS is a far from complete attempt to develop a database of all Internet users. Many UNIX systems support WHOIS. It is activated using the syntax

```
whois [-h hostname] username
```

If you use the optional hostname, be sure to supply the "-h" or it will be treated as a username.

If your system doesn't support WHOIS, you can access it by TELNETing to another system that does. A list of active WHOIS servers is available via anonymous FTP from site **sipb.mit.edu/pub/whois/whois-servers.list**.

WHOIS covers only about 80,000 of the millions of Internet users. However, it is the only such service available until a more comprehensive directory, the InterNIC list, becomes available.

InterNIC

The Internet's Network Information Center and AT&T are working to provide a master directory of all Internet users who want their addresses published. Although this system is still under development, you can access it by TELNETing to **ds.internic.net** and logging on as **guest**. You can add your name to their white pages directory by sending a message to **admin@ds.internic.net**. You can get further info about InterNIC by sending mail to **info@internic.net.**

USENET Tracking

One additional way to find e-mail addresses is to utilize the fact that the source address of all postings to USENET newsgroups is recorded in a directory. You can query this database by sending a message to the address **mail-server@pit-manager.mit.edu**. Leave the *Subject:* field blank, and in the body have a single line of format "send usenet-address/username"—for example, **send usenet-address/kochem.**

Tools for Retrieving Info

The sheer volume of information on the Internet is at once its greatest strength and its greatest weakness. While a piece of information you need is almost certainly out there, it can be almost impossible to find, hidden behind all the other information that you aren't looking for. This is a true needle-in-the-haystack situation.

So, it's not surprising that a lot of effort has gone into developing methods for searching for information. The measures of merit here are

➤ Completeness—If it's out there, will the search tool find it?

➤ Ease-of-use—How long does it take? How much user intervention is required?

The good news is that a lot of people have been working at it for a long time, and they have actually progressed a lot toward making information findable. We'll cover four primary tools in order of evolution, if not exact chronology. These tools are Archie, GOPHER, WAIS, and the World Wide Web.

Archie

Archie is a tool for searching a database of the names of files stored on a number of member FTP sites. The member sites periodically and automatically upload their directory structure and contents to a central Archie directory. By accessing the Archie tool, you can scan for files by their filename.

If your system has an Archie browser on it, just type "Archie" and then enter "help" to study the command set. The rather cryptic command set does support such things as exact and partial matches, and searches by filename extension. If your system does not have an Archie browser, you can TELNET to a server that does. One is at **archie.sura.net**. By the way, once you've located a particular file, there's a mechanism to activate an FTP transfer without leaving Archie.

Archie has shortcomings:

> ➤ It knows files only by name, not content.

> ➤ Not all FTP sites upload their contents to the Archie database.

> ➤ Not all hosts have the Archie search tool.

GOPHER

GOPHER is a menu-driven search tool for finding information on the Internet. On a UNIX command-line account, typing GOPHER brings up the menu shown in Figure 3.8.

Moving through the menu is quite straightforward. Just type the number of the menu item you're interested in, or use up and down arrows to make a selection. The combination of submenus is virtually unlimited. Many end in actual files, often text files, and you have the option to copy the file to your home system.

Note that there is almost always a top-level menu entry that says something like "access other GOPHER servers." No one GOPHER service knows about every file on the Internet, but by hopping from server to

**Figure 3.8
GOPHER main
menu.**

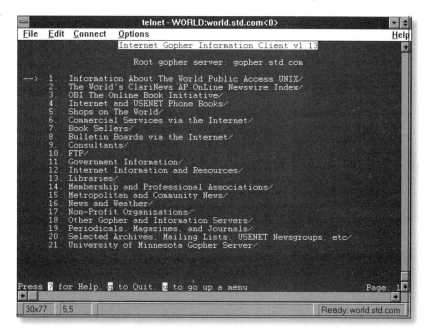

server you can cover almost the entire Internet; admittedly, it can take a long time.

Also note that GOPHER is somewhat backwards compatible with FTP. It has the ability to scan FTP sites and present files for downloading.

Besides letting you peruse the menu, GOPHER offers a search function. The search scans the titles in the menu tree and perhaps keywords, but it doesn't scan the document's contents. (This wouldn't work with executable or other binary files anyhow.)

A separate tool called "Veronica" indexes and searches all titles on all GOPHER servers. Veronica provides functions for GOPHER similar to those Archie provides for FTP sites. GOPHER sites periodically transmit their menu structures to regional (my inexact phrase) Veronica servers, which compile indexes. The separate Veronica servers then merge their databases into an overall collection. Veronica servers also provide a keyword browser. Most GOPHER menus provide a link to a Veronica server, usually under the "Other GOPHER Servers" menu item.

WAIS

WAIS (pronounced as in "ways and means") stands for Wide Area Information Service. It represents a step up searching's evolutionary ladder in that it searches through documents' contents. It has some features that narrow the search field, such as ranking finds by the number of field matches and limiting the number of finds reported. It also has tools for finding documents relevant to the documents it finds in any one search.

See Figure 3.9 for a view of a WAIS search on a UNIX system. WAIS interfaces are also available for other platforms such as Windows.

The WAIS server creates an index of keywords based on scanning the files it is covering. The index also has keywords manually assigned to files. For example, a graphic of a dog wouldn't have the text "dog" anywhere in its body or even its title, but the keyword "dog" can still be assigned to it.

Any given WAIS server typically covers a limited number of hosts (perhaps just one). This might be interpreted to mean that to search for a word you have to perform the search on every WAIS existing server. Fortunately this is not so. Each WAIS server has keywords associated with it. The entry level to WAIS lets you scan this database first to determine which servers best suit your search.

Like Veronica, WAIS servers can be accessed from GOPHER off the "Other GOPHER Servers" menu item.

**Figure 3.9
WAIS screen.**

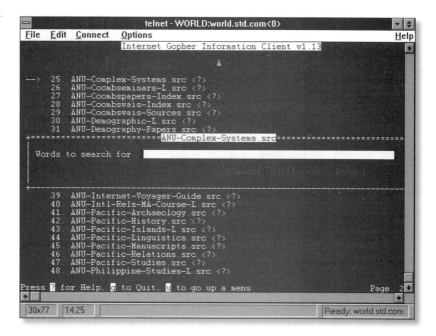

The World Wide Web

The World Wide Web is perhaps the first mechanism to cross the ease-of-use threshold so large numbers of people from varying backgrounds can benefit from the Internet. See Figure 3.10.

**Figure 3.10
Apple World
Wide Web home
page.**

CERN initially developed the Web as a mechanism to view hypertext documents and provide links between multiple documents on multiple hosts. Technologically it has grown to encompass true multimedia formats. The widespread availability of browsers, and multimedia-authoring tools, and the ability to create your own Web site have resulted in a complementary boom in both Web sites and Web users. The Web is expanding to include information of all types: business, educational, scientific, entertainment, and more.

Web Terminology and Operation

The World Wide Web is known by several names: WWW, w3, and the Web are often used interchangeably and mean the same thing.

Originally the Web went one major step beyond GOPHER, allowing a hypertext link between documents. This means that selecting a "hotword" in one document or on one screen jumps you to an entry point in another document. This link may be on the current host, or it may be to an entry point, or home page, on another host.

This frees you from the rigid structure of a menu tree, and even more importantly gives you access to the contents of documents (recall that Archie and Veronica only work with filenames or menu names). Also, Web sites and browsers typically have built-in search capabilities that equal or exceed the WAIS capabilities.

This additional freedom costs. Navigation can become harder. Even within any one site you may have difficulty keeping track of where you are and you may frequently encounter loops. At any point you may suddenly find yourself on a different site.

Also, the widespread proliferation of Web home pages makes it nearly impossible to effectively develop white or yellow pages.

Still, advantages greatly outweigh any newly acquired difficulties, and work continues to develop better searching and tracking features.

The basic hypertext format is defined in a semi-standard known as HTML (HyperText Markup Language). This format goes just beyond plain text and includes such text-formatting features as fonts, sizes, bold, and so on. Formatting has also expanded to include both images and sound. As you navigate the Web with a full-capability (multimedia) browser, you receive not just text information, but accompanying images and often sounds.

The name Mosaic is used a lot in reference to the Web. Mosaic is one of the most comprehensive of the many types of Web browsers available.

Versions are available for many platforms; it supports full multimedia capability; you may download it for free.

Web documents and browsers have exhibited fairly comprehensive backwards and forwards compatibility. Low-end text-only browsers appropriately filter out images and sound and make a best effort at reformatting text. Legacy features such as FTP and GOPHER are generally quite well represented within their given limitations.

About Addressing

You will see the phrase "URL" a lot. It stands for Uniform Resource Locator. In simplistic terms, it means addressing. Web sites are typically identified by some name like **http://www.ibm.com/**. Further extensions of the name identify subdirectories within sites. You typically don't need to keep track of this; the Web browser does it for you.

The address example is actually a subset of a more comprehensive naming structure. The **http** prefix identifies one resource type. **ftp://** and **gopher://** prefixes identify those types of sites.

About Bandwidth

It's all well and good to talk about a complete multimedia interface. However, bandwidth requirements can be significant. Recall that the bandwidth you have available depends upon your type of Internet connection. Your bandwidth may range from a low end of 9600 b/s for a dial-up line to 56 Kbits-to-megabits/sec if your company has its own IP gateway. The low end might be all right for text-only operations at home. (Don't even think about trying to operate with a lower-speed modem.) Graphics, audio, and motion require successively higher bandwidths. You can spend a lot of time sitting around watching the screen update. Most good browsers let you selectively shut off features like graphics if you find operation too slow.

Text-based Browsers

The earliest stages of Web development used text-based browsers only. In fact the very first ones were line at a time only. Lynx, one of the first screen-mode text-based browsers, remains widely available on UNIX and VMS systems.

See Figure 3.11 for a screen of a Lynx browser.

Because Lynx is text based, many of its screens may initially look like GOPHER screens. As you use arrow keys to move through them, you'll

**Figure 3.11
Lynx Web
browser.**

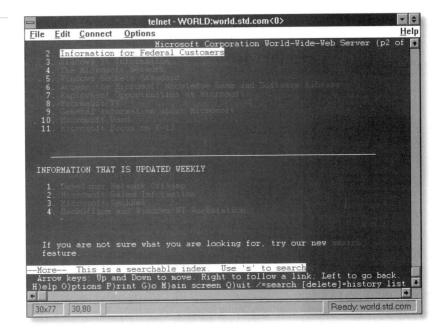

quickly notice that a highlight jumps to words in the middle of sentences. These are "hotkeys," links to other documents and sites. Pressing the carriage return or a different arrow key makes the jump. When you jump to a GOPHER site, you get a conventional GOPHER representation. When you jump to an FTP site, the screen presented looks a lot like a directory listing.

Besides the navigational features, it's important to know that at any point you can download the currently selected document. (This can be done by a file extract or by having it e-mailed to you at any address you select.)

Graphical Browsing Tools

The avalanche of interest in the Web has largely come about due to the widespread availability of good, multiplatform, graphical browsers that support text, graphics, and audio. Perhaps the most widely known is Mosaic, although many other good ones exist, and lots more are on the way.

Mosaic was initially developed by NCSA, the National Center for Supercomputing Applications. NCSA was established under a grant from the National Science Foundation, and Mosaic is available for free download. The Software Development Group (SDG) provides ongoing Mosaic support.

A large number of commercial versions of Mosaic are available. Mosaic is a cross-platform tool—versions are available for Windows, Macintosh, Amiga, and the UNIX operating systems. If you operate it over a dial-up line though, please note that the line has to support SLIP or PPP.

Many commercial companies are rushing to develop graphical Web browsers. Also, commercial online data services and Internet access providers are all working on making versions available over their systems. Figure 3.12 shows the Spry Mosaic browser available from CompuServe. This quite usable system makes easy Web access available to a very large audience.

Information about publicly available Mosaic and Mosaic files themselves are available from NCSA's anonymous FTP site at **ftp.ncsa.uiuc.edu**.

Many other graphical Web browsers are available. Cello, another freeware Windows browser, was developed by the Legal Information Institute with a grant from the National Center for Automated Information Research. You can obtain information about Cello by anonymous FTP to **ftp.law.cornell.edu**.

Figure 3.12 CompuServe's Spry Mosaic browser.

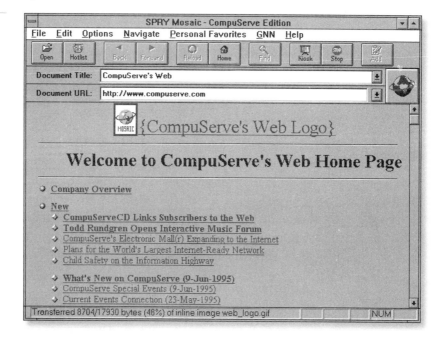

Hotspots—Some Key Sites

The following chapters of this book describe many locations of specific resources in the online universe, including, but not limited to, the Internet itself. This section describes a few general-purpose hotspots, sites that may have a lot of information appealing to a broad range of programming interests.

As you come to know more about the Internet, you become more acquainted with conducting searches for material for your specific needs. If you take the information in this chapter and combine it with the "must-have" Internet lists in the appendices, you will have an excellent foundation, or starter set, of Internet knowledge.

SimTel

This is entirely my own opinion, but the SimTel FTP archive site is probably the "mother of all file archives." This vast archive set includes MS-DOS and Windows programs, utilities, and informational files. (It also used to include Mac files, but there's now just a reference to another FTP site.) These files are almost entirely public domain and shareware. Their quality tends to be much higher than one might ordinarily expect. I believe this is because a significant fraction of uploads are by programmers posting files for other programmers, who are not necessarily trying to make a profit.

Coast to Coast Software Repository operates SimTel. Their principle of operation is to have a central file center, which many other organizations mirror. (See following material.) Many CD-ROM vendors offer partial versions of SimTel archives. Coast to Coast offers a more complete CD-ROM. (For information send e-mail to **cdrom@Mail.Coast.NET**.)

SimTel Contents

The MS-DOS section of SimTel has over 200 subdirectories containing thousands of files. Text editors and reformatters, print utilities, graphics tools, tools by language (C, BASIC, ASM, and so on), and many more are included. Table 3.3, SimTel MS-DOS Directories, is a listing of the directory titles; the directory names usually identify the contents fairly well. There is a comparable set of functionality under the section, although there are fewer directories (about 80).

Accessing SimTel

For security purposes you cannot access the SimTel file site directly. You access one of its many mirror sites. The primary mirror site is anonymous FTP at **oak.oakland.edu**, located, of course, in Rochester, Michigan.

(I assumed it was in California, but it isn't.) A partial list of other mirror sites is given in Table 3.4, SimTel Mirror Sites. There are something like 50 total mirror sites worldwide.

SimTel files may also be obtained by e-mail from various FTP mail servers or through the BITNET/EARN file servers. For details send e-mail to **listserv@SimTel.Coast.NET** with this command in the body of the message: get simtel-mailserver.info.

World Wide Web (WWW), Mosaic, and Netscape users can connect to the URL **http://www.acs.oakland.edu** to access the files on **OAK.Oakland.Edu**.

GOPHER users can access the collection through **Gopher.Oakland.Edu**.

When you do access a mirror site, from the top directory go to the SimTel subdirectory. There you'll find subdirectories for MS-DOS and Windows. The files are archived quite well. The file simibm.zip in the MS-DOS directory contains several useful index files including a complete directory index, with one-line descriptions, in both plain-text and comma-delimited text (for import to spreadsheets) formats. There is also a search utility.

Even without the simibm.zip file, the names of directories give a pretty good idea of what is in them, and each subdirectory contains a file 00-INDEX.TXT with one-line descriptions of contents.

Uploading to SimTel

A file labeled README.how-to-upload provides instructions for submitting files. You cannot upload files directly to SimTel. You are requested to send a description of your file, in a specified format, to an e-mail address. You are then given the name of a password-protected site that acts as an upload receiver for SimTel. Some basic checking is done against submission requirements. Your file is then posted on SimTel, and it will start propagating to its mirror sites. SimTel also posts an announcement message to the **newsgroup comp.MSDOS.announce**.

Table 3.3 SimTel MS-DOS Directories				
4dos	demacs	hamradio	notabene	statstic
ada	deskaccs	handicap	novell	stunnpc
ai	deskjet	hebrew	oberon	surfmodl
animate	deskpub	hercules	oemacs	swap
archiver	desqview	hypertxt	offline	sysinfo

**Table 3.3
SimTel MS-DOS
Directories
(Continued)**

arcutil	dirutil	iconlang	opus	sysutil
asm_mag	disasm	info	packet	tagbbs
asmutil	diskutil	infonet	paging	taxes
astrnomy	djgpp	install	pascal	teaching
at	dv_x	io_util	pathutil	telegard
autocad	editor	irit	pcboard	telix
awk	educatin	jdrbbs	pcmag	tex
bakernws	eel	ka9q	pctech	textutil
basic	ega	keyboard	pctecniq	tiff
batutil	electric	lan	pcvrmag	tsrutil
bbs	emulator	langtutr	perl	turbo_c
bbsdoor	engineer	laser	pgmutil	turbobas
bbslist	envutil	legal	pibterm	turbopas
bible	execomp	linguist	pktdrvr	turbovis
binedit	ezycom	litratur	plot	ubasic
biology	falken	logo	postscrp	uemacs
bootutil	fido	lotus123	printer	uucp
borland	filedocs	mac	procomm	ventura
c	fileutil	mapping	prodigy	vga
cad	finance	math	projmgr	virus
calculat	flowchrt	mathcopr	qbasic	visbasic
catalog	food	memutil	qedit	viscii
cdrom	formgen	menu	qemm	voice
celerity	forth	mfg	qmodem	voicmail
chemstry	fortran	microsft	qtrdeck	vpssoft
citadel	fossil	misclang	ramdisk	waffle
clipper	freemacs	modem	rbbs_pc	weather
clock	genealgy	modula2	recreatn	wildcat
cms_tape	geogrphy	mormon	rip	wordperf
compress	geology	mouse	satelite	worldmap

Table 3.3 SimTel MS-DOS Directories (Continued)	cpluspls	geos1x	msjournl	science	wpj_mag
	cron	geos2x	music	screen	wwiv
	crossasm	geosnews	naplps	security	x_10
	database	gif	ncsatln	simulatn	xlisp
	dbase	gnuish	netpage	sound	xwindows
	dbms_mag	graph	network	spredsht	zip
	ddjmag	graphics	neurlnet	sprint	zmodem
	decode	gtsmusic	nfs	starter	zoo

Table 3.4 SimTel Mirror Sites	St. Louis, MO:	uarchive.wustl.edu (128.252.135.4) tems/ibmpc/simtel
	Corvallis, OR:	achive.orst.edu (128.193.2.13) /mirrors/simtel/MSDOS /mirrors/simtel/win3
	Australia:	archie.au (139.130.4.6) micros/pc/oak
	England:	micros.hensa.ac.uk (148.88.8.84) /mirrors/simtel
	England:	src.doc.ic.ac.uk (146.169.2.10) /pub/packages/simtel /pub/packages/simtel-win3
	Finland:	ftp.funet.fi (128.214.248.6) /pub/MSDOS/Simtel
	France:	ftp.ibp.fr (132.227.60.2) /pub/pc/SimTel/MSDOS /pub/pc/SimTel/win3
	Germany	ftp.uni-paderborn.de (131.234.2.32) /SimTel/msdos /SimTel/win3
	Hong Kong:	ftp.cs.cuhk.hk (137.189.4.57) /pub/simtel/msdos /pub/simtel/win3
	Israel:	tp.technion.ac.il(132.68.1.10) /pub/unsupported /simtel/msdos

Table 3.4 SimTel Mirror Sites (Continued)	the Netherlands:	ftp.nic.surfnet.nl (192.87.46.3) /mirror-archive/software/simtel-msdos /mirror-archive/software/simtel-win3
	Poland:	ftp.cyf-kr.edu.pl (149.156.1.8) /pub/mirror/simtel/msdos
	South Africa:	ftp.sun.ac.za (146.232.212.21) /pub/simtel/msdos /pub/simtel/win3
	Sweden:	ftp.sunet.se (130.238.127.3) /pub/pc/mirror/SimTel/msdos/ pub/pc/mirror/SimTel/win3
	Switzerland:	ftp.switch.ch (130.59.1.40) /mirror/simtel/msdos/mirror/simtel/win3
	Taiwan:	NCTUCCCA.edu.tw (140.111.1.10) /PC/simtel
	Thailand:	ftp.nectec.or.th (192.150.251.33)

Other Key FTP Sites

There are a great many FTP sites archiving files for MS-DOS, Windows, and several other platforms. MODER.LST, a well-known list of MS-DOS/Windows archive sites, is archived on SimTel and many other sites. (See the appendices for directions on getting it.)

Here are a few of the many FTP sites you'll find cataloged on MODER.LST and elsewhere:

garbo.uwasa.fi

ftp.funet.fi

ftp.sunet.se

wuarchive.wustl.edu

ftp.uml.edu

ftp.cica.indiana.edu

ftp.cso.uiuc.edu

msdos.archive.umich.edu

archie.au

explorer.arc.nasa.gov

jplinfo.jpl.nasa.gov

Some key sites for Macintosh files are

mac.archive.umich.edu

sumex-aim.stanford.edu

wuarchive.wustl.edu

Note that wuarchive shows up for both Mac and MS-DOS/Windows. One of the larger sites, at present it accepts a maximum of 200 simultaneous FTP logins, and these are often all busy. SimTel, on the other hand, supports 450 logins, and I can usually log in with little problem.

CERN—Info about the Web

If SimTel is the "mother of all archive sites" it might be appropriate to refer to CERN as the "mother of all Web information."

CERN started the WWW and created all the original software. The Web site **http://info.cern.ch** remains a key location for obtaining information about WWW. This site contains introductory how-to information about the Web, the actual files that are needed to create a Web site, and much more information such as a listing of other Web sites.

Actually CERN has largely handed site maintenance to another organization, the W3 Consortium. This consortium consists of MIT and a European organization, INRIA, with some CERN collaboration. You can still access the site at the URL given above.

Much of the how-to info is located in either the "What's out there?" menu or a FAQ menu, both of which are accessible from the front page. "What's out there?" points to a subject index, "The WWW Virtual Library." It also points to a server list. The top page also includes a section on How to Get WWW Software for setting up sites or browsers.

YAHOO, AUDREY, and Web Directories of Home Pages

One difficult aspect of navigating the World Wide Web is that with so many new sites popping up, it is almost impossible to create a comprehensive and current directory of home pages.

The CERN list mentioned previously is certainly more comprehensive than many, but even it is probably not complete. An additional very useful list of about 1200 companies with Web sites is maintained at **http://www.zurich.ibm.com.**

Perhaps eclipsing all the above is the YAHOO site. Maintained at **http://www.yahoo.com**, this is a super list of over 30,000 Web home pages. It's actually a hypertext directory of other Web sites. Besides having a straightforward "tree" of Web directory pages, it also has a comprehensive search engine to find Web pages that meet desired criteria.

An interesting feature of YAHOO is that it lets people add to YAHOO references to home pages that they have found or created. In the submission queue in the top YAHOO page you can enter a description and URL for a site. The YAHOO maintainers verify the site and then add a link to it into their database.

Another extremely interesting Web site is at **http://www.fagg.uni-lj.si/** (also reachable via anonymous FTP at **audrey.fagg.uni-lj.si**). See Figure 3.13. Described as the Virtual Shareware Library (VSL), it catalogs some 60,000 free programs available from 15 large software archives and their Internet mirrors. You can access this library through a shareware search engine (SHASE). You can also link to this server from YAHOO via the SOFTWARE/ARCHIVES submenus.

Newsgroup Information Archive—rtfm

One last anonymous FTP site to mention is **rtfm.mit.edu**. This site archives a lot of information about newsgroups—FAQs for every group and many useful lists.

A large amount of information is stored in the subdirectories under **/pub/usenet-by-group**.

Figure 3.13 SHASE menu on AUDREY server.

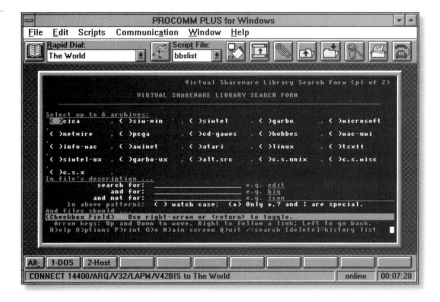

The number of files and subdirectories is so large that it may be cumbersome to navigate your way. If you know a specific path and filename, it may be manageable, but that's not usually the case when you're searching.

I'll share one mechanism I've used for searching this site. With some obvious modification this works on other sites also. Basically, it involves downloading the index and then using a text-scan utility.

If you can deal with downloading a 1.9 Mbyte file (that's the decompressed size), download the file index by name from the topmost directory of rtfm. Be careful to rename the file if your system doesn't support long UNIX names. This file gives a one-line listing of every file on rtfm and includes its full path.

A good text-scanning program to use is GREP. On many UNIX hosts, GREP is already installed as a common utility. Besides UNIX, versions of GREP are also available for almost every platform. A DOS version is available on SimTel under **\msdos\textutil**. GREP is a text-file search utility. If you just type the command "GREP" you get a help screen describing the command syntax. However, the general usage is

```
>grep search_string$ filename.
```

The file filename will be searched, and every line containing "search_string$" will be displayed on the screen. (On most systems you can redirect the output to a file in case there are too many matches.)

You can use GREP to conduct a fairly effective search for files. For example, searching for PDIAL (see the appendices) returns a result that PDIAL stores in two directories on rtfm and gives the full path.

A GREP scan of the rtfm index may also be useful for locating FAQs. This book frequently refers to FAQs, which serve as good primers on various topics. The "List of Periodic Informational Postings" document (see Appendix 2) includes references to FAQs on rtfm. However, the method for locating them is a little erratic. Sometimes a GREP search of the index is required. (Then again, your FTP program may have some form of search capability.)

A last note: I have been told that "rtfm" stands for "Read the Fine Manual." I suspect that this isn't exactly the actual name, but nonetheless rtfm is a fine library of manuals.

CHAPTER FOUR

ACCESS TO VENDORS

Electronic distribution has become a major mechanism of product support for computer-related vendors. And "product support" no longer just means answering questions when the customer gets stuck. The term has grown to include such features as

➤ Libraries of technical information, utilities, and source code with search mechanisms

➤ Lists of frequently asked questions (FAQs)

➤ Periodic updates to tool sets and libraries

➤ Current information on bug fixes and new product releases

➤ When you pose a question, you're no longer answered in a one-on-one exchange with the service rep; hundreds of fellow customers may participate and contribute.

This chapter describes the specific implementation of support resources from a number of major vendors who have an online presence. It provides an overview to demonstrate what is available from each and how its information is organized. Near the start of each section is a hotkey list. It describes some main points of access to that vendor—you can jump right in if you wish.

Some common threads run through the support mechanisms of some larger vendors.

Support Systems

Large vendors offer fee-based developers' support systems. Services may include periodic distribution of a large base of information and tools, as described above, on CD-ROM. One or more hard copy magazines may be distributed. Other benefits may include access to informational meetings and sometimes access to an internal network.

Information from the Internet

A significant fraction of the information base is usually available at no charge on the Internet, via a Web home page and/or an FTP site. Typically the content of the Web site is a superset of the FTP site. The contents of in-house publications are also available.

Online Data Services

A smaller subset of the information base is available on one or more online data services such as CompuServe, America Online, and, to a lesser extent, GEnie and Prodigy. However, the online services provide message centers or forums where you can share questions and opinions with company representatives and fellow customers. The forums also include an area for customers to upload software and useful information.

Dial-in for Downloading

The company may also offer a dial-in line for downloading files from the Technical Information Library. This makes a lot of the information available to people who don't have, or don't want to use, the Internet or the online services.

Newsgroups

The Internet may also have several newsgroups related to the company's products. Although this may not be officially run by or authorized by the company, it is not unusual to find a company's technical articles posted there (by the company) and company employees may engage in discussion threads.

Microsoft

Microsoft has a wide product line, so it's not surprising that they offer a wide range of support services. Their support information is delivered via almost every available online mechanism: Web and FTP sites, newsgroups on the Internet, a direct dial-in line, and multiple forums on every major online service provider.

Hotkeys

➤ *Web server:* **http://www.microsoft.com.** Go to the **/dev** subdirectory.

➤ *FTP site:* **ftp.microsoft.com.** Get the road map dirmap.txt in the top directory.

➤ *CompuServe:* Go to the forum entry point with "GO MICROSOFT."

➤ *America Online:* Go to the forum entry point with go-to-keyword, "MICROSOFT."

Overall Support Organization

The overall service program Microsoft Support Network has four areas: desktop applications, personal operating systems, advanced systems, and development products—the latter of which is of specific interest to programmers. (Although at some time you may benefit from the others also.)

Service Delivery

A number of service mechanisms are available, at varying costs, including having a personal support contact assigned to your company. The Microsoft Electronic Information Services organization delivers the online plans that programmers would be interested in.

What's Available

Two types of downloadable information are available: the Microsoft Knowledge Base and the Microsoft Software Library. Additionally, when accessing support via an online channel such as CompuServe, there are a number of points for question and answer support, with answers available from Microsoft representatives or other Microsoft customers. Amazing sources of help, both downloadable sources deserve a bit of explanation.

The comprehensive Microsoft Knowledge Base has more than 40,000 articles of technical information including answers to commonly asked technical support questions, bug lists, and tutorial information. (See Figures 4.1 and 4.2.) Microsoft's own support and development staff uses this source frequently. This database is available in many formats. It can be downloaded as a single Windows Help file and is relatively easy to use. (Note: Even the compressed version is several megabytes in size.) It can also be viewed online (via the Internet or an online data provider) and is usually provided with some sort of keyword-oriented browser. The Knowledge Base is provided as a part of some development products, such as the professional edition of some programming languages—for example, Visual Basic 3.0 Professional Edition.

**Figure 4.1
Screen from
the Microsoft
Knowledge Base.**

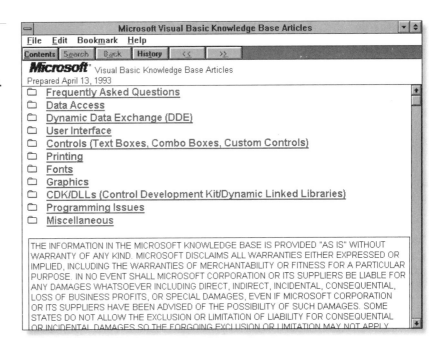

**Figure 4.2
Sample article
from the
Microsoft
Knowledge Base.**

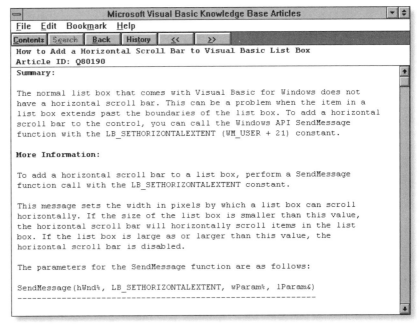

The Microsoft Software Library contains over 1500 sample programs, device drivers, patches, software updates, and programming aids. An index provides a one-line description of each. Many items also have an associated Microsoft Knowledge Base article with additional information.

How to Access

There are a number of methods to get at the Microsoft information.

➤ Online data services—Numerous support forums are maintained on CompuServe, America Online, and GEnie. (And on the Microsoft Network when it becomes available.) Microsoft is a strong presence on online services. As I noted before, the 50-plus Microsoft-related forums are the single largest family of forums on CompuServe.

➤ An Internet FTP site—When you do an anonymous FTP login (**ftp.microsoft.com**), there is a valuable file, dirmap.txt, in the top directory. This is an annotated directory tree of the first two levels of the site. The two main subdirectories of interest are DEVELOPR (Developer Tools and Information) and SOFT-LIB/MSLFILES. DEVELOPR contains further subdirectories for primary languages and tools including BASIC, FORTRAN, MASM, OLE, Visual BASIC, Visual C, Visual C++, Windows SDK, and WIN32DK 32-bit development kits. SOFTLIB/MSLFILES contains the Software Library files (over 1500 files).

➤ An Internet Web page—The Web home page (**http://www.microsoft.com**), basically a more user-friendly means to access the information available on the FTP site, offers some additional features like a browser for the Knowledge Base and the Software Library, and access to the more general product information.

➤ Download site—This dial-in BBS at 206-936-6735 offers the Microsoft Library.

➤ Subscription services—At least two plans for subscribing to peri-odical CD-ROMS offer, among other things, the Knowledge Base, the Software Library, and a newsletter. The Microsoft Developer Network is targeted at programmers. (Info at 800-759-5474.)

Other Support

A number of newsgroups on the Internet serve as question-and-answer forums or for posting relevant information about Microsoft development products. It is possible to have questions answered firsthand by Microsoft staff, although it may not be in an official capacity. Also, a large number of knowledgeable customers or fellow programmers out there represent an invaluable information source. Most Internet newsreader programs have a function that lets you search for newsgroups by keyword. For example, searching for BASIC on my newsreader turns up (among other things):

```
******157 unread articles in alt.lang.basic
******1222 unread articles in comp.lang.basic.visual
******107 unread articles in comp.lang.basic.visual.misc
******179 unread articles in comp.lang.basic.visual.3rdparty
******17 articles in comp.lang.basic.visual.announce
******283 unread articles in comp.lang.basic.visual.database
******1862 unread articles in comp.lang.basic.misc
```

These newsgroups are not limited to Microsoft, but in several Microsoft products account for the majority of the discussion.

Borland

Borland provides numerous levels of support at varying rates. Their chief means of distributing product information is via the Knowledge Base CD, which comes with many of the support options. A subset of this Technical Library is available on a Web site and an associated FTP site. Subsets are also available on online services like CompuServe, BIX, and GEnie.

Hotkeys

➤ *Web site:* **http://www.borland.com**. Go to submenu technical support or developer support.

➤ *FTP site:* **ftp.borland.com**

➤ *CompuServe:* GO BORLAND. Go to forum Development.

Service

Borland has numerous service plans ranging from 900 telephone service with per-minute charges up to dedicated consultants on a yearly basis. The Developer Connection Program is handled on a per-product basis and includes periodic product updates, access to prerelease software for evaluation, and a one-year subscription to a Knowledge Base CD. The Knowledge Base includes several thousand articles, FAQs, problem reports, and workarounds.

Access

A major part of the Knowledge Base is available at no charge on the Web site and the FTP site. Some major subsections of the FTP directory tree of interest are (under **/pub**)

DEVINFO	(Developer Information)
TECHINFO	(Technical Information)
DEVCORNR	(Developers Corner)
TECHDOCS	(Technical Files and Documents)
LANGUAGE	(Computer Language Products)
C++	(Borland C/C++)
Patch	(Borland C/C++ Patch Files)
DELPHI	(DELPHI Language)
Pascal	(Pascal)
TOOLS	(Programming Language Tools)

When you access the FTP site from the Web site, you can access a full listing of the tree structure. At the top of the FTP site, the files index.txt and index.zip give a complete list of all technical information files, with a one-line description.

Technical information can also be downloaded from a BBS line at 408-431-5096.

There is also a fax retrieval line at 800-822-4269.

About a dozen CompuServe forums are on Borland, all accessed via GO BORLAND. These do not appear to contain the Technical Information Library, but a good deal of similar information is there. There is a very active series of messaging areas not necessarily supported by Borland representatives. However, there is a customer service area specifically for posting messages to Borland representatives. And the service reps do tend to read the general message areas also.

Apple

Apple offers a number of fee-based developer support and training programs. These consist of certain core services plus an information and tool base distributed quarterly on CD-ROM, as well as several journals. Access is granted to an internal online Apple support network. Much material in the developer programs is available at no charge through a Web site and an FTP site. Apple also offers some of its courses online via the Internet. A subset of the information base is available on the online services, the more comprehensive (today) being on America Online.

Hotkeys

➤ *Web site:* **http:/www.info.apple.com**. Go to submenu Developer.

➤ *FTP site:* **ftp.info.apple.com**. Go to subdirectory Developer.

➤ *CompuServe:* Enter the Apple Forums with GO APPLE.

➤ *America Online:* Enter the Mac Operating Systems area with keyword MOS and go to the Development Forum.

Service Structure

Apple's primary way to support people developing programs to run on their platforms is via four fee-based developers' programs:

➤ Macintosh Associates Program—A self-support program including ongoing technical information and services. A main feature is the Developer CD Series—a series of three CD-ROMs updated monthly in rotation (estimated cost: $350 per year).

➤ Macintosh Partners Program—A more comprehensive version than the Associates Program, with additional information about system software and an e-mail question-and-answer center. In addition, this version focuses on PowerPC, QuickTime, QuickDraw GX, PowerTalk, System 7.5 APIs, and Apple development tools (estimated cost: $1500 per year).

➤ Newton Associates Program & Newton Partners Program— Similar to the Macintosh programs.

➤ Apple Multimedia Program—Some technical resources but also a high content of industry and marketing information about the multimedia industry (estimated cost: $300 per year).

All these programs feature a series of core services including such things as purchasing access to special development hardware, a Third-Party Compatibility Test Lab, a Developer Handbook, and an Orientation Kit. (Information about joining is available at the Developer Hotline 408-974-4897 or via e-mail: **devsupport@applelink.apple.com**.)

Apple also supports its developers via two networks: an access-controlled internal network (AppleLink) and a more public network, Eworld.

Internet Access to Apple Resources

Apple maintains the Web server and the FTP site at the addresses listed above. Access is free. Although you can't get a duplicate of everything in the service programs, you can get a lot. Here's a partial list:

➤ Complete text of two Apple publications—*Apple Directions* and "develop" (*The Apple Technical Journal*).

➤ Technical documentation—Complete text of technical books, Macintosh technical notes, Macintosh developer notes, technology overviews, ABS technical notes, numerous Apple standards (i.e., file formats and so on), and much more.

➤ Sample code—Complete sample code and applications including system software, utilities, and a Tool Chest. The Tool Chest contains language-specific development information and utilities. C++, Dylan, and LISP are covered.

➤ Many individual technical files and code files are actually stored on the FTP site, but you can see them in a more user-friendly manner (and also download them) from the Web site.

The Web site points to, although it does not actually contain, another FTP site that holds a list of Apple FAQs.

Online Services

Apple is heavily represented on America Online. In the computing area there is a subarea for Apple Forums for several aspects of Mac and Apple II support. At present those two areas are geared more towards applications. A separte area, the Developers Forum in the Mac OS area (keyword MOS), is specifically targeted at developers.

Features of the Development Forum on AOL include

➤ A FAQ list called the Mac Development Q&A (MDV Q&A). The FAQ has subareas on getting started in Macintosh programming, programming books, the Apple support features, and other documentation.

➤ A series of special-interest groups including game design, groupware, PDA-development, and AppleScript.

➤ A numner of libraries of code and information

➤ A messaging area

CompuServe activities focus on providing access to the Technical Information Library. A browser/searcher is provided. At present there is no messaging area.

Non-Apple Support

Two mechanisms that are not operated by Apple are worth noting.

There are numerous Internet newsgroups related to Apple. A quick browse on my newsreader turns up about 30 newsgroups under **comp.sys.mac.***, the **comp.binaries.***, and other groups.

A significant Apple users group on CompuServe operates several forums. The Micronetworked Apple Users Group (MAUG(R)) is operated by MCU Inc. This organization provides extensive information about using Apple computers and developing programs on them. This area provides a comprehensive messaging area.

IBM

With IBM's vast range of products and services, it is impractical to list here all the services available. Instead, this section lists items of interest.

This is a starter kit of sorts. Once you're familiar with IBM's Web search page, it becomes easy to look up numerous topics of interest.

The Web

The Web address is straightforward enough: **http://www.ibm.com**. Of the six menu selections on the Web home page, three are of specific interest:

➤ Products, Services, and Support—This selection leads you to a multipage tree structure of product areas.

➤ Technology and Research—This area covers technology updates and also carries an online version of IBM technical journals.

➤ Finding Your Way Around—This is a good search engine for locating anything in the IBM database.

Products and Services

In the products and services area, the following subset of the directory tree is related directly to programming:

* AS/400 Advanced Series Business Computing Systems
    + AS/400 software
        o Application development
        o Network communications
        o Operating system
*Large-scale computing systems
    + Large-scale computing software
        o Application development
* Personal computing systems
    + Personal computing software
        o Application development
        o Operating systems (OS/2 WARP)
* RS/6000 computing systems
    + RS/6000 software
        o AIX operating system
        o Other software

Finding Your Way Around

If you go into the search engine in this area and look up "library" you will locate, along with about 100 other entries, a path to the IBM Personal Computer File Library. (There is probably a more direct way to get there.) This is a large library of downloadable software in the general areas OS/2, DOS, networking, and miscellaneous.

Searching FTP Sites

Searching for "FTP sites" brings you to these useful entries:

➤ A list of IBM PC FTP sites

➤ An IBM PC Internet resource list

➤ A useful index of companies that have Web sites

Searching for Development Resources

A search for "development" brings you to lists of numerous services for developers, including the IBM Developers Connection. This includes subscription programs for CD-ROM and updates for tools and information.

Other Keywords

Other keywords or phrases that may provide topics of interest are "user groups," "OS/2," "DOS," and "RISC." I'm sure you get the idea.

Symantec

Symantec support centers on forums run on their own dial-in BBS, and on CompuServe and America Online. A Web server and FTP site provide limited promotional material and patches.

Hotkeys

➤ *America Online:* Go to Keyword SYMANTEC. Go to the Development Tools Forum.

➤ *CompuServe:* GO SEMANTEC and select the forum for Development Tools.

➤ *Direct Dial:* Company BBS at 503-484-6699 (2400 baud) or 503-484-6669 (9600 and 14,400 baud)

Services

The largest amount of information is available on America Online. Go into the support area, and you'll find subareas for all Symantec major products and one in particular for development tools.

Use separate menus to select Mac-based tools (Think and Thin C, C++ for MPW, Visual Architect, and Think Class Libraries) and PC-based tools (Zortech, Multiscope Debuggers, Optilink, C++ for DOS and Windows, and Symantec Enterprise Developer). Each area has both a series of libraries and message areas. The libraries contain info posted both by Symantec and by customers.

A similar structure applies on CompuServe. Entering GO SYMANTEC brings you to the main Symantec area. About 10 forums are listed—one for development tools and the others for application products and other information. Development tools consist of a message area and approximately 12 forums—one for each major tool product. The libraries, in essence, form a technical library, with not as many articles as Microsoft or Apple.

Messages can be exchanged with Symantec and its customers on technical support issues.

Symantec maintains a dial-in BBS that functions similarly to the CompuServe and America Online Forums.

The Web server (**http://www.symantec.com**) and FTP site (**ftp.symantec.com**) at this point do not have the full content of information that is available from online services. They appear to serve as distribution points for bug fixes and utilities. However, it is very likely that with time both will develop into a complete technical library.

The company also maintains two fax-on-demand lines:

➤ Technical tips and documents at 503-984-2490

➤ Marketing and product information at 800-544-4403

Watcom and Powersoft

Watcom's well-organized Web site at **http://www.watcom.com** provides fundamental information on its products and also links to the Web home pages of several related vendors.

At the top page are three very useful submenus on C/C++ Tools, VX-REXX, and FAQ.

The C/C++ tutorials area lists about a dozen tutorials online on C/C++ programming. Internet paths to each are given, but you can also directly download them from the Web home page. Many tutorials are also posted frequently to Internet newsgroups including **comp.lang.c**, **comp.lang.c++**, **news.answers**, and **comp.answers**.

The C/C++ tutorials area also lists many useful books and provides short reviews.

The tutorials area of the VX-REXX menu fulfills a similar role.

The FAQ lists many useful technical articles (all downloadable) about Watcom's products.

The Web home page lets you jump to FTP sites for both Watcom and Powersoft. Links are provided to Web or FTP sites of many other vendors including Sybase, Microsoft, IBM, and CD-ROM.

Vendor Directory

This is a mini-directory of several vendors who maintain services that are available via some form of Internet connection or a dial-in BBS.

All these vendors maintain contact points on either CompuServe or America Online, and often both.

New vendors come online every week, especially with the proliferation of Web home pages. One very good directory of companies on the Internet is available at the Web page maintained by IBM on **http://www.zurich.ibm.com**. From this site you can download a list of more than 1200 companies that have Web home pages. Both the companies and their URLs are given.

You may also be able to locate elusive sites by making educated guesses. Most vendors establish Internet names that contain some variant on their business name:

➤ Anonymous FTP site names often start with **ftp** followed by the vendor's name and **.com**—for example, **ftp.microsoft.com**. Occasionally you will find TELNET access the same way.

➤ World Wide Web addressing follows a similar method starting with **www**—for example, **http://www.intel.com/**.

➤ Besides just using their name directly, companies may use their initials—for example, Standard Microsystems Corporation's is **smc.com**.

Unfortunately finding some companies will be quite a bit harder— Quarterdeck Corporation uses **qdeck.com**. (You can't win 'em all!)

If all else fails, try calling the company directly and asking. (Not very high-tech, but it works.)

And, as incredible as it sounds, not everybody is even on the Internet yet.

American Cybernetics

Address: 1830 W. University Dr., Ste. 112, Tempe, AZ 85281

Main Phone: 602-968-1945

Fax Phone: 602-966-1654

Wats Phone: 800-899-0100

BBS Phone: 602-968-1082

Apple Computer Corp.

Address: 20525 Mariani Ave., Cupertino, CA 95014

Main Phone: 408-974-6952

Fax Phone: 408-974-6412

Wats Phone: 800-776-2333

E-mail Address: Internet: FTP: **ftp.info.apple.com;**
WWW: **http://www.apple.com**

Autodesk Inc.

Address: 2320 Marinship Way, Sausalito, CA 94965

Main Phone: 415-331-0356

Fax Phone: 415-331-8093

Wats Phone: 800-525-2763

BBS Phone: 415-289-2270

Borland International Inc.

Address: 100 Borland Way, Scotts Valley, CA 95066-3249

Main Phone: 408-438-8400

Fax Phone: 408-439-9262

Wats Phone: 800-331-0877

BBS Phone: 408-431-5096

E-mail Address: Internet: **customer-support@borland.com;**
CIS: **76703,3033**

Aleternate e-mail Address: Internet: FTP: **ftp.borland.com;**
WWW: **http://www.borland.com**

Clark Development Co., Inc.

Address: 3950 S. 700 East, Ste. 303, Salt Lake City, UT 84107-2173

Main Phone: 801-261-1686

Fax Phone: 801-261-8987

Wats Phone: 800-356-1686

BBS Phone: 801-261-8976

Clear Software Inc.

Address: 385 Elliot St., Newton, MA 02164

Main Phone: 617-965-6755

Fax Phone: 617-965-5310

Wats Phone: 800-338-1759

BBS Phone: 617-965-5406

Computer Associates International

Address: 711 Stewart Ave., Garden City, NY 11530

Main Phone: 516-227-3300

Fax Phone: 516-227-3937

Wats Phone: 800-645-3003

Alternate Info: CA-Clipper Technical Support

Alternate Phone: 310-348-4400

Alternate Fax: 310-348-4401

Creative Programming Consult.

Address: PO Box 112097, Carrollton, TX 75011-2097

Main Phone: 214-245-9139

Fax Phone: 214-245-9717

Wats Phone: 800-336-1166

BBS Phone: 214-245-9518

E-mail Address: Internet: **cpc@onramp.net**

Aleternate e-mail Address: WWW: **http://www.onramp.net/~cpc/home.mtml**

Crescent Software Inc.

Address: 11 Bailey Ave., Ridgefield, CT 06877

Main Phone: 203-438-5300

Fax Phone: 203-431-4626

Wats Phone: 800-352-2742

E-mail Address: CIS: **70662,2605**

Crystal Services Inc.

Address: 1050 W. Pender St., #2200, Vancouver, BC V6E 3S7 Canada

Main Phone: 604-681-3435

Fax Phone: 604-681-2934

Wats Phone: 800-663-1244

BBS Phone: 604-681-9516

Data Techniques Inc.

Address: 1000 Business Ctr. Dr., Ste. 120, Savannah, GA 31405

Main Phone: 912-651-8003

Fax Phone: 912-651-8021

Wats Phone: 800-955-8015

BBS Phone: 912-651-8015

DiagSoft Inc.

Address: 5615 Scotts Valley Dr., Ste. 140, Scotts Valley, CA 95066

Main Phone: 408-438-8247

Fax Phone: 408-438-7113

Wats Phone: 800-342-4763

BBS Phone: 408-438-8997

Digital Equipment Corp.

Address: 146 Main St., Maynard, MA 01754

Main Phone: 508-493-5111

Fax Phone: 508-493-8780

Wats Phone: 800-344-4825

BBS Phone: 800-234-1998

E-mail Address: Internet: WWW: **http://www.dec.com**

Distinct Corp.

Address: 14395 Saratoga Ave., Ste. 120, Saratoga, CA 95070

Main Phone: 408-741-0781

Fax Phone: 408-741-0795

E-mail Address: Internet: **mktg@distinct.com**

Frontier Technologies Corp.

Address: 10201 N. Port Washington Rd., Mequon, WI 53092

Main Phone: 414-241-4555

Fax Phone: 414-241-7084

BBS Phone: 414-241-7083

E-mail Address: Internet: **info@FrontierTech.com;**
                         WWW: **http://www. frontiertech.com**

FTP Software Inc.

Address: 2 High St., North Andover, MA 01845

Main Phone: 508-685-3300

Fax Phone: 508-794-4488

Wats Phone: 800-336-1166

E-mail Address: Internet: **info@ftp.com;** WWW: **http://www.ftp.com**

Genus Microprogramming Inc.

Address: 1155 Dairy Ashford, Ste. 200, Houston, TX 77079

Main Phone: 713-870-0737

Fax Phone: 713-870-0288

Wats Phone: 800-227-0918

BBS Phone: 713-870-0601

GPF Systems Inc.

Address: 30 Falls Rd., Moodus, CT 06469

Main Phone: 203-873-3300

Fax Phone: 203-873-3302

Wats Phone: 800-831-0017

BBS Phone: 203-873-3304

Greenleaf Software Inc.

Address: 16479 Dallas Pkwy., Ste. 570, Dallas, TX 75248

Main Phone: 214-248-2561

Fax Phone: 214-248-7830

Wats Phone: 800-523-9830

BBS Phone: 214-250-3778

Greenview Data Inc.

Address: PO Box 1586, Ann Arbor, MI 48106

Main Phone: 313-996-1300

Fax Phone: 313-996-1308

Wats Phone: 800-458-3348

BBS Phone: 313-996-1304

E-mail Address: CIS: **71333,3656**

Hewlett-Packard

Address: 19310 Pruneridge Ave., Cupertino, CA 95014

Main Phone: 208-323-2551

Wats Phone: 800-752-0900

BBS Phone: 408-553-3500

E-mail Address: Internet: WWW: **http://www.hp.com**

Hummingbird Communications Ltd.

Address: 2900 John St., Unit 4, Markham, Ontario L3R 5G3 Canada

Main Phone: 905-470-1203

Fax Phone: 905-470-1207

E-mail Address: Internet: **sales@hcl.com**; WWW: **http://www.hcl.com**

IBM Corp.

Address: Old Orchard Rd., Armonk, NY 10605

Main Phone: 301-564-2000

Wats Phone: 800-426-2468

BBS Phone: 404-835-6600

E-mail Address: Internet: WWW: **http://www.ibm.com**

Intel Corp.

Address: 5200 N.E. Elam Young Pkwy., Hillsboro, OR 97124-6497

Main Phone: 503-629-7354

Fax Phone: 503-629-7227

Wats Phone: 800-538-3373

BBS Phone: 503-645-6275

E-mail Address: Internet: FTP: **ftp.intel.com**; WWW: **http:/www.intel.com**

Knowledge Dynamics Corp.

Address: PO Box 780068, San Antonio, TX 78278

Main Phone: 210-979-9424

Fax Phone: 210-979-9004

Wats Phone: 800-331-2783

BBS Phone: 210-979-8837

E-mail Address: CIS: **76416,3214**

LEAD Technologies Inc.

Address: 8701 Mallard Creek Rd., Charlotte, NC 28262

Main Phone: 704-549-5532

Fax Phone: 704-548-8161

Wats Phone: 800-637-4699

BBS Phone: 704-549-9045

Liant Software Corp.

Address: 959 Concord St., Framingham, MA 01701-4613

Main Phone: 508-872-8700

Fax Phone: 508-626-2221

Wats Phone: 800-237-1873

BBS Phone: 206-236-6485

E-mail Address: Internet: **sales@lpi.liant.com**

Lifeboat Publishing

Address: 1163 Shrewsbury Ave., Shrewsbury, NJ 07702

Main Phone: 908-389-0037

Fax Phone: 908-389-9227

Wats Phone: 800-447-1955

BBS Phone: 908-389-9783

Metagraphics Software Corp.

Address: 269 Mount Hermon Rd., Box 66779, Scotts Valley, CA 95066

Main Phone: 408-438-1550

Fax Phone: 408-438-5379

Wats Phone: 800-332-1550

BBS Phone: 408-438-5368

Microsoft Corp.

Address: One Microsoft Way, Redmond, WA 98052-6399

Main Phone: 206-882-8080

Fax Phone: 206-883-8101

Wats Phone: 800-541-1261

BBS Phone: 206-637-9009

E-mail Address: Internet: FTP: **ftp.microsoft.com**

Novell Inc.

Address: 122 E. 1700 South, Provo, UT 84606-6194

Main Phone: 801-429-7000

Fax Phone: 801-377-6742

Wats Phone: 800-453-1267

BBS Phone: 801-429-3030

E-mail Address: Internet: **gopher.novell.com;**
WWW: **http://www.novell.com**

Alternate e-mail Address: Internet: FTP: **ftp.novel.com**

Opt-Tech Data Processing

Address: PO Box 678, Zephyr Cove, NV 89448

Main Phone: 702-588-3737

Fax Phone: 702-588-7576

BBS Phone: 702-588-1076

PKware Inc.

Address: 9025 N. Deerwood Dr., Brown Deer, WI 53223-2437

Main Phone: 414-354-8699

Fax Phone: 414-354-8559

BBS Phone: 414-354-8670

E-mail Address: CIS: **75300,730;**
Internet: **PKWARE.Inc@mixcom.com**

Pocket Soft Inc.

Address: 7676 Hillmont St., Ste. 195, Houston, TX 77040

Main Phone: 713-460-5600

Fax Phone: 713-460-2651

Wats Phone: 800-826-8086

Powersoft Corp.

Address: 561 Virginia Rd., Concord, MA 01742

Main Phone: 508-287-1500

Fax Phone: 508-369-3997

Wats Phone: 800-937-7693

Qualitas Inc.

Address: 7101 Wisconsin Ave., Ste. 1386, Bethesda, MD 20814

Main Phone: 301-907-6700

Fax Phone: 301-907-0905

Wats Phone: 800-733-1377

BBS Phone: 301-907-8030

Quarterdeck Office Systems

Address: 150 W. Pico Blvd., Santa Monica, CA 90405

Main Phone: 310-314-3222

Fax Phone: 310-314-4217

Wats Phone: 800-354-3222

BBS Phone: 310-314-3227

E-mail Address: Internet: WWW: **http://www.qdeck.com**

SemWare Corp.

Address: 4343 Shallowford Rd., Ste. C3A, Marietta, GA 30062-5022

Main Phone: 404-641-9002

Fax Phone: 404-640-6213

BBS Phone: 404-641-8968

E-mail Address: CIS: **75300,2710**

Sequiter Software Inc.

Address: 9644-54th Ave., Ste. 209, Edmonton, Alberta T6E 5V1 Canada

Main Phone: 403-437-2410

Fax Phone: 403-436-2999

BBS Phone: 403-437-2229

E-mail Address: CIS: **71321,1306**

Sun Microsystems Inc.

Address: 2550 Garcia Ave., Mountain View, CA 94043

Main Phone: 415-960-1300

Fax Phone: 415-856-2114

Wats Phone: 800-786-0404

E-mail Address: Internet: WWW: **http://www.sun.com**

Symantec Corp.

Address: 10201 Torre Ave., Cupertino, CA 95014

Main Phone: 408-253-9600

Fax Phone: 408-253-4092

Wats Phone: 800-441-7234

BBS Phone: 408-973-8598

E-mail Address: Internet: WWW: **http://www.symantec.com**

TeraTech Inc.

Address: 100 Park Ave., Ste. 360, Rockville, MD 20850

Main Phone: 301-424-3903

Fax Phone: 301-762-8185

Wats Phone: 800-447-9120

BBS Phone: 301-762-8184

Watcom International Corp.

Address: 415 Phillip St., Waterloo, Ontario N2L 3X2 Canada

Main Phone: 519-886-3700

Fax Phone: 519-747-4971

Wats Phone: 800-265-4555

BBS Phone: 519-884-2103

E-mail Address: Internet: **tech@watcom.on.ca**

Zinc Software Inc.

Address: 405 S. 100 East, Ste. 201, Pleasant Grove, UT 84062

Main Phone: 801-785-8900

Fax Phone: 801-785-8996

Wats Phone: 800-638-8665

BBS Phone: 801-785-8997

E-mail Address: Internet: **info@zinc.com**; WWW: **http://www.zinc.com**

CHAPTER FIVE

USER GROUPS

User groups have been around as long as there have been users. From the very beginning they served as a point of communication for all levels of computer users as well as vendors. A significant portion of the user community consists of programmers. Services available compare to the wide range of libraries and message centers available on the major online services. User groups go a step further by offering many live educational activites in their geographic area.

The majority of user groups started out as local bulletin board systems. Over a decade many have taken on national dimensions, either by themselves or with other user groups.

The thousands of user groups in the United States run the gamut from general purpose to specific focus. Some larger groups offer support for a wide range of computer types and interests. On the other hand, groups formed to address fairly specific topics or technologies, like OS/2 user groups, have popped up like mushrooms.

This chapter first discusses methods for locating user groups. Then it samples some of the more well known groups.

Finding User Groups

The age-old advice, "keep you eyes and ears open," is an effective way to find user groups in your area. If you're in a major computer store ask at the service desk. You may find notices posted there also. Ask at work or on your company bulletin board.

Fortunately, there are more organized alternatives to the Sherlock Holmes approach.

➤ *Computer Shopper* magazine compiles a list of user groups, drawing on the groups that submit their names and relevant information for publication. The list is updated monthly and published on CompuServe in the COMPSHOPPER Forum. Its filename is use.zip and it decompresses to about 100 Kbytes.

➤ The Association of Personal Computer User Groups (APCUG) provides some user group services. A primary service is an automated dial-in directory of user groups: You punch in area codes you're interested in and hear a recording of contact information for groups in that area. The telephone number is 914-876-6678. The association also sells a maillist of user group addresses listing key contacts. You can reach APCUG by sending e-mail to Marilyn Henry [**73147,1170**] or **MCI:apcug**, or writing to APCUG, Ste. 700, 1730 M St. N.W., Washington, DC 20036.

➤ IBM maintains a list of OS/2 user groups on their World Wide Web server. You can access their list by going to the Finding Your Way Around menu of the home page (**http://www.ibm.com**) and searching for "user groups."

➤ America Online has areas for approximately six major user groups. On AOL, go into the COMPUTING AREA of the main menu, and select "user groups." Additionally, AOL maintains a database of about 400 user groups and provides a search engine based on location and interest keywords.

A number of Internet newsgroups serve as user groups or help locate user groups. A quick scan of the list of current newsgroups identifies these:

COMP.ORG.DECUS   DIGITAL EQUIPMENT COMPUTER
                                        USERS' SOCIETY NEWSGROUP

COMP.ORG.LISP-USERS	ASSOCIATION OF LISP USERS RELATED DISCUSSIONS
COMP.ORG.SUG	TALK ABOUT/FOR THE SUN USERS' GROUP
COMP.OS.PARIX	FORUM FOR USERS OF THE PARALLEL OPERATING SYSTEM PARIX
COMP.STD.LISP	USER GROUP (ALU) SUPPORTED STANDARDS (MODERATED)
COMP.SYS.ACORN.ANNOUNCE	ANNOUNCEMENTS FOR ACORN AND ARM USERS (MODERATED)
COMP.SYS.APPLE2.USERGROUPS	ALL ABOUT APPLE II USER GROUPS
COMP.SYS.MAC.ANNOUNCE	IMPORTANT NOTICES FOR MACINTOSH USERS (MODERATED)
COMP.OS.LINUX.MISC	LINUX-SPECIFIC TOPICS NOT COVERED BY OTHER GROUPS
COMP.SYS.AMIGA.INTRODUCTION	GROUP FOR NEWCOMERS TO AMIGAS
COMP.UNIX.QUESTIONS	UNIX NEOPHYTES GROUP

The following pages cover some groups that are notable because of their membership size, range of services, or accessibility. No judgment is made about their quality or the quality of groups not covered.

Boston Computer Society

The Boston Computer Society (BCS) is one of the oldest, largest, and most well respected organizations of computer users. With approximately 24,000 members, the BCS provides special activities for many different computer or computer-related interests. The group is also open to creating new activitity groups as interest arises.

It is not unusual for BCS to sponsor 100 actvities a month. Most BCS meetings and seminars are held in the Boston and Greater New England area, but there are a growing number of local BCS chapters around the country.

The BCS implements a number of bulletin board services in the Boston area and also maintains a forum on America Online. Individual

Table 5.1 **Boston Computer** **Society Bulletin** **Boards**	BCS Information Center	617-290-5726
	BCS Atari	617-567-8642
	BCS Commodore/Amiga	617-729-7340
	BCS Computer-Aided Pub	617-864-3375
	BCS Construction	617-290-5726
	BCS IBM (members)	617-466-8740
	BCS IBM (non-members)	617-466-8730
	BCS IBM/Merrimack Valley	508-682-6263
	BCS NeXT	617-864-3375
	BCS New Media	617-729-7340
	BCS Texas Instruments	617-331-4181
	BCS ZI-TEL (CPM/MS-DOS)	617-965-7046
	BCS Macintosh	617-864-3375
	BCS Networking	617-290-5726

BCS members or activists also can be reached on their bulletin boards via Internet e-mail (address = **firstname.lastname@bcsinfo.bcs.org**).

A programming-related subset of BBSs supported by BCS is shown in Table 5.1. The Information Center line is a good place to start. They also have a voice line at 617-290-5700.

Note that many BBSs are open only to members. The Info Center and the IBM BBSs are available to the public, after a sign-up process. Becoming a member costs about $50 per year and gives you access to all BBSs.

It's worth taking a look at the contents of some individual BBSs.

The IBM Board

Figure 5.1 shows the top menu of the IBM users' group board. Besides general housekeeping, two main areas of interest are the (M)essage area and the (F)iles area.

The files area covers numerous subjects, but of particluar interest is the programming area, which includes two journal archives. Here's the complete topics list.

Figure 5.1
Top menu of BCS
IBM board.

```
============================================================
The BCS Programming Language Area

    File area #1 ...   WINDOWS Development Files Area

    File area #2 ...   C User Journal Source Code Listings!

    File area #3 ...   Windows/DOS Developer's Source Code!

    File area #4 ...   "C" Language Utilities Area

    File area #5 ...   "C" Language Compilers Area

    File area #6 ...   Pascal Language Utilities Area

    File area #7 ...   BASIC Language Utilities Area

    File area #8 ...   Assembly Language Utilities Area

    File area #9 ...   COBOL Language Utilities Area

    File area #10 ... Miscellaneous Utilities Area

    File area #11 ... NEW Programming Files

============================================================
```

The messages area contains very active discussion areas for all board topics, including the programming topics.

BCS on America Online

BCS maintains a forum in the computing area on America Online. Go into the user groups area and click the button for user group contacts. The material here is not quite as extensive as that of the BCS BBS, but still it offers a lot, including message areas and a software library.

Micronetworked Apple Users Group (MAUG)

MAUG, a complete users group, runs as a subsystem on CompuServe instead of a stand-alone bulletin board. With a truly national and even worldwide membership, it differs from dial-in systems whose memberships tend to be fairly local. This means, for example, that hundreds of programmmers may be logged onto the developers area at once.

On CompuServe, use GO MAC to go to the Macintosh/Apple area. This brings up several choices including some MAUG features:

1 Visit the MAUG Forums

2 The MAUG Newsletter

3 MAUG Spotlight File of the Month

4 Vendor Support Forums

5 FileFinder

6 Apple News Clips

7 ZiffNet/MacUser/ZMAC Forums

8 Macintosh User Survey

Only items 1 through 3 are associated with MAUG. The Newsletter and Spotlight File are rather self-explanatory and useful. When you go into the MAUG forums (choice 1) you can enter either a Macintosh/Newton or an Apple II area. Both have numerous features on applications, tips, and news, but most important (to this book, anyhow) is that they both have specific areas for program developers. The Mac developers area (also reachable via GO MACDEV) contains:

Mac Developers Forum+Libraries Menu

1 Forum Business/Help

2 BASIC

3 Assembly Language

4 C and Pascal

5 Object Oriented

6 Other Languages

7 Apple System Tools

8 Apple System Files

9 Dev. Environments

10 Scripting Month

11 Learn Programming

12 A/UX

13 Tools/Debuggers

14 MacTech Magazine

15 Metrowerks

These libraries contain a very comprehensive set of files on all topics listed. Additionally, the messaging area is very active.

The Apple II area has a similar structure, with appropriately modified library topics:

```
Apple II Programmer Forum+

1 Forum Business/Help

2 S'ware from Apple

3 BASIC Tools

4 Pascal and C Tools

5 Machine Lang. Tools

6 Other Lang. Tools

7 GS Toolbox Tools

8 Hardware Helps

9 HyperStudio

10 Sound/Music

11 HyperCard GS
```

MAUG is a registered trademark of MCU Inc. Besides accessing the forums on CompuServe, you can reach them at

U.S. Mail: MCU Inc., PO Box 520, Bethpage, NY 11714

CompuServe Mail: **76703,401**

Berkeley Mac Users Group (BMUG)

BMUG is a non-profit membership group with over 12,000 Macintosh users in more than 50 countries. BMUG began as a small group in 1984, shortly after the introduction of the Macintosh. BMUG accepts no advertisements or support from any for-profit companies and has no affiliation with Apple.

Features and Services

BMUG offers numerous features and services including

➤ A newsletter—400 pages, published twice a year.

➤ Bulletin boards—The Planet BMUG and SouthBay Planet BBSs in the San Franciso area and the BMUG Boston BBS provide many messaging areas and software libraries. Message activities on many forums are cross-linked to all three BBSs.

➤ Technical help line—Advice and support for almost any hardware or software problem.

➤ Software libraries—Approximately four hundred 800 Kbyte discs are online and may be ordered via CD-ROM.

➤ Meetings—BMUG holds a weekly Mac meeting and frequent (almost daily) meetings on various topics.

➤ You can dial into the BBSs; initial enrollment is free. Use the name newuser when you're prompted for an ID. Once you're in, you'll find both message areas and about a dozen or so file areas. The file area for program development has the following submenus:

```
1 Scripting Files

2 Languages and Updates

3 Apple Technical Notes

4 Source Code

5 Developer's Tools
```

Contacting BMUG

You can contact BMUG by several methods.

Electronic Address: Internet: **bmuginfo@bmug.org**
America Online: BMUG or BMUG1
Eworld: BMUG or BMUG1
AppleLink: UG0001
CompuServe: **73237,501**
Prodigy: HCHT96B
The WELL: **bmug**

Telephone: Announcement Line: 510-549-2684 Ext. 8
Business Office: 510-549-2684
Fax: 510-849-9026
Planet BMUG (BBS): 510-849-2684

Telephone (continued): BMUG Boston (BBS): 617-356-6336
SouthBay Planet (BBS): 408-777-1720

By Mail: BMUG Inc., 1442A Walnut St., #62, Berkeley, CA 94709-1496

Membership

BMUG offers a variety of membership plans for individuals, families, organizations, and businesses. Fees range from about $30 for a six-month individual membership to several thousand dollars for a corporate yearly membership.

CHAPTER SIX

PUBLICATIONS

Computer-related magazines can be a great resource for programmers. They cover a wide range of subject matter in news, product reviews, code examples, technical tips, and much more. Computer magazines lead the periodicals industry in establishing an online presence. This participation has increased the benefits these magazines provide: code is downloadable, databases can be searched for subjects, and the writing staff is often accessible.

Presently magazines are available online in several forms, each with strengths and features:

➤ Forums on online data services let you contact the writing staff and often offer libraries of useful or related code and selected reprints.

➤ Computer databases contain the text of articles and sometimes entire issues. These typically have a search engine that works on one or many magazines. These services are offered on a fee basis.

➤ Internet archive sites established by a number of magazines provide whole issues, selected articles, or code examples. Although these have no search engine, access is inexpensive.

This chapter gives several examples of some of the more interesting and more accessible magazine resource sites.

Computer- and Programming-related Magazine Forums on CompuServe

Computer magazines are available at these CompuServe forums:

AI EXPERT Forum	AIEXPERT
Dr. Dobb's Journal Forum	DDJFORUM
Computer Life	LIFE
DBMS Magazine Forum	DBMSFORUM
Data-Based Advisor Forum	DBADVISOR
Electronic Gamer™	EGAMER
Internet World Forum	IWORLD
LAN Magazine Forum	LANMAG
NetGuide Magazine	NETGUIDE
PC Computing	PCCOMP
PC MagNet	PCMAGNET
PC Plus/PC Answers	PCPLUS
PC World Online Forum	PWOFORUM
Windows Magazine Forum	WINMAG
Windows Sources Forum	WINSOURCES
Ziff Computer Shopper Forum	COMPSHOPPER

Computer- and Programming-related Magazines Archived on ZIFFNET

ZIFFNET maintains a computer-publications database of over 200 magazines; many have full-text articles going back to the mid-1980s. You can access ZIFFNET from either CompuServe or Prodigy. Then use the database Computer DataBase Plus. There is a surcharge.

The following list is a subset of the magazines archived in the database. An asterisk follows the names of full-text publications. There may be gaps in the dates of coverage.

AI Expert (1989–present)*

Aldus Magazine (1990–present)

AT&T Technical Journal (1987–1993; ceased abstracting)

Byte

C Users Journal (1991–1994; became *C/C++ Users Journal*)*

Communications News*

CommunicationsWeek (1988–present)

Computer

Computer Gaming World (1994–present)*

Computer Graphics World*

Computer Security Journal (1988–present)

Computer Shopper (1991–present)*

Computer Weekly*

Computerworld

Data Communications

Database Programming & Design (1991–present)*

Data-Based Advisor (1989–present)*

Datamation*

DBMS*

DEC Professional*

Digital Systems Journal (1992–; formerly *VAX Professional*)*

Dr. Dobb's Journal (1989–present; formerly *Dr. Dobb's Journal of Software Tools* and *Dr. Dobb's Journal of Software Tools for the Professional Programmer*)*

EDN*

Hewlett-Packard Journal*

Home Office Computing (1990–present)*

HP Professional (1991–present)*

IBM Journal of Research and Development

IBM System User (1989–present)*

IEEE Computer Graphics and Applications

IEEE Software

IEEE Spectrum

IEEE Transactions on Computers

IEEE Transactions on Software Engineering

Journal of Object-Oriented Programming (1989–present)

Journal of Systems and Software, The

LAN Computing (1991–present)*

LAN Magazine (1989–present)*

LAN Times (1989–present)*

MacUser*

MacWEEK (1988–present)*

Macworld

Microsoft Systems Journal (1988–present)*

Multimedia World (1994–present)

NetWare Technical Journal (1989–1990, 1993–; publication temporarily suspended)

Network Computing (1994–present)

Network World (1988–present)

Newsbytes (1989–present)*

Open Computing (1994–; formerly *UNIX World*)

OS/2 Professional (1993–present)

PC-Computing (1988–present)*

PC Laptop Computers Magazine (1994–present)

*PC Magazine**

PC User (1989–present)*

*PC Week**

*PC World**

Software Development (1994–present)

Software Magazine (1988–; formerly *Software News*)*

Software News (1987; now *Software Magazine*)

*UNIX Review**

Visual BASIC Programmers Journal (1994–present)

Windows Magazine (1993–present)

Windows Sources (1993–present)*

Windows Tech Journal (1994–present)

Windows-DOS Developer's Journal (1991–present; formerly *TECH Specialist*)

Computer- and Programming-related Publications with Forums on America Online

The computing and software area on America Online has a publications and reference area that covers both magazines, newsletters, and radio/TV-related sources. This section covers only the magazines and newsletters.

Magazines with Forums on America Online

Some major computer-related magazines with forums on America Online are:

Connect Magazine

Family PC Magazine

Home Office Computing

HomePC Magazine

Inside Technology

Mac Shareware 500

MacHome Journal

Macintosh Bible

MacTech Magazine

Macworld Magazine

Mobile Office Computing

Multimedia World

PC World

Windows Magazine

Windows Shareware 500

Wired Magazine

WordPerfect Magazine

Newsletters Available on America Online

America Online also has a number of computer-related newsletters online. These are all in the Hardware Forum of Computing Area.

Bits and Bytes Online—A magazine focusing on corporate America.

Computer Underground Digest—An forum for sharing information among computer enthusiasts, including the presentation and debate of diverse views.

Computing Connection—A computing and software magazine published by the staff of AOL.

The Hack Report—A monthly release covering pirated, hacked, or otherwise dangerous programs on the shareware market.

Novell Digest—Discusses Novell Netware and related products.

RAndY's RumOR RaG—Rumors and gossip about the hardware and software of the computer industry.

Sound Blaster Digest—Reviews, informative text, and other features about Creative Labs' Sound Blaster music card. Includes program examples, sound samples, songs, etc.

Virus-L—A mail forum for discussing computer virus issues.

Z*NET PC—News of the PC and related communities.

Magazines Archived on the Internet

This rather cryptic list is from an FTP site on the Internet where selected magazines are archived. This site focuses more on code examples than articles. You can access the site via anonymous FTP to **ftp.uu.net/published**.

```
byte

cybernews

db-prog-design

dbms

dr-dobbs

open-systems-today

pc-tech

pc-techniques

UNIX-review

UNIX-today

UNIX-world

windowsdos
```

These magazines are archived at **efn.org/pub**:

VB Tech Journal
Windows Tech Magazine

Miscellaneous Magazine Contacts

Several miscellaneous magazines are also online.

BBS Magazine

Publisher: Callers Digest

Internet—info: **info@bbscd.com**

Boardwatch Magazine

Publisher: Boardwatch Magazine

Internet mail subscriptions: **subscriptions@boardwatch.com**

BBS: 303-973-422

Internet Web Page: **http://www.boardwatch.com**

BYTE Magazine

Publisher: McGraw-Hill

Internet Anonymous FTP: **ftp.uu.net /published/byte**

BIX BBS, TELNET: **x.25.bix.com**

BBS: 603-24-9820

C/C++ Users Journal

Publisher: R&D Publications Inc.

CompuServe Forum: go SDFORUM, Library 7

Internet Anonymous FTP: **ftp.uu.net**

C++ Report

Publisher: SIGS Publications Inc.

Internet: **stan@fa.disney.com** to contact the editor

Dr. Dobb's Journal

Publisher: Miller Freeman Inc.

CompuServe Forum: go DDJ

Internet Anonymous FTP: **ftp.mv.com /pub/ddj**

DOS World

Publisher: Business Computing Publishers

BBS: 603-924-3181

CompuServe Mail: **75300,2361**

DV-Digital Video Magazine

Publisher: TechMedia Publishing Inc.

Internet Mail: **subs@dv.com**

Internet World

Publisher: Meckler Media Corporation

Internet Mail: **meckler@jvnc.net**

CompuServe Mail: **70373,616**

LINUX Journal

Publisher: SSC

Internet Mail: **subs@ssc.com**

NetGuide Magazine

Publisher: CMP Publications

Internet Web Page: **http://techweb.cmp.com/win/current**

Online Access

Publisher: Chicago Fine Print Inc.

CompuServe Mail: **74514,3363**

America Online: READOA

Prodigy: THK14PC

Internet Mail, Request Files: **file.name@oamag.com**

BBS: 404-924-3665

Open Computing

Publisher: McGraw-Hill

Internet Mail: **circ@uworld.com**

PC Graphics & Video

Publisher: Advanstar Communications

CompuServe: **73312,1142**

America Online: JVEDITOR

Software Development Magazine

Publisher: Miller Freeman Inc.

CompuServe Forum: go SDFORUM

CompuServe Mail: **71572,341**

VB Tech Journal

Publisher: Oakley Publishing

Internet Anonymous FTP: **efn.org/pub/VBTech**

Visual BASIC Programmers Journal

Publisher: Fawcette Technical Publications

MCI Mail: JFawcette

VR World

Publisher: MecklerMedia Corporation

Internet Mail: **meckler@jvnc.net**

CompuServe Mail: **70373,616**

Windows Magazine

Publisher: CMP Publications

Internet Web Page: **http://techweb.cmp.com/win/current**

Windows/DOS Developers Journal

Publisher: R&D Publications Inc.

CompuServe Forum: go SDFORUM, Library 7

Internet Anonymous FTP: **ftp.uu.net**

CHAPTER SEVEN

PROGRAMMING LANGUAGES

Assembler

Although some form of assembly language tool set exists for every computing platform, the largest number available online deal with PC platforms—in particular, the products from Microsoft (MASM) and Borland (Turbo ASM, or TASM).

Vendor Support Sites

Several hardware or software vendors maintain FTP or WWW sites with information on assembly programming. This section lists the more prominent ones.

Intel

Use anonymous FTP to **ftp.intel.com**. Go to the subdirectories for Intel386, Intel486, and Pentium.

Microsoft

Use anonymous FTP to **ftp.microsoft.com/developr/masm** (also reachable via the WWW at **http://www.microsoft.com**). This site contains an assembler-centric subset of the Microsoft Knowledge Base and an area for unsupported tools.

Borland

Use anonymous FTP to **ftp.borland.com/pub/techinfo/techdocs/language/turboasm** (also reachable via the WWW at **http://www.borland.com**). This site holds several hundred useful articles and code samples.

Shareware and Freeware Tools and Libraries

The following shareware libraries are available at the SimTel anonymous FTP site and its mirrors (**SimTel/msdos/asmutil**). (In fact, you probably can find these libraries at other repositories.)

➤ A86 is Eric Isaacson's shareware x86 assembler that supports up to the 286 instruction set. Besides the assembler (filename a86vV372.zip), a debugger (d86v372.zip) and a tool to convert MASM to A86 (a86cnvrt.zip) are available.

➤ ASMLIB PROGRAMMER'S TOOLKIT (asmlibB37.zip), by Douglas Herr, contains 450 medium-model subroutines and an editor.

➤ THE ASSEMBLY WIZARD'S LIBRARY (asmwiz16.zip), by Thomas Hanlin.

➤ UCR Standard Library for Assembly Language Programmers, by Randall Hyde and others (includes sources).

➤ ALIB, by Jeff Ownens (includes sources).

Internet Maillists

The maillist TopSoft provides information on programming in assembler and related topics.

Contact: **ts-request@atlas.chem.utah.edu** (Tony Jacobs)

Description: Freeware from the Macintosh Programming Users Group

BITNET ListServer Maillists

To subscribe to a maillist, send a mail message to **listserv@bitnic.bitnet**. Leave the *Subject:* field blank. In the body of the message, write: **SUBSCRIBE listname**, where listname is a name in the first column of the following list.

```
ASSEMBLER-LIST 370      Assembly Programming Discussion List

ASSMPC                  Assembly for the IBM PC

TASM-L                  Borland Turbo Assembler and Debugger
                        List
```

Newsgroups

```
comp.lang.asm.x86           General 80x86 assembly
                            language programming

comp.os.os2.programmer.tools  OS/2 compilers, assemblers,
                            and interpreters
```

Online Data Services

A number of resources are available from the major commercial online data service providers.

CompuServe Forums

```
Borland C++/DOS Forum       BCPPDOS

Micro Focus Forum           MICROFOCUS

MS Language Forum           MSLANG

PC Programming Forum        PCPROG
```

America Online Forums

In the Development Forum (in the COMPUTING AREA) are software libraries; you can select choices [for either Assembly or Tutorials.]

BIX Conference

Go into the programming area and access the conference assembler, where there are numerous [topics on 80xxx, 68xxx, 65xx, and general assembler programming.]

Periodic Postings and FAQs

FAQs with an archive-name given are available on the anonymous FTP server **rtfm.mit.edu.**

Subject: **comp.lang.asm.x86** FAQ (*)

Newsgroups: **comp.lang.asm.x86, comp.lang.asm370,** [**comp.lang.basic.misc,** comp.answers, and news.answers]

From: **mikeaver@prairienet.org** (Michael J. Averbuch)

Archive-name: **assembly-language/x86-faq**

BASIC

BASIC is one of the most widely used languages—in part, because it was shipped along with the OS on many PCs. The language has evolved along many paths:

➤ Compiled and interpreted versions are available for a number of platforms.

➤ Visual versions have become very popular—for Windows and non-Windows environments—and are present in several applications (such as word processors and databases), providing a sort of macro-language for defining higher-level functions.

Newsgroups

Some online resources associated with BASIC cover anything called BASIC, others narrowly focus on one style, and still others are separated by platform. This section provides a road map to some of the key resource locators. (Note: There are a number of Internet newsgroups associated with BASIC implementations.)

The Visual styles of BASIC are covered in the following newsgroups:

comp.lang.basic.visual	Microsoft Visual BASIC & App BASIC for Windows and DOS
comp.lang.basic.visual	Third-party Add-ins for Visual BASIC
comp.lang.basic.visual.announce	Official information on Visual BASIC (moderated)
comp.lang.basic.visual.database	Database aspects of Visual BASIC
comp.lang.basic.visual.misc	Visual BASIC in general

To complicate matters, **comp.language.visual** is a newsgroup that has little to do with Visual BASIC. If you post a question there about Visual BASIC, you will promptly get back one or more messages asking that you refrain from doing so—at least I did.

Non-Visual styles of BASIC are addressed in two newsgroups: **alt.lang.basic** and **comp.lang.basic.misc**. Although these groups may pick up an occasional note about Visual BASIC, they deal primarily with other BASIC flavors and platforms. In fact, the most common topic is QuickBASIC on PCs, but you can find discussions on GW-BASIC, a few freeware compilers, and BASIC for other platforms (such as Atari, Macintosh, and UNIX).

FAQs

Visual BASIC newsgroups have a well-defined family of archived FAQs (including General FAQ, VB/DOS FAQ, VB/Win FAQ, VB/Win Commercial VBX List, and VB/Win Shareware VBX List) at **rtfm.mit.edu/pub/usenet/comp.lang.basic.visual/**. The non-Visual BASICs are FAQed in a less standard method—the exact WWW locator is **http://www.fys.ruu.nl/~bergman/basic.html**. (**http://www.fys.ruu.nl** is the home page for a German university; **~bergman**, a personal home page, serves as a toggle switch that enables you to select an English-language menu; and **basic.html** is a menu item.)

Resources for "Basic" BASIC

Several non-Visual BASIC programming tool sets and file archives are available.

Compilers and Interpreters

The WWW page at **http://www.fys.ruu.nl/~bergman/** provides information on a number of commercial products for several platforms. It also holds several shareware or freeware compilers:

Generic

Bywater BASIC 1.1 (filename bwb110s.zip)—The source code in ANSI C of a BASIC compiler

basic.p.Z.—A BASIC interpreter written in Pascal

MS-DOS

ASIC 4.00 (filename asic400.zip)

BASICBASIC (wbasic14.zip)

TSRBASIC

UBASIC

UNIX

basic.tar.Z.—A public domain version of DEC's MU-BASIC mixed with Microsoft BASIC

Macintosh

Chipmunk BASIC (filename chipmunk-basic-3.1.0-sit.hqx)—An interpreter for 68k Macs and PPC and accelerated for Power Macs

Commodore Amiga

ACE BASIC compiler—A freeware Amiga BASIC compiler that produces 68000 assembly source code. (A link is provided to an ACE home page for more information.)

Code Repositories

General	**oak.oakland.edu/SimTel/msdos/basic** and **Garbo.uwasa.fi/pc/programming**
QuickBASIC	**oak.oakland.edu/SimTel/msdos/qbasic** and **x2ftp.oulu.fi/pub/books/msdos/docs/winer.zip**
PowerBASIC	**south.pacific.net/pub/pc/dse** and **ftp.eskimo.com/future**

In addition, several places on CompuServe and America Online hold large stores of code and utilities.

Resources for Visual BASIC

Many Visual BASIC tools and files are available.

Tools

The largest supply of information is the Microsoft Knowledge Base, available at **ftp.microsoft.com**, Microsoft's anonymous FTP site.

Code Repositories

FTP Sites

ftp.cica.indiana.edu:/pub/pc/win3/programr/vbasic—A large source of Visual BASIC files, utilities, example programs, VBXs, and so forth.

ftp.microsoft.com—Some more useful directories are /Softlib/MSLFILES (which contains the Microsoft Knowledge Base), /MSDN/VBTECH, and /DEVTOOLS/LANG/VB/PUBLIC (which includes assorted VB files and updates).

VB-centric BBSs

The Centre Programmers Unit BBS (in Pennsylvania); telephone: 814-353-0566

Atlanta Visual BASIC BBS; telephone: 404-872-0311

Online Data Services

Both CompuServe and America Online have extensive code repositories and messaging areas.

Internet Maillists

MACPROG

Contact: **listserv@wuvmd.wustl.edu**

Description: Programming languages, Mac techniques

STOS

Contact: **ae-a@minster.york.ac.uk**

Description: Discussion of STOS BASIC for the Atari ST computer family

BITNET List Server Maillists

To subscribe to a maillist, send a mail message to **listserv@bitnic.bitnet**. Leave the *Subject:* field blank. In the body of the message, write: **SUBSCRIBE listname**, where listname is a name in the left column below.

```
VBDATA-L        Discussion for Microsoft Visual BASIC
                Data Access

VISBAS-L        Visual BASIC List
```

Online Data Services

BASIC programming is heavily supported on the major commercial online data services.

CompuServe Forums

Apple II Prog. Forum	APPROG
Atari ST Prod. Forum	ATARIPRO
CA Micro Germany Forum	CAMICRO
Commodore Applications Forum	CBMAPP
Mac Developers Forum	MACDEV
MS BASIC Forum	MSBASIC
MS CE Systems Forum	MSCESYSTEM
MS Central Europe Services	MSEURO
MS Central Forum	MSCE
MS Language Forum	MSLANG
MS Press(FREE)	MSP
MS Software Library	MSL
PC New User's Forum	PCNEW
PC Vendor B Forum	PCVENB
PC Vendor J Forum	PCVENJ
Texas Instruments Forum	TIFORUM
VBPJ Forum	VBPJFORUM
Windows Components B Forum	ADTC
Windows 3rd Party C Forum	WINAPC

America Online Forums

The computing area has numerous resources for BASIC programmers, including programming forums, software libraries, and messaging areas for BASIC or Visual BASIC under the Multimedia and Windows forums. Moreover, the Development Forum has a specific conference on Visual BASIC programming that includes a messaging area, a software library, and industry contacts. The Developer Forum is also the contact point for Programmer's University—a series of interactive courses for many languages, including BASIC.

BIX Conference

Go into the programming area and access the menu choice "7 o basic" (the BASIC conference).

C and C++

Although UNIX may be the most prevalent OS on Internet hosts, and although MS-DOS/Windows may be the dominant OS on desktops, the C family of languages is the common denominator across many OSs. C programmers ranging from beginning programmers to advanced hackers can find a large number of resources on all online media—that is, the Internet and online data services.

The best places to start a search for information are the Internet newsgroups and their associated FAQs. Some key FAQS are briefly described in this section. (Detail paths for all the FAQs are given at the end of this chapter.)

The LEARN C/C++ TODAY FAQ gives a lot of good introductory information about C, including its history. It also

➤ Lists the more commonly used C/C++ compilers for popular platforms and OSs (including UNIX, MS-DOS/Windows, Apple).

➤ Describes over a dozen tutorials and interactive teaching tools available on the Internet. For example, check out the following:

Title: Programming in C

Filename: CE.html
URL: **http://www.cm.cf.ac.uk/Dave/C/CE.html**

Title: TUTOR v3.10

Filename: CTUTORDE.zip
URL: **ftp://oak.oakland.edu/simtel/msdos/c/ctutorde.zip**

Title: C++ on the WWW

Filename: C++.html

URL: **http://uu-gna.mit.edu:8001/uu-gna/text/cc/index.html**

➤ Reviews about a dozen commercially available books on C and C++.

comp.lang.c FAQ addresses many commonly encountered questions, ranging from beginner to advanced. The frequently asked questions are sorted into approximately 17 topics, such as Arrays and Pointers, Memory Allocation, C Preprocessor, System Dependencies, and FORTRAN-to-C Converters.

The available C++ libraries FAQ describes publicly and commercially available C and C++ libraries. It also provides directions for accessing them.

Internet Maillists

Subscribe by sending mail to the contact shown and receive information about C and C++ programming.

c2man

Contact: **listserv@research.canon.oz.au**

Description: Discussion of c2man, which parses comments from C and C++ programs to develop manuals and information files.

Arjuna

Contact: **arjuna-request@mailbase.ac.uk**

Description: Discussion of Arjuna programming tools, used for constructing distributed applications in C++.

cwarrior

Contact: **listserv@netcom.com**

Description: Discussion of Metrowerks CodeWarrior Macintosh development tools. CodeWarrior includes C, C++, and Pascal compilers; a class library; and associated tools.

info-ccc

Contact: **uunet!xurilka!info-ccc-request** (Luigi Perrotta)

Description: The Concurrent C and Concurrent C++ programming languages.

TurboVision

Contact: **listserv@vtvm1.cc.vt.edu**

Description: TurboVision is a library that comes with Borland C++ and Pascal compilers. To enroll, send the message **subscribe turbvis your name**.

BITNET List Server Maillists

To subscribe to a maillist, send a mail message to **listserv@bitnic.bitnet**. Leave the *Subject:* field blank. In the body of the message, write: **SUBSCRIBE listname**, where listname is a name in the left column below.

```
COMPUT-L    Discussion of issues affecting academic
            computing on the OSU C+

TCPLUS-L    TURBO C++ discussion group
```

FTP Sites

Key FTP sites are **ftp.microsoft.com**, the Microsoft site (home of the Microsoft Knowledge Base), and **ftp.borland.com**, Borland's support site.

The indicated files at **ftp://usc.edu/pub/C-numanal/numcomp-free-c.gz** and **ftp://ftp.math.psu.edu/pub/FAQ/numcomp-free-c** provide a directory to other FTP and WWW sites containing numerical C and C++ libraries.

The official site for GNU Software is **prep.ai.mit.edu**. Other sites include:

wuarchive.wustl.edu:/systems/gnu

labrea.stanford.edu

ftp.digex.net:/pub/gnu

ftp.kpc.com:/pub/mirror/gnu

f.ms.uky.edu:/pub3/gnu

jaguar.utah.edu:/gnustuff

ftp.hawaii.edu:/mirrors/gnu

vixen.cso.uiuc.edu:/gnu

mrcnext.cso.uiuc.edu:/pub/gnu

ftp.cs.columbia.edu:/archives/gnu/prep

col.hp.com:/mirrors/gnu

gatekeeper.dec.com:/pub/gnu

ftp.uu.net:/systems/gnu

The following sites have a significant amount of C or C++ software or information:

ftp.clarkson.edu

ftp.css.cdc.com

ftp.fuw.edu.pl

ftp.ifi.unizh.ch

ftp.igd.fhg.de

ftp.irisa.fr

ftp.morningstar.com

ftp.netlib.org

ftp.umu.se

ftp.uni-erlangen.de

iamftp.unibe.ch

isgate.is

isy.liu.se

sics.se

sun.soe.clarkson.edu

vela.acs.oakland.eduwilbur.stanford.edu

Newsgroups

These permanent newsgroups are accessible via most network news-reader programs:

```
comp.lang.c              Discussion about C

comp.lang.c++            Discussion about C++

comp.std.c               Discussion about C language
                         standards

comp.std.c++             Discussion about C++ language
                         standards

comp.lang.objective-c    Discussion about the Objective-C
                         language
```

Online Data Services

C and C++ programming are supported on the major commercial online data service providers.

CompuServe Forums

```
BORLAND                          BORLAND

Borland C++ for Win/OS2 Forum    BCPPWIN

Borland C++/DOS Forum            BCPPDOS

CA Micro Germany Forum           CAMICRO

IBM Software Solutions Forum     SOFSOL

Macmillan Publishing Forum       MACMILLAN

MS CE Systems Forum              MSCESYSTEM

MS Central Europe Services       MSEURO

MS Language Forum                MSLANG

PC Programming Forum             PCPROG

PC Vendor E Forum                PCVENE

PC Vendor H Forum                PCVENH

PowerBuilder Forum               PBFORUM

Powersoft Forum                  PSFORUM

Powersoft Support                POWERSOFT

TopSpeed Corporation Forum       CLARION

UNIX Forum                       UNIXFORUM
```

```
Watcom Forum                        WATFORUM

Windows Components B Forum          ADTC
```

America Online Forums

The COMPUTING AREA on America Online has numerous resources for C and C++ programmers, including entries in the software libraries. Moreover, the Development Forum has a reference area for several C and C++ topics. The Developer Forum is also the contact point for Programmer's University—a series of interactive courses for many languages, including C and C++.

BIX Conference

In the programming area, access the conference o c.plus.plus.

Periodic Postings and FAQs

FAQs with an archive-name given are available on the anonymous FTP server **rtfm.mit.edu**.

Subject: FAQ for g++ and libg++, * version [Revised *]

Newsgroups: **gnu.g++.help**, **comp.lang.c++**, **news.answers**, and **comp.answers**

From: **jbuck@synopsys.com** (Joe Buck)

Comment: Two versions are being posted: plain text (plain) and texinfo (texi). Note: Archive-names (in parentheses) are in the g++-FAQ archive directory.

Archive-name: g++-FAQ/texi

Subject: C++ FAQ: posting #*/*

Newsgroup: **comp.lang.c++**

From: **cline@sun.soe.clarkson.edu** (Marshall Cline)

Summary: Please read before posting to **comp.lang.c++**.

Subject: Available C++ libraries FAQ

Newsgroups: **comp.lang.c++**, **comp.answers**, and **news.answers**

From: **nikki@trmphrst.demon.co.uk** (Nikki Locke)

Summary: Lists available C++ libraries—public domain and commercial

Archive-name: C++-faq/libraries
Comp-lang-c++-archive-name: C++-faq/libraries

Subject: Comp.Object FAQ Version * (*) Announcement

Newsgroups: **comp.lang.c++, comp.lang.eiffel, comp.lang.smalltalk, comp.lang.clos, comp.lang.ada, comp.databases.object, comp.lang.sather, comp.lang.misc, comp.software-eng, comp.sw.components, comp.lang.modula3, comp.lang.objective-c, comp.sys.next.programmer, comp.langoberon, comp.object.logic, comp.lang.scheme, comp.answers,** and **news.answers**

From: **rjh@geodesic.com** (Bob Hathaway)

Summary: Lists FAQ and available systems for object-oriented technology
Archive-name: **object-faq/announce**

Subject: LEARN C/C++ TODAY

Newsgroups: **comp.lang.c, comp.lang.c++, news.answers,** and **comp.answers**

From: **carpenterv@vms.csd.mu.edu** (V. S. Carpenter)

Summary: Lists tutorials/resources
Archive-name: **C-faq/learn-c-cpp-today**

Subject: Diffs to Index of free C or C++ source code for numerical computation

Newsgroups: **comp.lang.c, comp.lang.c++, sci.math.num-analysis, sci.comp-aided,** and **sci.op-research**
From: **ajayshah@cmie.ernet.in**

Subject: Part * of *: Free C, C++ for numerical computation

Newsgroups: comp.lang.c, comp.lang.c++, sci.math.num-analysis, sci.comp-aided, and sci.op-research

From: ajayshah@cmie.ernet.in

FORTRAN

This section centers on several incarnations of FORTRAN:

➤   FORTRAN 77—A FORTRAN standard. Also known as F77.

➤   FORTRAN 90—A newer superset of F77. Also known as F90.

➤   Versions of FORTRAN for use on massively parallel processors. High Performance FORTRAN (HPF), a language for programming massively parallel architectures, is a standard.

➤   C—Although C isn't a flavor of FORTRAN, many people are interested in converting FORTRAN programs to C or vice versa. Also, one of the primary suppliers of FORTRAN tools, NAG, uses C as an intermediate language.

Public Domain Compiler

BC-FORTRAN 1.3b is a FORTRAN 77 compiler for PCs; it is possibly the only freeware compiler available. A freeware student version exists—available via anonymous FTP to **ftp.uni-stuttgart.de/pub/systems/pc/lang/fortran/compiler/bcf77.zip**—but it is not to be used in any commercial environment. The instruction file is in German, but an English translation is available by request from doylecm@HYDRA.ROSE-HULMAN.EDU.

Source Code Editors, Checkers, and Reformatters

➤   FWEB is a tool for concurrently developing source code and documentation. It may be obtained from **ftp.sunet.se/pub/text-processing/TeX/web**.

➤   EMACS and xemacs modes for FORTRAN 90 may be obtained by anonymous FTP to **mailbase.ac.uk/pub/lists/comp-fortran-90/files/**.

➤ From its compiler (version 2.1), NAG has extracted a syntax verifier that supports Sun 3, Sun 4, Sgi, RS/6000, DECstation, Solaris, and Linux environments. To use this tool, which is implemented interactively over the WWW, connect to **http://www.nag.co.uk:70/0/Forms/f90_interface.html**.

➤ TOOLPACK is a large set of tools for code analysis and transformation. It is available by anonymous FTP to **perelandra.cms.udel.edu/pub/Lang/Toolpack/**.

➤ FORCHECK is a Windows-based FORTRAN checking tool. A demo version is available at **oak.oakland.edu/pub/msdos/fortran/fckdemo1.zip** and other SimTel mirrors.

FORTRAN 77-to-FORTRAN 90 Converters

Two tools available are CONVERT (via anonymous FTP to **jkr.cc.rl.ac.uk/pub/MandR/convert.f90**) and ftof90.c (via anonymous FTP to **ftp.ifremer.fr/pub/ifremer/fortran90/ftof90.c**).

FORTRAN-to-C Converter

f2c, which converts F77 code to C, is available as source code by anonymous FTP to **netlib.att.com/dist/f2c**. This tool was jointly developed by people from Bell Labs, Bellcore, and Carnegie Mellon University.

Tutorials, Help

Paths indicated are FTP or WWW sites.

```
ftp.mcc.ac.uk/pub/mantec/Fortran90
A FORTRAN 90 course
```

```
nsc.liu.se/pub/bibliotek/f77to90.txt
"FORTRAN 90 for the FORTRAN 77 programmer"
```

```
ftp://ftp.cs.unm.edu/pub/smith_quetzal/Fortran90_Tutorial/
A FORTRAN 90 tutorial
```

```
http://asis01.cern.ch/CN/CNTUT/f90/Overview.html
A FORTRAN 90 tutorial
```

```
http://www.fortran.com/fortran/u_gd.html
A programmer's guide to FORTRAN 90
```

```
http://www.fortran.com/fortran/free.html
List of free software
```

```
http://www.fortran.com/fortran/u_iso1539.html
FORTRAN 90 standard documentation

http://cui_www.unige.ch/OSG/Langlist/Free/free-toc.html
List of compilers/tools
```

Code Repositories

```
http://www.nag.co.uk:70/1h/nagware/Examples
NAG repository of contributed code

http://www.fortran.com/fortran/market.html
The FORTRAN Market ("One place to find all information,
products, and services related to FORTRAN")
```

Massively Parallel Development

Draft standards for HPF are available via anonymous FTP at several sites in multiple formats:

titan.cs.rice.edu/public/HPFF/draft/

think.com/public/HPFF/hpf-v10-final.ps.Z

ftp.gmd.de/hpf-europe/hpf-v10-final.ps.Z

theory.tc.cornell.edu/pub/hpf-v10-final.ps.Z

minerva.npac.syr.edu/public/hpf-v10-final.tar.Z

In addition, a review of products related to parallel systems programming is available via anonymous FTP to **bulldog.wes.army.mil/pub/report.ps.Z.**

Vendor Directory

Following are Internet contact points for several FORTRAN-related vendors:

```
Apogee Software Inc.
info@apogee.com

Applied Parallel Research Inc.
forge@netcom.com and
ftp://ftp.netcom.com/pub/forge/home.html

CRAY
http://www.cray.com/ and craysoft@cray.com
```

DEC
http://www.digital.com/info.html, and info@digital.com

Fujitsu Open Systems Solutions Inc.
info@ossi.com

Lahey Computer Systems Inc.
sales@lahey.com

NA Software Ltd.
f90doc@nasoftwr.demon.co.uk

NAG Inc.
infodesk@nag.com

NAG Users Association
nagua@nag.co.uk

Pacific-Sierra Research Corp.
info@psrv.com

ParaSoft Corp.
f90-info@parasoft.com

PGI
sales@pgroup.com

Quetzal Computational Associates
quetzal@aip.org

Unicomp Inc.
walt@fortran.com

Internet Maillists

The following maillists provide information on FORTRAN and related topics.

DISSPLA

Contact: **DISSPLA@taunivm.tau.ac.il**

Description: The DISSPLA (Display Integrated Software System and Plotting LAnguage) [high-level FORTRAN graphics subroutine library.]

[comp-fortran-90]

Contact: **mailbase@mailbase.ac.uk**

Description: Covers FORTRAN 90 and HPF. To enroll, send the message **join comp-fortran-90 firstname lastname**

MasPar

Contact: **mp-users-request@thunder.mcrcim.mcgill.edu** (Lee Iverson)

Description: Discussion of hardware/software issues regarding the MasPar MP-1 [parallel SIMD machines (programmable in FORTRAN).]

BITNET List Server Maillists

To subscribe to a maillist, send a mail message to **listserv@bitnic.bitnet**. Leave the *Subject:* field blank. In the body of the message, write: **SUBSCRIBE listname**, where listname is a name in the left column below.

```
PFUG-L      Parallel FORTRAN Users' Group newsletter

VFORT-L     VS-FORTRAN discussion list
```

FTP Sites

Numerous sites contain FORTRAN code or informational files, including the following:

ftp.che.utexas.edu

ftp.netlib.org

ftp.npac.syr.edu

ftp.physics.mcgill.ca

ftp.uni-stuttgart.de

ftp.uniovi.es

gopher.iqm.unicamp.br

info.mcs.anl.gov

leif.thep.lu.se

lifshitz.ph.utexas.edu

rusmv1.rus.uni-stuttgart.de

softlib.cs.rice.edu

venus.eng.buffalo.edu

zebra.desy.de

Newsgroup

The newsgroup **comp.lang.fortran** discusses FORTRAN.

Online Data Services

FORTRAN is addressed in numerous places on the major commercial online data services, including the following CompuServe forums:

MS Language Forum	MSLANG
PC Vendor H Forum	PCVENH
PowerBuilder Forum	PBFORUM
Powersoft Forum	PSFORUM
Powersoft Support	POWERSOFT
STARBASE PUBLIC FORUM	STR-4
Watcom Forum	WATFORUM

Periodic Postings and FAQs

Subject: FORTRAN FAQ

Newsgroups: **comp.lang.fortran**, **comp.answers**, and **news.answers**

From: **khb@chiba.Eng.Sun.COM** (Keith Bierman)

Archive-name: **fortran-faq**

Pascal

Pascal has many adherents, though other programming languages enjoy vaster supplies of supporting information and products. One of the best ways to obtain information about Pascal is to contact Borland's support site (available on the WWW at **http://www.borland.com** or via anonymous FTP to **ftp.borland.com**), where you can find a lot of files and information on both Pascal and DELPHI, the Pascal-related visual programming product.

Internet Maillists

The following maillists provide information on Pascal and related topics.

INFO-M2

Contact: **listservUCF1VM.CC.UCF.EDU**

Description: The Modula-2 programming language, which extends the Pascal foundation.

INFO-PASCAL

Contact: INFO-PASCAL-REQUEST@**arl.mil**

Description: General discussion of Pascal

cwarrior

Contact: **listserv@netcom.com**

Description: Discussion of Metrowerks CodeWarrior Macintosh development tools. CodeWarrior includes C, C++, and Pascal compilers; a class library; and associated tools.

TurboVision

Contact: **listserv@vtvm1.cc.vt.edu**

Description: TurboVision is a library that comes with Borland C++ and Pascal compilers. To enroll, send the message **subscribe turbvis your name.**

BITNET List Server Maillists

To subscribe to a maillist, send a mail message to **listserv@bitnic.bitnet.** Leave the *Subject:* field blank. In the body of the message, write: **SUBSCRIBE listname**, where listname is a name in the left column below.

```
ADV-PAS      List for advanced Pascal users

HSPASCAL     Amiga High-Speed Pascal discussion
```

```
PASCAL-L     Pascal discussion list
```

FTP Sites

The following sites have some Pascal files:

clutxclarkson.edu

flinux.tu-graz.ac.at

ftp.cwi.nl

ftp.dur.ac.uk

ftp.mechnet.liv.ac.uk

ftp.netlib.org

ftp.psg.com

ftp.uniovi.es

garbo.uwasa.fi

gondwana.ecr.mu.oz.au

kampi.hut.fi

ucselx.sdsu.edu

Newsgroup

There is only one central newsgroup on Pascal: **comp.lang.pascal**.

Online Data Services

The following forums provide information, support, and files about Pascal.

CompuServe Forums

```
Apple II Prog. Forum        APPROG

BORLAND                     BORLAND

Borland DELPHI Forum        DELPHI

Mac Developers Forum        MACDEV

PC Programming Forum        PCPROG

Portable Prog. Forum        CODEPORT

STARBASE PUBLIC FORUM       STR-4
```

```
Texas Instruments Forum      TIFORUM

TopSpeed Corporation Forum   CLARION

Windows Components B Forum   ADTC
```

America Online Forums

The COMPUTING AREA on America Online has resources for Pascal programmers, including a software library specifically dedicated to Pascal. Moreover, the Development Forum includes a reference article on beginning Pascal programming. The Developer Forum is also the contact point for Programmer's University—a series of interactive courses for many languages, including Pascal.

BIX Conference

Go into the programming area and access the conference dedicated to Pascal.

Periodic Postings and FAQs

I am not aware of a Pascal FAQ. The following FAQ is posted regularly to the Pascal newsgroup, however:

Subject: SuperVGA/VESA programmer's notes

Newsgroups: **comp.graphics**, **comp.lang.pascal**, **comp.answers**, and **news.answers**

From: **myles@giaec.cc.monash.edu.au**

Frequency: Every two months

FORTH

FORTH is an extensible programming language; in other words, you can create new instructions and structures from the language's basic building blocks.

FORTH was originally created over 20 years ago to provide a form of higher-level language for lower-end machines, particularly microcontrollers. Over time FORTH has been ported to just about every type of processing platform, including 8051/8031, PCs, 32-bit protected-mode PCs, Windows 3.1, Windows NT, OS/2, 68HC16, C, UNIX, Sun, Macintosh, Amiga, Atari ST, Transputers, Tandy TRS-80, Apple II, 68000 boards, miscellaneous DSP chips, and VMS.

FAQ

The FORTH FAQ, archived at **rtfm.mit.edu/pub/usenet/news.answers/ForthFaq/**, has an excellent description of where to get commercial and freeware FORTH implementations, libraries, and information.

FORTH Interest Group

The FORTH Interest Group (or FIG) actively promotes FORTH. The group maintains a FORTH Round Table on GEnie, where it maintains a significant archive of FORTH code. (The archive is also mirrored at the anonymous FTP site **asterix.inescn.pt/pub/forth**.)

You can contact the FIG at

FORTH Interest Group
PO Box 2154
Oakland, CA 94621
Telephone: 510-89FORTH
Fax: 510-535-1295

FORTHnet

FORTHnet is a virtual network on FORTH; it consists of a cooperative cross-posting of FORTH-related articles on four network mechanisms:

➤ FIG's Round Table on GEnie

➤ USENET's **comp.lang.forth**

➤ BITNET's **list server maillist FIGI-L**

➤ Assorted BBSs, including

```
ACFB (Australia Connection FORTH Board)
Telephone: 03-809-1787 in Australia
            (61-3-809-1787 international)

FORTH Systeme GmbH BBS
Telephone: (Country Code 49) 7667-556 (Breisach,
            Germany)
```

```
                       FORTH-BBS Munich
                       Telephone: 089-8714548 in Germany
                                  (49-89-8714548 international)

                       Grapevine (Grapevine RIME hub)
                       Telephone: 501-753-8121 to register (Little Rock,
                                  Arkansas)

                       Interface BBS
                       Telephone: 707-544-9661 (Santa Rosa, California)

                       LMI BBS (Laboratory Microsystems Inc.)
                       Telephone: 310-306-3530 (Marina del Ray, California)

                       RCFB (Real-Time Control FORTH Board)
                       Telephone: 303-278-0364 (Golden, Colorado)
```

Other FTP Sites   ftp.tu-graz.ac.at/pub/FreeBSD/ports-2.0/lang

ftp.belwuede

sunserver.embnet.dkfz-heidelberg.de/pub/msdos

ftp.fht-mannheim.de/pub/languages

ftp.fht-mannheim.de/pub/msdos/languages

ftp.tu-dresden.de/ftpext3/FreeBSD/FreeBSD-current/ports/lang

ftp.inf.tu-dresden.de/pub/incoming/ms-dos/program

ftp.informatik.tu-muenchen.de/pub/comp/os/bsd/FreeBSD/
FreeBSD-current/ports/lang

ftp.informatik.tu-muenchen.de/pub/comp/platforms/pc/msdos/
programming

ftp.informatik.tu-muenchen.de/pub/comp/platforms/pc/windows/
programming

forte.mathematik.uni-bremen.de/pub/unix/languages

ftp.uni-kl.de/pub0/apple2/languages

rs1.rrz.uni-koeln.de/pc/msdos/programming

athene.uni-paderborn.de/pcsoft/msdos

athene.uni-paderborn.de/pcsoft2/atari/lang

gigaserv.uni-paderborn.de/ftp/disk4/atari/lang

gigaserv.uni-paderborn.de/pcsoft2/atari/lang

rrzs3.rz.uni-regensburg.de/pub/freeware/software/dos/sprachen

rrzs3.rz.uni-regensburg.de/pub/pcsoft/msdos

rrzs3.rz.uni-regensburg.de/pub/pcsoft2/atari/lang

ftp.cs.uni-sb.de/pub/lang

ftp.uni-stuttgart.de/pub/programming

ftp.uni-stuttgart.de/pub/systems/acorn/riscos/lang

ftp.uni-stuttgart.de/pub/systems/pc/lang

ftp.uni-stuttgart.de/pub/systems/sun/sug/sug_tape_90/sug85/languages

ftp.uni-stuttgart.de/pub/unix/programming

ftp.uni-trier.de/pub/pc/msdos-koeln/programming

ftp.uni-trier.de/pub/unix/systems/sun/sug/sug_tape_90/sug85/languages

ftp.umcs.maine.edu/pub/msdos/compilers

rtfm.mit.edu/pub/usenet-by-hierarchy/comp/lang

nic.funet.fi/pub/languages

nic.funet.fi/pub/msdos/languages

ftp.ibp.fr/pub/parallel/languages

ftp.ibp.fr/pub/parallel/software/compilers

ftp.ibp.fr/pub/parallel/vendors/inmos/archive-server

ftp.ibp.fr/pub3/pc/SimTel/msdos

ftp.jussieu.fr/pub/parallel/languages

ftp.jussieu.fr/pub/parallel/software/compilers

ftp.jussieu.fr/pub/parallel/vendors/inmos/archive-server

ftp.mcs.anl.gov/pub/FreeBSD/ports-2.0/lang

ftp.elte.hu/software/language

teseo.unipg.it/pub/msdos/languages

lysita.lysator.liu.se/pub/languages

lysita.lysator.liu.se/pub/religion/zen/hacking

ftp.luth.se/pub/FreeBSD/FreeBSD-current/ports/lang

ftp.luth.se/pub/FreeBSD/ports-2.0/lang

Online Data Services

FORTH receives some support on the major commercial online data services:

BIX	In the Programming conference, access the conference 14 (forth / FORTH programming)
CompuServe	Creative Solutions/FORTH Forum—GO FORTH
GEnie	The FORTH Round Table

LISP

LISP (LISt Processing language) is a widely used language for artificial intelligence (AI). Since LISP's origination in 1956, numerous versions of LISP have been developed—for general-purpose and AI-specific platforms (i.e., those platforms from LISP Machines Inc. and Symbolics). The following are some forms of LISP:

LISP1.5
The original LISP dialect

BBNLISP

Interlisp (originally BBNLISP) and MacLISP
LISP diverges into two dialects

NIL (New Implementation of LISP)
LISP for the VAX

```
S-1 LISP
LISP for the Mark IIA supercomputer

Franz LISP
Dialect of MacLISP; LISP for UNIX

Scheme

Flavors and LOOPS
Object-oriented programming LISP

SPICE-LISP
Dialect of MacLISP; LISP for the SPICE workstation

PSL (Portable Standard LISP)
LISP for a variety of platforms

Common LISP
Unofficial description of common elements found in previ-
ous LISP implementations

CLtL1
Published de facto standard for Common LISP

CLtL2
Unofficial snapshot of work in progress by ANSI standards
committee X3J13
```

Because of LISP's long history, multiplatform evolution, and progress towards standardization, a very large body of LISP information, tools, and code is available.

FTP Sites

Following are FTP sites relevant to LISP, including sources of code, and LISP implementations.

Sources of Code

There are a number of major FTP archives of LISP information and publicly distributable code. Some of the key ones are as follows:

```
ftp.cs.cmu.edu:/user/ai/lang/lisp/
The Common LISP Repository, which is part of the
Carnegie Mellon University Artificial Intelligence
Repository, includes more than 250 Mbytes of freely
```

distributable source code. This repository can be searched by keyword via e-mail. For information, send a message with the *Subject:* field blank and the word **help** in the body to ai+query@cs.cmu.edu. This repository is mirrored at ftp.sunet.se:/pub/lang/lisp/. It also may be accessed via the WWW at http://www.cs.cmu.edu/Web/Groups/AI/html/repository.html.

nervous.cis.ohio-state.edu:/pub/lispusers/clos/
The CLOS Code Repository.

cambridge.apple.com:/pub/MCL2/contrib/
The Macintosh Common LISP Repository contains user-contributed code for MCL. This repository is also available via the WWW at http://www.cambridge.apple.com.

cambridge.apple.com:/pub/clim
The CLIM Library contains user-contributed code for the CLIM environment.

ftp.ai.mit.edu:/pub/
The MIT AI Lab contains a library of many LISP resources, especially the clmath set of math routines.

nervous.cis.ohio-state.edu:/pub/lispusers/medley/
The LISPUsers Archives is a collection of programs for the Medley development environment.

gatekeeper.pa.dec.com:/pub/micro/amiga/lisp/
A repository of Amiga LISP implementations.

Common LISP Implementations

ftp.informatik.uni-kiel.de:/pub/kiel/apply/
clicc-0.6.4.tar.gz
CLiCC (Common LISP to C Compiler).

ma2s2.mathematik.uni-karlsruhe.de:/pub/lisp/clisp/
CLISP is a Common LISP implementation.

ftp.cs.cmu.edu:/afs/cs.cmu.edu/project/clisp/release
Access to CMU CL (CMU Common LISP) requires that you log

in with username anonymous; password is your e-mail address. You must cd directly to the source directory with a single command.

ftp.di.unipi.it:/pub/lang/lisp/
ECoLISP, a Common LISP implementation, compiles LISP functions into C functions.

ftp.cli.com:/pub/gcl/
GCL (GNU Common LISP).

rascal.ics.utexas.edu:/pub/
KCL (Kyoto Common LISP) is free but requires a license. Commercial version is also available.

ftp.cs.cmu.edu:/user/ai/lang/lisp/impl/powerlsp/v1_10/
powerlsp.hqx
PowerLISP is a Common LISP development environment for the Macintosh.

ftp.cs.cmu.edu:/user/ai/lang/lisp/impl/reflisp/
RefLISP is a small LISP interpreter for many platforms.

cdr.stanford.edu:/pub/wcl/
WCL is an implementation of Common LISP for SPARC-based workstations.

ftp.cs.cmu.edu:/user/ai/lang/lisp/impl/xlisp/
XLISP is a free implementation that is portable to many platforms.

Miscellaneous FTP Sites

A number of other FTP sites hold additional LISP information and code:

arp.anu.edu.au

atheist.tamu.edu

ccrma-ftp.stanford.edu

clutxclarkson.edu

cmns.think.com

cs.indiana.edu

cs.orst.edu

das.harvard.edu

donau.et.tudelft.nl

etlport.etl.go.jp

ftp.3com.com

ftp.center.osaka-u.ac.jp

ftp.cs.rochester.edu

ftp.cs.umn.edu

ftp.cs.yale.edu

ftp.csrl.aoyama.ac.jp

ftp.daimi.aau.dk

ftp.diku.dk

ftp.gmdde

ftp.icsi.berkeley.edu

ftp.iesd.auc.dk

ftp.ijs.si

ftp.ncc.up.pt

ftp.ucdavis.edu

ftp.uni-erlangen.de

ftp.uni-muensterde

ftp.wimsey.bc.ca

laplace.stat.ucla.edu

lib.stat.cmu.edu

ncbi.nlm.nih.gov

nebula.cs.yale.edu

rascal.ics.utexas.edu

think.com

titan.ksc.nasa.gov

umnstat.stat.umn.edu

Newsgroups

The following maillists provide information on multimedia, CD-ROM, and related topics:

comp.lang.clos	Discussion of Common LISP Object System
comp.lang.lisp	Discussion of LISP
comp.lang.lisp.mcl	Discussion of Macintosh Common LISP
comp.lang.scheme	Scheme programming language
comp.org.lisp-users	Association of LISP Users discussions
comp.std.lisp	Users group (ALU)-supported standards (moderated)

BIX Conference

In the programming area, go into the menu entry for LISP.

Periodic Postings and FAQs

Subject: Garnet Toolkit FAQ

Newsgroups: **comp.windows.garnet, comp.answers,** and **news.answers**

From: **bam+@cs.cmu.edu** (Brad Myers)

Summary: Garnet user interface development environment for LISP.
Archive-name: **garnet-faq**

Subject: FAQ: Object-oriented Programming in LISP */* [monthly posting]

Newsgroups: **comp.lang.lisp, comp.lang.clos, news.answers,** and **comp.answers**

From: **mkant+@cs.cmu.edu** (Mark Kantrowitz)

Summary: Questions about CLOS, PCL, and object-oriented programming in LISP

Archive-name: **lisp-faq/part5**

Subject: LISP FAQ */* [monthly posting]

Subject: FAQ: LISP Implementations and Maillists */* [monthly posting]

Subject: FAQ: LISP FTP Resources */* [monthly posting]

Subject: FAQ: LISP Window Systems and GUIs */* [monthly posting]

Newsgroups: **comp.lang.lisp, news.answers**, and **comp.answers**

From: **mkant+@cs.cmu.edu** (Mark Kantrowitz)

Comment: The following articles are currently being posted: LISP FAQ (part1_part3); LISP Implementations and Mailing Lists (part4); LISP FTP Resources (part6); LISP Window Systems and GUIs (part7). Note: Archive-names (in parentheses) are in the lisp-faq archive directory.

Summary: Introductory matter and bibliography of introductions and references.

Archive-name: **lisp-faq/part1**

Subject: **comp.lang.lisp.mcl** FAQ

Newsgroups: **comp.lang.lisp.mcl**

From: **straz@cambridge.apple.com** (Steve Strassmann)

Subject: Scheme FAQ [monthly posting]

Subject: FAQ: Scheme Implementations and Mailing Lists */* [monthly posting]

Newsgroups: **comp.lang.scheme, comp.lang.lisp, news.answers, comp.answers**

From: **mkant+@cs.cmu.edu** (Mark Kantrowitz)

Archive-name: scheme-faq/part1

Ada

Ada is the specified language for software developed for the Department of Defense. There have been two major revisions of Ada: Ada 83 and Ada95. (Note: Ada95 is backwards compatible with Ada83.)

Ada has some quality-control features not ordinarily available for computer languages, including the following:

➤ A formal process for verifying compliance of any compiler against the Ada standard

➤ Procedures for benchmarking performance of Ada tools

➤ A formal clearinghouse for the distribution of Ada standards and information—the Ada Information Clearinghouse (AdaIC). The Ada Joint Program Office (AJPO) is another key organization in the definition and distribution of Ada information.

The Ada Information Clearinghouse (AdaIC)

You can contact the Ada Information Clearinghouse (AdaIC) at

Ada Information Clearinghouse
PO Box 46593
Washington, DC 20050-6593
Telephone: 800-232-4211, 703-685-1477
Fax: 703-685-7019

The AdaIC publishes a quarterly report, covering such topics as the following:

➤ Ada validated compilers

➤ Ada news and current events

➤ Ada usage

➤ Online sources of Ada information

➤ Ada compiler validation and evaluation

➤ Ada software, tools, and interfaces

➤ Ada regulations, policies, and mandates

➤ Ada historical information

Most if not all AdaIC reports may be obtained by anonymous FTP to **ftp://sw-eng.falls-church.va.us/public**. Some key entries on the site are

```
/public/AdaIC/tools/compilers/83val/val-comp.txt
List of validated compilers
```

```
/public/AdaIC/docs/standard/95lrm_rat/v6.0
Ada95 reference manual
```

```
/public/AdaIC/docs/standard/83lrm
Ada83 reference manual
```

```
/public/AdaIC/docs/usage/cauwg.txt
Report on commercial uses of Ada (reported by the
Commercial Ada Users Working Group [CAUWG], of the
Association for Computing Machinery's Special Interest
Group on Ada [ACM SIGAda]
```

```
/public/AdaIC/docs/usage
Database of commercial Ada projects
```

Public Domain Compilers/ Interpreters

Although there exist several versions of public Ada systems for different platforms, the two primary types are as follows:

```
Ada/Ed An Ada83 interpreter available for PCs, UNIX
machines, Amiga, and Atari systems. UNIX and 386/486 DOS
versions may be obtained at ftp://cs.nyu.edu/pub/adaed.
```

```
GW-Ada/Ed, an enhanced version of Ada/Ed for 386/486 DOS
machines and Macintoshes, is available at
ftp://wuarchive.wustl.edu/pub/languages/ada/compiler/
adaed/gwu.
```

GNAT (GNU New York University Ada Translator) An Ada95 compiler available for UNIX, DOS, OS/2, and NT 386/486 systems. It may be obtained at `ftp://cs.nyu.edu/pub/gnat` and `ftp://wuarchive.wustl.edu/pub/languages/ada/compiler/gnat`.

Note: Ada/Ed and GNAT are publicly available but have copyright and usage restrictions.

FTP Sites

`wuarchive.wustl.edu`
PAL (Public Ada Library), formerly Ada Software Repository

`ftp.cs.kuleuven.ac.be` in pub/Ada-Belgium
Ada-Belgium

`sw-eng.falls-church.va.us`
AdaIC (mirrored by the PAL)

`source.asset.com`
ASSET / STARS (Software Technology for Adaptable, Reliable Systems) (Note: Does not accept anonymous FTP. You can request a free account from info@source.asset.com.)

`ajpo.sei.cmu.edu`
"All the ADA you could ask for"

`anna.stanford.edu`
Anna (Annotated Ada) software and docs

`bugs.nosc.mil`
ADA math

`ftp.cnam.fr`

`ftp.cs.chalmers.se`

`ftp.cs.kuleuven.ac.be`
Ada-Belgium FTP archive with a.o. PAL on CD-ROM and GnuAda 9X compiler mirror

ftp.gwu.edu
Small-Ada

ftp.seas.gwu.edu

geocub.greco-prog.fr

gogol.cenatls.cena.dgac.fr

info.mcs.anl.gov

wilbur.stanford.edu
YACC grammars for ADA, C++, and SQL

BBSs

ACM SIGAda Performance Issues Working Group
412-268-7020

AdaIC BBS
703-604-4624; call 800-444-1458 to register for access

Air Force Software Technology Support Center (STSC) BBS
801-774-6509

Embedded Systems Programming Magazine BBS
415-905-2689

Naval Computer Telecommunications Command
804-444-7841; (DSN 564-7841)

Software Inc.
608-251-5121

WWW Sites

http://info.acm.org/sigada/
ACM SIGAda (ACM Special Interest Group on Ada)

http://lglwww.epfl.ch/Ada/
HBAP (Home of the Brave Ada Programmers)

http://wuarchive.wustl.edu/languages/ada/userdocs/html/
Welcome.html
PAL (Public Ada Library)

```
http://www.cs.kuleuven.ac.be/~dirk/ada-belgium/
Ada-Belgium
```

```
http://www.sei.cmu.edu/FrontDoor.html
SEI (Software Engineering Institute), a federally funded
research and development center at Carnegie Mellon
University.
```

Internet Maillists

The following maillists provide information on Ada and related topics.

ada-belgium

Contact: **ada-belgium-request@cs.kuleuven.ac.be**

Description: Ada-related discussions. Posting access limited to members of Ada-Belgium. For information, send empty message with *Subject:* = **help**

ada-belgium-info

Contact: **ada-belgium-info-request@cs.kuleuven.ac.be**

Description: Announcements of Ada-Belgium. For information, send empty message with *Subject:* = **help**

ADA-SW

Contact: ADA-SW-REQUEST@WSMR- SIMTEL20.ARMY.MIL

Description: Accessing and contributing software to the Ada repository on the SimTel archive site.

ada-train

Contact: **listserv@wunet.wustl.edu** (Richard Conn)

Description: Ada programming, design, and software engineering training.

pal-announce

Contact: **listserv@wunet.wustl.edu** (Richard Conn)

Description: PAL announcements.

posix-ada

Contact: **umd5!grebyn!posix-ada-request**

From: **posix-ada-request@grebyn.com** (Karl Nyberg)
Description: Discuss Ada binding of the POSIX standard.

x-ada

Contact: **x-ada-request@expo.lcs.mit.edu**
Description: Discuss Ada interface to the X Windows system.

**BITNET
List Server
Maillist**

To subscribe to a maillist, send a mail message to **listserv@bitnic.bitnet**.
Leave the *Subject:* field blank. In the body of the message, write:
SUBSCRIBE INFO-ADA.

Newsgroup

The maillist **comp.lang.ada** provides information on Ada and related
topics.

**BIX
Conferences**

BIX has two conferences under the programming area:

```
o ada          Ada language conference

o ada.vrs      Ada 9x standardization project
```

**Periodic
Postings and
FAQs**

FAQs with an archive-name given are available on the anonymous FTP
server **rtfm.mit.edu.**

Subject: Ada FAQ: **comp.lang.ada** (part * of *)

Subject: Ada FAQ: Programming with Ada (part * of *)

Subject: Ada FAQ: The Ada WWW Server

Newsgroups: **comp.lang.ada, comp.answers, news.answers**

From: **Magnus.Kempe@di.epfl.ch** (Magnus Kempe)

Reply To: **Magnus.Kempe@di.epfl.ch** (Magnus Kempe)

Subject: Public Ada Library (with VHDL support) FAQ

Newsgroups: **comp.lang.ada, comp.lang.vhdl, comp.answers, news.answers**

From: **conn@wuarchive.wustl.edu** (Richard Conn)

Summary: PAL FAQ

Archive-name: computer-lang/Ada/pal-vhdl-faq

Subject: **comp.lang.ada** FAQ */*

Newsgroups: **comp.lang.ada, news.answers, comp.answers**

From: **cla-faq@ajpo.sei.cmu.edu** (Ada Information Clearinghouse)

Summary: **comp.lang.ada FAQ** (Note: Does not get into programming questions.)

Archive-name: comp-lang-ada/cla-faq1

Subject: Comp.Object FAQ Version * (*) Announcement

Newsgroups: **comp.lang.c++, comp.lang.eiffel, comp.lang.smalltalk, comp.lang.clos, comp.lang.ada, comp.databases.object, comp.lang.sather, comp.lang.misc, comp.software-eng, comp.sw.components, comp.lang.modula3, comp.lang.objective-c, comp.sys.next.programmer, comp.lang.oberon, comp.object.logic, comp.lang.scheme, comp.answers,** and **news.answers**

From: **rjh@geodesic.com** (Bob Hathaway)

Summary: Lists FAQ and available systems for object-oriented technology

Archive-name: **object-faq/announce**

Vendor Directory

Note: Several of these contacts are individual mailboxes and may have changed by the time of publication.

Convex	allison@convex.com
Cray	det@cray.com
DDC-I	sale@ddci.dk
DEC	http://www.digital.com/home.html
Green Hills Software Inc.	support@ghs.comHarris
IBM/Ada	malcho@torolab6.vnet.ibm.com
Intermetrics	http://www.inmet.com/
Irvine Compiler Corp. (ICC)	info@irvine.com
OC Systems Inc.	http://ocsystems.com/
R. R. Software	rbrukardt@bix.com
Rational Software Corp.	product_info@rational.com
Tartan	customer-support@tartan.com and info@tartan.com
Thomson Software Products	adasupport@alsys.com and marketng@alsys.com

CHAPTER EIGHT

GENERIC OPERATING SYSTEMS AND ENVIRONMENTS

This chapter addresses generic operating systems and development environments that run on multiple computing platforms. UNIX and OS/2, for example, run on several different platforms, so they are covered here. Windows and DOS, on the other hand, run almost exclusively on Intel-IBM architecture systems. Similarly, Apple's various computing platforms (Apple II, Mac, Newton, and so on) each have a fairly unique development environment. Also, VMS runs only on DEC machines. Chapter 9 covers these and other platform-specific operating systems.

OS/2

The following sections cover sitelists, maillists, and other information sources to OS/2.

FTP Sites

These are some leading sites for obtaining OS/2 shareware and freeware applications and utilities.

Site	Directory
ftp-os2.cdrom.com	pub/os2
ftp-os2.nmsu.edu	os2
software.watson.ibm.com	pub/os2
mtsg.ubc.ca	os2
access.usask.ca	pub/archives/os2
luga.latrobe.edu.au	pub/os2
funic.funet.fi	pub/os2
pdsoft.lancs.ac.uk	micros/ibmpc/os2
ftp.uni-stuttgart.de	soft/os2
src.doc.ic.ac.uk	computing/systems/os2
zaphod.cs.uwindsor.ca	pub/local/os2
ftp.luth.se	pub/pc/os2
ftp.informatik.tu-muenchen.de	pub/comp/os/os2

Also, the **ftp-os2.cdrom.com** library is available on CD-ROM from Walnut Creek (510-947-5996).

Newsgroups   A number of focused Internet newsgroups monitored by OS/2 experts from IBM serve as primary ways to get help or information about OS/2. Look through the relevant FAQs first (see "Periodic Postings and FAQs" on page 167). If your question isn't answered there, a post to the right newsgroup might result in an answer.

`comp.binaries.os2`	Binaries for use under the OS/2 ABI (moderated)
`comp.os.os2.advocacy`	Supporting and flaming OS/2
`comp.os.os2.announce`	Notable news and announce-ments related to OS/2 (moderated)
`comp.os.os2.apps`	Discussions of applica-tions under OS/2

comp.os.os2.beta	All aspects of beta releases of OS/2 systems software
comp.os.os2.bugs	OS/2 system bug reports, fixes, and workarounds
comp.os.os2.games	Running games under OS/2
comp.os.os2.misc	Miscellaneous topics about the OS/2 system
comp.os.os2.multimedia	Multimedia on OS/2 systems
comp.os.os2.networking.misc	Miscellaneous OS/2 networking issues of OS/2
comp.os.os2.networking.tcp-ip	TCP/IP under OS/2
comp.os.os2.programmer.misc	Programming OS/2 machines
comp.os.os2.programmer.oop	Programming system objects (SOM, WPS, etc.)
comp.os.os2.programmer.porting	Porting software to OS/2 machines
comp.os.os2.programmer.tools	Compilers, assemblers, interpreters under OS/2
comp.os.os2.setup	Installing and configuring OS/2 systems

World Wide Web Sites

These are key WWW sites for OS/2 information:

gopher://index.almaden.ibm.com
IBM's OS/2 Warp GOPHER site

http://www.ibm.com
The main home page for IBM Corp.

http://www.ibm.net
The IBM Global Network home page (includes information on OS/2 Warp and its Internet connection)

```
http://www.mit.edu:8001/activities/os2
The OS/2 home page at MIT
```

User Groups

There are so many OS/2 user groups that it's not practical to list them all. You can obtain a comprehensive list from WWW at **http://www.austin.ibm.com/pspinfo/ibmpcug.html**.

You can add a group to this list by mailing its description to **ibmpcug@vnet.ibm.com**.

BBSs

These BBSs have large libraries of OS/2 files as well as a more complete worldwide OS/2 BBS listing.

BBS	Number
Fernwood	203-483-0348
The Bin BBS	206-451-1905
OS/2 Source BBS	303-744-0373
Denver OS/2 BBS	303-755-6859
Inside Technologies BBS	313-283-1151
OS/2 Woodmeister	314-446-0016
Pyramid/2	415-494-7497
Gateway/2	314-554-9313
Bay Area OS/2	510-657-7948
OS/2 San Diego	619-558-9475
OS/2 Las Vegas	702-433-5535
OS/2 Shareware	703-385-4325
Greater Chicago Online	708-895-4042
OS/2 Exchange BBS	904-739-2445
Abaforum (Barcelona)	+34-3-589.38.88
IBM UK	+44-256-336655
OS/2 UK	+44-454-633197

BBS	Number
IBM Denmark	+45-42-88-72-22
Copenhagen UG BBS	+45-48-24-45-80
OS/2 Norway	+47-22-38-09-49
IBM Norway	+47-66-99-94-50
IBM Germany	+49-7034-15-2160
OS/2 Australia	+61-2-241-2466
Soft/2 Shareware (Adelaide)	+61-8-370-7339

BITNET List Server Maillists

To subscribe to a maillist, send a mail message to **listserv@bitnic.bitnet**. Leave the *Subject:* field blank. In the body of the message, write: **SUBSCRIBE listname**, where listname is one of the names in the first column.

```
OS2-L           IBM OS/2 Unedited Discussion List

OS2USERS        OS/2 Users Discussion List

TEAMOS2HELP-L   Team OS/2 Help Desk

TEAMOS2-L       Team OS/2 Members Discussion List

TEAMOS2LDR-L    Team OS/2 Event and Area Leaders
                Discussion List
```

Online Data Services

Commercial online data services offer a large number of support resources for OS/2.

CompuServe Forums

CompuServe's IBMOS2 (GO IBMOS2) is IBM's official non-IBM online service for OS/2 user and developer support. OS/2 developers can contact the IBM Developer Assistance Program on CompuServe with GO OS2DAP. Additional forums have information or services related to OS/2:

```
Borland C++ for Win/OS2 Forum   BCPPWIN

CD-ROM Forum                    CDROM
```

Developer Relations Forum	MSDR
Dr. Dobb's Journal Forum	DDJFORUM
IBM Desktop Forum	IBMDESK
IBM OS/2 B Vendors Forum	OS2BVEN
IBM OS/2 Developer 1 Forum	OS2DF1
IBM OS/2 Developer 2 Forum	OS2DF2
IBM OS/2 Help Database	OS2HELP
IBM OS/2 Service Pak	OS2SERV
IBM OS/2 Support Forum	OS2SUPPORT
IBM OS/2 Users Forum	OS2USER
IBM OS/2 Vendor Forum	OS2AVEN
IBM PSM Deutschland Forum	OS2UGER
IBM VoiceType Forum	VOICETYPE
MS Knowledge Base	MSKB
PC Utilities/Systems Forum	PCUTIL
PC Vendor A Forum	PCVENA
PC Vendor F Forum	PCVENF
PC World Online	PCWORLD
PowerBuilder Forum	PBFORUM
Powersoft Forum	PSFORUM
Powersoft Support	POWERSOFT
Support Directory	SUPPORT
Symantec Dev. Tools Forum	SYMDEVTOOL
Symantec Norton Util. Forum	SYMUTIL
TopSpeed Corporation Forum	CLARION
Watcom Forum	WATFORUM
Zenith Data Systems Forum	ZENITH

America OnLine

A number of resources in the OS/2 Forum in AOL's computing area support OS/2 development and usage:

- ➤ A software library

- ➤ A message board

- ➤ An industry connection to product suppliers

- ➤ OS/2 newsletters, including a developer's periodical

- ➤ An OS/2 reference guide

BIX Forums

The programmers conference area on BIX supports two OS/2 areas:

o `ibm.os2`   *OS/2 operating system*

o `os2.pro`   *OS/2 Professional Magazine* online

Other Online Data Services

The OS/2 Warp Roundtable (keyword OS2) is available on GEnie, and a dedicated OS/2 Warp forum (GO CUS 41) is available on DELPHI.

Periodic Postings and FAQs

FAQs with an archive-name listed are available on the anonymous FTP server **rtfm.mit.edu**.

Subject: OS/2 Frequently Asked Questions List Rel. * (* of *)

Subject: OS/2 Users' Frequently Asked Questions List Edition *

Newsgroups: **comp.os.os2.misc, comp.answers, news.answers**

From: **sip1@kimbark.uchicago.edu** (Timothy F. Sipples)

From: **klund@MIT.EDU**

Reply To: **tsipple@vnet.ibm.com** (FAQ comments address)

Subject: Team OS/2 Frequently Asked Questions

Newsgroups: **comp.os.os2.advocacy, comp.answers, news.answers**

From: **C.J.Scarborough@durham.ac.uk** (Christian Scarborough)

Archive-name: **Team-OS2-FAQ**

Summary: A collection of information relevant to the informal grassroots organization, Team OS/2; dedicated to promoting IBM's PC operating system, OS/2, to friends, family, workmates, and others.

Subject: OS/2 Users' Frequently Asked Questions List Edition *

Newsgroups: **comp.os.os2.misc, comp.answers, news.answers**

From: **klund@MIT.EDU**

Reply To: **tsipple@vnet.ibm.com**(FAQ Comments address)

Archive-name: **os2-faq/user/part1**

Summary: Lists common questions (and answers) about the IBM OS/2 Warp operating system. Everyone interested in OS/2 Warp should read this, from the new and curious to the long-time power user.

Subject: OS/2 New User Introduction (Revised * * *)

Newsgroups: **comp.os.os2.misc, comp.os.os2.apps, comp.os.os2.setup, comp.os.os2.beta, news.answers, comp.answers**

From: **phaniraj@badlands.nodak.edu** (V. Phaniraj)

Archive-name: **os2-faq/new-user/part1**

Subject: FAQ: OS/2 Programming FAQ

Newsgroup: **comp.os.os2.programmer.misc**

From: **andreas@traci.almroth.pp.se** (Andreas Almroth)

X Windows

This section covers the X style of windows programming, including two commonly used standard systems: Motif and OpenLook.

Internet Maillists

The following maillists provide information on X Windows and related topics.

bx-talk

Contact: **majordomo@qiclab.scn.rain.com** (Darci L. Chapman)

Description: Support for users of Builder Xcessory (BX), a graphical user interface builder for Motif applicatons.

GLEList

Contact: **listproc@tbone.biol.scarolina.edu**

Description: User support for GLE graphics package (a graphics package for scientists). Supported on several platforms (PCs, VAXes, and UNIX). To enroll, send message **sub glelist your name** to **tproc@tbone.biol.scarolina.edu**.

metacard-list

Contact: **listserv@grot.starconn.com**

Description: Discusses the MetaCard product from MetaCard Corporation, an application development system similar to Apple's HyperCard.

.XWIN-L

Contact: **listserv@vm3090.ege.edu.tr**

Description: X Windows protocol and X Windows programming.

FTP and WWW Sites

The Motif WWW page MW3: Motif, located on the World Wide Web at **http://www.cen.com/mw3/**, connects you to a large number of Motif resources on the Web, which cover such topics as FAQs, toolkits, code examples, commerical products, organizations, and many related topics.

A few other key WWW sites are related to Motif:

`http://www.x.org//`	X Consortium
`http://www.nads.de/EXUG/EXUG.html`	European X user group
`http://www.osf.org/`	OSF home page
`http://www.let.rug.nl/FWF/`	Free Widget Foundation (FWF)

A key FTP site for OpenLook information is **export.lcs.mit.edu**. XView (Sun's toolkit for X11) is available here, along with a lot of other information.

Newsgroups

You can access these permanent newsgroups via most network newsreader programs.

`comp.windows.x.motif`	Discussion of the X Motif System
`comp.windows.open-look`	Discussion of OpenLook
`comp.windows.x`	Discussion about the X Windows System
`comp.windows.x.announce`	X Windows System announcements (moderated)
`comp.windows.x.apps`	Getting and using, not programming, applications for X Windows
`comp.windows.x.i386unix`	The XFree86 Windows System and others
`comp.windows.x.intrinsics`	Discussion of the X toolkit
`comp.windows.pex.`	PEX extension of X Windows System

Periodic Postings and FAQs

FAQs with an archive-name listed are available on the anonymous FTP server **rtfm.mit.edu**.

Subject: Motif FAQ (Part * of *)

Newsgroups: **comp.windows.x.motif, comp.answers, news.answers**

From: **ksall@cen.com** (Ken Sall)

Archive-name: **motif-faq/part1**

Summary: Motif Frequently Asked Questions (with answers).

Subject: OpenLook GUI FAQ */*:

Newsgroups: **comp.windows.open-look, alt.toolkits.xview, comp.windows.news, alt.sys.sun, alt.toolkits.intrinsics, comp.answers, alt.answers, news.answers**

From: **lee@sq.sq.com** (Liam Quin)

Archive-name: **open-look/01-general**

Summary: Overview of OpenLook graphical user interface.

UNIX

UNIX (more exactly, "the UNIXes") is one of the most widely covered topics in the online world. About 80,000 people frequently read the UNIX newsgroups' information. Certainly a major factor in this popularity is that historically the vast majority of Internet sites have been UNIX-based machines. Also, there are at least as many variations of UNIX as there are operating systems and computing platforms. Consequently a large number of Internet newsgroups and FAQs address the various UNIX flavors.

An excellent starting point for locating any UNIX information is the **comp.unix.questions** newsgroup and the new users FAQ series. The newsgroup and FAQ feature

- ➤ A catalog of all UNIX newsgroups

- ➤ A primer on UNIX usage and programming topics

- ➤ A history of UNIX

- ➤ An evolutionary tree of various UNIX styles

- ➤ Brief notes on the well-known commercial UNIXes

The primary Internet UNIX newsgroups are

`comp.bugs.2bsd`	Reports of UNIX* version 2BSD related bugs
`comp.bugs.4bsd`	Reports of UNIX version 4BSD related bugs
`comp.bugs.4bsd.ucb-fixes`	Bug reports/fixes for BSD UNIX (moderated)
`comp.bugs.misc`	General UNIX bug reports and fixes (incl V7, uucp)
`comp.security.unix`	Discussion of UNIX security
`comp.sources.unix`	Postings of complete, UNIX-oriented sources (moderated)
`comp.std.unix`	Discussion for the P1003 committee on UNIX (moderated)
`comp.sys.3b1`	Discussion and support of AT&T 7300/3B1/UNIXPC
`comp.unix.admin`	Administering a UNIX-based system
`comp.unix.advocacy`	Arguments for and against UNIX and UNIX versions
`comp.unix.aix`	IBM's UNIX version
`comp.unix.amiga`	Minix, SYSV4, and other *nix on an Amiga
`comp.unix.aux`	The Apple Macintosh II UNIX version
`comp.unix.bsd`	Discussion of Berkeley Software Distribution UNIX
`comp.unix.dos-under-unix`	MS-DOS running under UNIX by whatever means

comp.unix.internals	Discussions on hacking UNIX internals
comp.unix.large	UNIX on mainframes and in large networks
comp.unix.misc	Various topics that don't fit elsewhere
comp.unix.osf.misc	Various aspects of Open Software Foundation products
comp.unix.osf.osf1	The Open Software Foundation's OSF/1
comp.unix.pc-clone.16bit	UNIX on 286 architectures
comp.unix.pc-clone.32bit	UNIX on 386 and 486 architectures
comp.unix.programmer	Q&A for people programming under UNIX
comp.unix.questions	UNIX neophytes group
comp.unix.shell	Using and programming the UNIX shell
comp.unix.sys3	System III UNIX discussions
comp.unix.sys5.misc	Versions of System V that pre-date Release 3
comp.unix.sys5.r3	Discussions of System V Release 3
comp.unix.sys5.r4	Discussions of System V Release 4
comp.unix.ultrix	Discussions about DEC's Ultrix
comp.unix.unixware	Discussion about Novell's UNIXWare products
comp.unix.user-friendly	Discussion of UNIX user-friendliness
comp.unix.wizards	For only true UNIX wizards (moderated)

`comp.unix.xenix.misc`	General discussions regarding XENIX (except SCO)
`comp.unix.xenix.sco`	XENIX versions from the Santa Cruz Operation
`comp.windows.x.i386unix`	The XFree86 Window System and others

Almost all these newsgroups have one or more FAQs containing a large amount of information. See the section "Periodic Postings and FAQs" for directions to FAQs on the **rtfm.mit.edu** server.

Internet Maillists

Several maillists provide information on UNIX and related topics.

DECnews-UNIX

Contact: **decnews-unix-request@pa.dec.com** (Russ Jones)

Description: Information for the Digital UNIX community.

To enroll, send a message with subject line **subscribe abstract.** Include your name and telephone number in the body of the message.

groupname

Contact: **majordomo@Warren.MentorG.COM**

Description: This maillist for UNIX sysadmins in the New Jersey area is a lot like a regional version of Usenix's SAGE or LISA groups.

info-gnu

Contact: **info-gnu-request@prep.ai.mit.edu**

Description: Progress reports on the GNU Project, a freeware UNIX-compatible software system.

info-MOON

Contact: **moon-request@one.it**

Description: Info for MOON (Managing Objects On Network) users.

info-prime

Contact: **info-prime-request@eeyore.usc.edu**

Description: Discussion list for users and administrators of Prime Computer's 50-series and EXL series (UNIX).

MachTen

Contact: **MachTen-request@tenon.com** (Leonard Cuff)

Description: Discussions of MachTen, a Mach/BSD UNIX for Macintoshes.

metacard-list

Contact: **listserv@grot.starconn.com**

Description: Discussions of the MetaCard product from MetaCard Corporation, an application development system similar to Apple's HyperCard.

ORA-NEWS

Contact: **listproc@online.ora.com**

Description: Announcements from the publisher O'Reilly & Associates.

rc

Contact: **rc-request@Hawkwind.utcs.toronto.edu** (Chris Siebenmann)

Description: Discussions of the rc shell.

security

Contact: **uunet!zardoz!security-request** (Neil Gorsuch)

Contact: **security-request@cpd.com**

Description: Notification of UNIX security flaws and related security topics. Membership is restricted. Enrollment requests must be mailed from a system administration account and must include the recipient's full name and the address to send the list to.

smail3-users

Contact: **smail3-users-request@cs.athabascau.ca** (Lyndon Nerenberg)

Description: For administrators of smail3.X-based mailers.

starserver

Contact: **starserver-request@engr.uky.edu** (Wes Morgan)

Description: For owners, operators, and administrators of AT&T StarServer systems.

STD-UNIX

Contact: STD-UNIX-REQUEST@uunet.uu.net comp.std.unix

Description: Discussion of UNIX standards.

Univel

Contact: **univel-request@telly.on.ca**

Description: For users, developers, and others interested in the products of the Novell subsidiary Univel, which producees UNIX system software for PC systems.

UNIX-SW

Contact: UNIX-SW-REQUEST@WSMR-

Description: Announces availablity of new UNIX/C language software on the WSMR-SIMTEL20.ARMY.MIL repository.

**BITNET
List Server
Maillist**

To subscribe to a maillist, send a mail message to **listserv@bitnic.bitnet**. Leave the *Subject:* field blank. In the body of the message, write: SUBSCRIBE **listname**, where listname is a name in the first column.

```
NADUNX-D      German Node Administrators (NAD) UNIX

UNIX-SRC      UNIX-Sources Mailing List

UNIX-TR       UNIX Tartisma ve Yardimlasma Listesi

UNIX-WIZ      UNIX-Wizards Mailing List
```

FTP Sites

It is almost impossible to find an anonymous FTP site that does not have some information or files relevant to UNIX. While having a lot of information available is usually an advantage, looking for something specific is often a "needle in a haystack" situation.

Fortunately, the newsgroup **comp.sources.wanted** can help you locate UNIX sources. Also, to access a file with guidelines on locating sources, use anonymous FTP to **rtfm.mit.edu** and access the file **/pub/usenet/comp.sources.wanted/How_to_find_sources(READ_THIS_ BEFORE_POSTING)**. The next sections list some FTP sites known for their collections of sources.

AIX

U.S. SITES:

acd.ucar.edu

acsc.acsc.com

aixpdslib.seas.ucla.edu

byron.u.washington.edu

lightning.gatech.edu

tesla.ee.cornell.edu

EUROPEAN SITES:

ftp-aix.polytechnique.fr

ftp.uni-stuttgart.de

ftp.zrz.TU-Berlin.DE

iacrs1.unibe.ch

nic.funet.fi

A/UX

abs.apple.com

afsg.apple.com

aux.support.apple.com

dolphin.csudh.edu

dunkin.Princeton.EDU

ftp.fenk.wau.nl

jagubox.gsfc.nasa.gov

nada.kth.se

rascal.ics.utexas.edu

redstar.dcs.qmw.ac.uk

wc208.residence.gatech.edu

wuarchive.wustl.edu

UNIXWare

Novell has an anonymous FTP service at **ftp.novell.com**, and Novell Germany has a site at **ftp.novell.de://pub/unixware/usle**.

Xenix

SCO provides support-level supplements (SLS) at **ftp.sco.com** and **ftp.uu.net**.

Online Data Services

Commercial online data services provide a large amount of information and support for the UNIXes.

CompuServe Forums

Several CompuServe forums have information on and support for various aspects of UNIX:

Dr. Dobb's Journal Forum	DDJFORUM
Media Newsletters($)	MEDIANEWS
NCSA InfoSecurity Forum	NCSAFORUM
NCSA Virus Vendor Forum	NCSAVEN
NeXT Forum	NEXTFORUM
Novell Vendor A Forum	NVENA
PC Vendor D Forum	PCVEND
PC Vendor F Forum	PCVENF
PDP-11 Forum	PDP11
Santa Cruz Operation Forum	SCOFORUM
STACKS Magazine Forum	STACKS
SunSoft Forum	SUNSOFT
The Mask UNIX Download Area	MASK
UNIX Forum	UNIXFORUM
UNIX Vendor A Forum	UNIXAVEN
UNIXWare Forum	UNIXWARE
VAX Forum	VAXFORUM
Xerox Office Solutions Forum	XRXOFFICE
Xerox Software Forum	XRXSW
Zenith Data Systems Forum	ZENITH

BIX Forums

BIX has two conferences related to UNIX in the programming area.

o amiga.unix	UNIX on the Amiga
o unix	The UNIX conference

Periodic Postings and FAQs

Because so many FAQs are available for UNIXes, all of them are presented here to make locating FAQs easier.

UNIX BBS Software Frequently Asked Questions

FAQ: **biz.sco.*** **newsgroups/mlists** (periodic posting)

FAQ: SCO UNIX newsgroups and mailing lists

X on Intel-based UNIX Frequently Asked Questions (FAQ)

Public UNIX Rechner in Deutschland

GNU software on prep

[**misc.books.technical**] *A Concise Guide to UNIX Books*

aus.org.auug - Frequently Asked Questions (last modified: *)

Waffle Frequently Asked Questions (FAQ)

WINE (WINdows Emulator) Frequently Asked Questions

V*INF1: Introduction to **comp.sources.unix**

V*INF2: List of sources in the **comp.sources.unix** archives

COMP.SYS.IBM.PC.RT: AIX V2 FAQ - Index

COMP.SYS.IBM.PC.RT: AIX V2 FAQ - OS Specific Hardware, Part * of 1

COMP.SYS.IBM.PC.RT: AIX V2 FAQ - Software questions, Part * of 3

COMP.SYS.IBM.PC.RT: AIX V2 FAQ - Question/Answer, Part * of 2

COMP.SYS.IBM.PC.RT: AIX V2 FAQ - Porting software, Part * of 1

FAQ: Sun Computer Administration Frequently Asked Questions

AIX Frequently Asked Questions (Part * of *)

FAQ for A/UX 2.0.1

Apple A/UX FAQ List (*/*)

BSDI BSD/386 Ported Software List Part */*

Frequently Asked Questions (FAQ) for **comp.unix.msdos**

So You Want to Be a UNIX Wizard? (The Loginataka)

vi editor FAQ (Frequently Asked Question List), Part */2

Programming for Internationalization FAQ

UNIX - Frequently Asked Questions (*/*) (frequent posting)

Welcome to **comp.unix.questions** (frequent posting)

Changes to "Welcome to **comp.unix.shell**" (frequent posting)

Z-shell Frequently Asked Questions

rc shell Frequently Asked Questions

Csh Programming Considered Harmful

UNIX shell differences and how to change your shell (monthly posting)

Welcome to **comp.unix.shell** (frequent posting)

Solaris 2 Porting FAQ

Solaris 2 Frequently Asked Questions (FAQ) *

Known Bugs in the USL UNIX distribution

PC-Clone UNIX Hardware Buyer's Guide

PC-Clone UNIX Software Buyer's Guide

ULTRIX and DEC OSF/1 AXP Common Frequently Asked Questions (FAQ)

ULTRIX Frequently Asked Questions (FAQ)

DEC OSF/1 AXP Frequently Asked Questions

comp.unix.unixware Frequently Asked Questions (FAQ) list

comp.unix.user-friendly Frequently Asked Questions (FAQ)

Intro to **comp.unix.wizards**—read before posting! (last change: *)

Welcome to **comp.unix.xenix.sco** (changes from previous version)

Welcome to **comp.unix.xenix.sco** (monthly FAQ posting)

Subject: UNIX BBS Software Frequently Asked Questions

Newsgroups: **alt.bbs.unixbbs, alt.bbs, alt.answers, news.answers**

From: **tree@bbs.dsnet.com** (system administrator)

Summary: BBS Software for use with UNIX-like operating systems

Archive-name: **unix-faq/bbs-software/faq**

Subject: FAQ: **biz.sco*newsgroups/mlists** (periodic posting)

Subject: FAQ: SCO UNIX newsgroups and mailing lists

Newsgroups: **comp.unix.sco.announce, comp.unix.sco.misc, comp.unix.xenix.sco, comp.unix.pc-clone.32bit, comp.answers, news.answers**

From: **edhew@xenitec.on.ca** (Ed Hew)

Subject: X on Intel-based UNIX Frequently Asked Questions

Newsgroups: **comp.windows.x.i386unix, comp.unix.pc-clone.32bit, comp.unix.bsd, comp.windows.x, comp.answers, news.answers**

From: **steve@ecf.toronto.edu** (Steve Kotsopoulos)

Archive-name: **x-faq/Intel-UNIX-X-faq**

Summary: X options for Intel-based UNIX (SYSV/386, BSD, Linux, Mach)

Subject: Public UNIX Rechner in Deutschland

Newsgroups: **de.etc.lists, de.answers, news.answers**

From: **wsb@behre.han.de** (Wolfgang Sander-Beuermann)

Archive-name: **de-pub-unix**

Summary: Lists public UNIX sites in Germany, accessible by modem. Like the newsgroup, it is in German.

Subject: GNU software on prep

Newsgroup: **gnu.misc.discuss**

From: **julian@uhunix.uhcc.hawaii.edu** (J. Cowley)

Subject: (**misc.books.technical**) *A Concise Guide to UNIX Books*

Newsgroups: **misc.books.technical, alt.books.technical, biz.books.technical, comp.unix.questions, comp.unix.wizards, comp.unix.admin, misc.answers, comp.answers, alt.answers, news.answers**

From: **sko@Helix.net** (Samuel Ko)

Archive-name: **books/unix**

Summary: Lists recommended books and documents on UNIX and related subjects

Subject: **aus.org.auug**—Frequently Asked Questions (last modified: *)

Newsgroups: **aus.org.auug, news.answers**

From: **pjw@csis.dit.csiro.au** (Peter Wishart)

Archive-name: **auug-faq**

Summary: Answers Frequently Asked Questions about AUUG Inc., an Australian users group for UNIX and open systems. It covers questions about membership, history, contacts, and other useful information.

Subject: Waffle Frequently Asked Questions (FAQ)

Newsgroups: **comp.bbs.waffle, comp.answers, news.answers**

From: **cbwfaq@alpha3.ersys.edmonton.ab.ca** (Comp.Bbs.Waffle FAQ)

Archive-name: **waffle-faq**

Archive-name: **faq**

Summary: Waffle is a BBS, a UUCP, mail, and a news package for MS-DOS and UNIX Comp-bbs-waffle.

Subject: WINE (WINdows Emulator) Frequently Asked Questions

Newsgroups: **comp.emulators.announce, comp.emulators.ms-windows.wine, comp.os.386bsd.announce, comp.os.linux.answers, comp.windows.x.i386unix, comp.answers, news.answers**

From: **pdg@primenet.com** (Dave Gardner)

Archive-name: **windows-emulation/wine-faq**

Summary: Lists Frequently Asked Questions (and their answers) about WINE, the WINdows Emulator project. Anyone who wants to know more about the development of this programming project, which will allow users to run MS Windows binary programs under certain UNIXes and UNIX clones, should read this.

Subject: V*INF1: Introduction to **comp.sources.unix**

Newsgroup: **mp.sources.unix**

From: **comp-sources-unix@bloom-beacon.mit.edu**

Subject: V*INF2: Lists sources in the **comp.sources.unix** archives

Newsgroup: **comp.sources.unix**

From: **comp-sources-unix@bloom-beacon.mit.edu**

Subject: COMP.SYS.IBM.PC.RT: AIX V2 FAQ—Index

Subject: COMP.SYS.IBM.PC.RT: AIX V2 FAQ - OS-specific hardware, Part * of 1

Subject: COMP.SYS.IBM.PC.RT: AIX V2 FAQ - Software questions, Part * of 3

Subject: COMP.SYS.IBM.PC.RT: AIX V2 FAQ - Questions and answers, Part * of 2

Subject: COMP.SYS.IBM.PC.RT: AIX V2 FAQ - Porting software, Part * of 1

Newsgroups: **comp.sys.ibm.pc.rt, comp.unix.aix, comp.answers, news.answers**

From: **faq-rt@antimatr.hou.tx.us** (Mark Whetzel)

Archive-name: **ibm-rt-faq/aix-v2/index**

Summary: Posts the Master Index to Frequently Asked Questions (and their answers) on issues related to using AIX V2.2.x on IBM RT (Model 615x) computers

Subject: FAQ: Sun Computer administration Frequently Asked Questions

Newsgroups: **comp.sys.sun.admin, comp.sys.sun.misc, comp.unix.solaris, comp.answers, news.answers**

From: **montjoy@thor.ece.uc.edu** (Rob Montjoy)

Archive-name: **comp-sys-sun-faq**

Summary: Answers questions that appear in **comp.sys.sun.***

Subject: AIX Frequently Asked Questions (Part * of *)

Newsgroups: **comp.unix.aix, comp.answers, news.answers**

From: **jwarring@amsinc.com** (Jeff Warrington)

Archive-name: **aix-faq/part1**

Summary: Lists Frequently Asked Questions about AIX, IBM's version of UNIX, and their answers

Subject: FAQ for A/UX 2.0.1

Newsgroup: **comp.unix.aux**

From: **jim@jagubox.gsfc.nasa.gov** (Jim Jagielski)

Summary: Posts latest frozen FAQ for A/UX 2.0.1

Subject: Apple A/UX FAQ List (*/*)

Newsgroups: **comp.unix.aux, news.answers, comp.answers**

From: **jim@jagubox.gsfc.nasa.gov** (Jim Jagielski)

Archive-name: **aux-faq/part1**

Summary: Post latest FAQ for A/UX

Subject: BSDI BSD/386 ported software list Part */*

Newsgroup: **comp.unix.bsd**

From: **smm@iedv7.acd.com** (Steve McCoole)

Subject: Frequently Asked Questions (FAQ) for **comp.unix.msdos**

Newsgroup: **comp.unix.msdos**

From: **fnx!vpix-faq@uunet.UU.NET** (VP/IX FAQ maintainance)

Subject: So You Want to Be a UNIX Wizard? (The Loginataka)

Newsgroups: **comp.unix.questions, alt.folklore.computers, news.answers**

From: **esr@ccantares.wcupa.edu** (Eric S. Raymond)

Archive-name: **unix-faq/loginataka**

Subject: Lists vi editor Frequently Asked Question, Part */2

Newsgroups: **comp.unix.questions, comp.editors, comp.answers, news.answers**

From: **ellidz@midway.uchicago.edu** (E. Larry Lidz)

Archive-name: **editor-faq/vi/part2**

Summary: Lists of Frequently Asked Questions about the vi editor and their answers

Subject: Programming for internationalization FAQ

Newsgroups: **comp.unix.questions, comp.std.internat, comp.software.international, comp.lang.c, comp.windows.x, comp.std.c, comp.answers, news.answers**

From: **mike@vlsivie.tuwien.ac.at**

Archive-name: **internationalization/programming-faq**

Summary: Discusses how to write programs that can handle different language conventions, character sets, and so on. Applicable to all character set encodings with particular emphasis on ISO-8859-1.

Subject: UNIX - Frequently Asked Questions (*/*) (frequent posting)

Newsgroups: **comp.unix.questions, comp.unix.shell, comp.answers, news.answers**

From: **tmatimar@isgtec.com** (Ted Timar)

Archive-name: **unix-faq/faq/part1**

Subject: Welcome to **comp.unix.questions** (frequent posting)

Newsgroups: **comp.unix.questions, news.answers, comp.answers**

From: **tmatimar@isgtec.com** (Ted Timar)

Archive-name: **unix-faq/unix/intro**

Subject: Gives information about newsgroups and mailing lists

Newsgroups: **comp.unix.sco.announce, comp.unix.sco.misc, comp.unix.xenix.sco, comp.unix.pc-clone.32bit, comp.answers, news.answers**

From: **edhew@xenitec.on.ca** (Ed Hew)

Archive-name: **biz-sco-faq**

Summary: Contains **biz.sco** newsgroups and mailing lists and information on how to subscribe (and why)

Subject: Changes to "Welcome to **comp.unix.shell**" (frequent posting)

Newsgroups: **comp.unix.shell, comp.answers, news.answers**

From: **tmatimar@isgtec.com** (Ted Timar)

Archive-name: **unix-faq/shell/diff**

Subject: Z-shell Frequently Asked Questions

Newsgroups: **comp.unix.shell, comp.answers, news.answers**

From: **pws@amtp.liv.ac.uk** (Peter Stephenson)

Archive-name: **unix-faq/shell/zsh**

Summary: Gives questions and answers about zsh, a powerful (and free) UNIX shell

Subject: rc shell Frequently Asked Questions

Newsgroups: **comp.unix.shell, comp.answers, news.answers**

From: **alan@lowell.edu** (Alan Watson)

Archive-name: **unix-faq/shell/rc**

Comp-UNIX-shell-archive-name: **rc-FAQ**

Summary: Answers Frequently Asked Questions about rc, a clean, portable, and freely available shell for UNIX systems

Subject: Csh Programming Considered Harmful

Newsgroups: **comp.unix.shell, comp.unix.questions, comp.unix.programmer, comp.answers, news.answers**

From: **tchrist@mox.perl.com** (Tom Christiansen)

Archive-name: **unix-faq/shell/csh-whynot**

Subject: Explains UNIX shell differences and how to change your shell (monthly posting)

Newsgroups: **comp.unix.shell, comp.unix.questions, news.answers, comp.answers**

From: **bnb@gryphon.demon.co.uk** (Brian Blackmore)

Archive-name: **unix-faq/shell/shell-differences**

Subject: Welcome to **comp.unix.shell** (frequent posting)

Newsgroups: **comp.unix.shell, news.answers, comp.answers**

From: **tmatimar@isgtec.com** (Ted Timar)

Archive-name: **unix-faq/shell/intro**

Subject: Solaris 2 porting FAQ

Newsgroups: **comp.unix.solaris, comp.answers, news.answers**

From: **meyer@frostbite-falls.uoregon.edu** (David M. Meyer, 503-346-1747)

Archive-name: **Solaris2/porting-FAQ**

Summary: Lists Frequently Asked Questions (and their answers) about porting BSD applications to ANSI/SVID/SVR4 systems in general and Solaris 2 in particular

Subject: Solaris 2 Frequently Asked Questions (FAQ) *

Newsgroups: **comp.unix.solaris, comp.sys.sun.admin, comp.answers, news.answers**

From: **casper@fwi.uva.nl** (Casper H. S. Dik)

Archive-name: **Solaris2/FAQ**

Summary: Lists Frequently Asked Questions (and answers) about Sun Microsystem's Solaris 2.x system in general. See also the FAQs archived as Solaris2/Porting and Solaris2/x86.

Subject: Known bugs in the USL UNIX distribution

Newsgroups: comp.unix.sys5.r4, comp.unix.pc-clone.32bit, comp.bugs.sys5, news.answers

From: esr@ccantares.wcupa.edu (Eric S. Raymond)

Archive-name: usl-bugs

Subject: PC-Clone UNIX hardware buyer's guide

Newsgroups: comp.unix.sys5.r4, comp.unix.pc-clone.32bit, comp.sys.intel, comp.os.linux.announce, news.answers

From: esr@ccantares.wcupa.edu (Eric S. Raymond)

Archive-name: pc-unix/hardware

Summary: Gives tips on how and where to buy UNIX hardware

Subject: PC-clone UNIX software buyer's guide

Newsgroups: comp.unix.sys5.r4, comp.unix.pc-clone.32bit, comp.unix.bsd, comp.os.linux.announce, news.answers

From: esr@ccantares.wcupa.edu (Eric S. Raymond)

Archive-name: pc-unix/software

Summary: Contains a buyer's guide to UNIX versions for PC-clone hardware

Subject: ULTRIX and DEC OSF/1 AXP Common Frequently Asked Questions (FAQ)

Newsgroups: comp.unix.ultrix, comp.sys.dec, comp.unix.osf.osf1, comp.answers, news.answers

From: lionel@quark.enet.dec.com (Steve Lionel)

Archive-name: **dec-faq/common**

Summary: Lists Frequently Asked Questions (and their answers) about the ULTRIX and DEC OSF/1 AXP operating systems from Digital Equipment Corporation

Subject: ULTRIX Frequently Asked Questions (FAQ)

Newsgroups: **comp.unix.ultrix, comp.sys.dec, news.answers, comp.answers**

From: **lionel@quark.enet.dec.com** (Steve Lionel)

Archive-name: **dec-faq/ultrix**

Summary: Lists Frequently Asked Questions(and their answers) about the ULTRIX operating system from Digital Equipment Corporation

Subject: DEC OSF/1 AXP Frequently Asked Questions

Newsgroups: **comp.unix.ultrix, comp.unix.osf.osf1, comp.sys.dec, vmsnet.alpha, comp.answers, news.answers**

From: **lionel@quark.enet.dec.com** (Steve Lionel)

Archive-name: **dec-faq/osf1**

Summary: Lists Frequently Asked Questions (and their answers) about the DEC OSF/1 AXP operating system from Digital Equipment Corporation

Subject: **comp.unix.unixware** Frequently Asked Questions (FAQ)

Newsgroups: **comp.unix.unixware, comp.unix.sys5.r4, news.answers, comp.answers**

From: **vlcek@byteware.com** (James Vlcek)

Archive-name: **unix-faq/unixware/general**

Summary: Answers questions frequently asked about Novell's UNIXWare product

Subject: **comp.unix.user-friendly** Frequently Asked Questions (FAQ)

Newsgroups: **comp.unix.user-friendly, comp.answers, news.answers**

From: **cuuf@wfu.edu**

Archive-name: **unix-faq/user-friendly**

Subject: Introduces **comp.unix.wizards**. Read this before posting! (last change: *)

Newsgroups: **comp.unix.wizards, news.answers, comp.answers**

From: **fitzgb@mml0.meche.rpi.edu** (Brian Fitzgerald)

Archive-name: **unix-faq/wizards-faq**

Summary: Explains the purpose of the **comp.unix.wizards** newsgroup. Anyone who wishes to post here should read this.

Subject: Welcome to **comp.unix.xenix.sco** (changes from previous version)

Newsgroups: **comp.unix.xenix.sco, news.answers**

From: **chip@chinacat.unicom.com** (Chip Rosenthal)

Archive-name: **sco-xenix-diff**

News-answers-archive-name: **sco/xenix-diff**

Subject: Welcome to **comp.unix.xenix.sco** (monthly FAQ posting)

Newsgroups: **comp.unix.xenix.sco, news.answers**

From: **chip@chinacat.unicom.com** (Chip Rosenthal)

Archive-name: **sco-xenix**

News-answers-archive-name: **sco/xenix**

Summary: Answers Frequently Asked Questions

Linux

Linux, a freeware UNIX-like Operating System, is written to comply with the POSIX specification but also has extensions for SYSV and BSD. It presently runs only on IBM architecture systems having the EISA or ISA bus and a 386 or higher processor. Efforts are underway to port it to 68x and other platforms. Linus Torvalds (**torvalds@kruuna.helsinki.fi**) from Finland wrote the Linux kernel with other volunteers.

Two excellent files provide information about Linux, INFO-SHEET and META-FAQ, available at the primary archive sites. They describe Linux, point to numerous useful sites and files, and tell how to obtain source files.

Internet Mailists

The next two sections provide information on Linux and related topics.

Linux-Activists

Contact: **linux-activists-request@niksula.hut.fi** (Ari Lemmke)

Description: For Linux operating system use/hacking.

linux-postgres

Contact: **linux-postgres-request@native-ed.bc.ca**

Description: For the Linux port of the POSTGRES database system.

BITNET ListServer Maillists

To subscribe to a maillist, send a mail message to **listserv@bitnic.bitnet**. Leave the *Subject:* field blank. In the body of the message, write: SUBSCRIBE **listname**, where listname is a name in the first column.

```
LINUX-IL      LINUX-IL—Linux Software discussions &
              announcements of Isra+
```

FTP Sites

The primary archive sites for Linux, **tsx-11.mit.edu**, **sunsite.unc.edu**, and **ftp.funet.fi**, are mirrored at many other sites. Go to **tsx-11.mit.edu//pubs/linux/docs** to obtain the files INFO-SHEET and

META-FAQ for info about obtaining and using Linux. Table 8.1 shows the overall directory structure of tsx-11.

To find Linux information on the World Wide Web, go to the major WWW page **http://sunsite.unc.edu/mdw/linux.html**. You'll see the Linux Documentation Project home page, which provides links or other referrals to all relevant FAQs and a series of how-tos.

**Table 8.1
Linux Archive
Directory
Structure**

```
------------------------------------------

Linux — The free 386 UNIX clone is here!

------------------------------------------


Welcome to TSX-11's Linux FTP site!


Directory structure


docs          documentation (such as it is)

docs/LDP      Linux Documentation Project work. A series
              of books on Linux, at various stages of
              completion

sources       Linux sources, categorized as system
              sources (including libc.a), system programs
              sources, usr.bin sources, and library
              sources

binaries      Various binary files for Linux. (Use the
              tar and compress programs on the root disk
              or in binaries/usr.bin to unpack these.)

packages      Packaged programs, like GCC, Ada, OI,
              FORTRAN, Emacs, and others

ALPHA         Software not yet considered stable by its
              author(s)

BETA          Software considered a little better by its
              author(s)

patches       Patches to Linux (typically, but not
              always, patches to system sources, such as
              patches that add new features to the
```

**Table 8.1
Linux Archive
Directory
Structure
*(Continued)***

```
                   kernel). Check ALPHA and BETA for many
                   newer patches; most are old.

ports              Patches to make other programs compile on a
                   Linux system

mail-archive       Archive of the Linux-Activists mailing list

info               Various informational files that Linux
                   hackers may find useful

attic              Old version of programs
```

Newsgroups

Permanent newsgroups are accessible via most network newsreader programs.

```
comp.os.linux.admin                  Installing and adminis-
                                     tering Linux systems

comp.os.linux.advocacy               Benefits of Linux com-
                                     pared to other operating
                                     systems

comp.os.linux.announce               Important announcements
                                     to the Linux community
                                     (moderated)

comp.os.linux.answers                FAQs, how-tos, READMEs,
                                     and so on about Linux
                                     (moderated)

comp.os.linux.development            Ongoing work on the
                                     Linux operating system

comp.os.linux.development.apps       Writing Linux applica-
                                     tions, porting to Linux

comp.os.linux.development.system     Linux kernels, device
                                     drivers, and modules

comp.os.linux.hardware               Hardware compatibility
                                     with the Linux operating
                                     system
```

`comp.os.linux.help`	Questions and advice about Linux
`comp.os.linux.misc`	Linux-specific topics not covered by other groups
`comp.os.linux.networking`	Networking and communications under Linux
`comp.os.linux.setup`	Linux installation and system administration
`comp.os.linux.x`	Linux X Windows system servers, clients, libraries, and fonts

Periodic Postings and FAQs

Because so many FAQs are available for Linux and related topics, only a brief listing is given here to help you locate specific topics.

Friendly Online Support for Linux

X on Intel-based UNIX Frequently Asked Questions (FAQ)

WINE (WINdows Emulator) Frequently Asked Questions

LILO FAQ, version *

Linux FTP and BBS List #* (LONG)

Linux BBS list #*

Linux Electronic Mail HOWTO

Linux UUCP HOWTO

Linux News HOWTO

Linux Ethernet HOWTO (part */*)

Linux Printing HOWTO (Part */*)

Linux INFO-SHEET

Linux META-FAQ

Linux XFree86 HOWTO

Linux * HOWTO

Linux HOWTO Index

Linux NET-2 HOWTO (part */*)

Welcome to the **comp.os.linux.*** hierarchy!

Linux Frequently Asked Questions with Answers (FAQ: */*)

Changes to Linux Frequently Asked Questions with Answers

PC-clone UNIX Hardware Buyer's Guide

PC-clone UNIX Software Buyer's Guide

Subject: Friendly online support for Linux

Newsgroup: **comp.os.linux.misc**

From: lilo <TaRDiS@Mail.UTexas.EDU>

Subject: X on Intel-based UNIX Frequently Asked Questions [FAQ]

Newsgroups: **comp.windows.x.i386unix, comp.unix.pc-clone.32bit, comp.unix.bsd, comp.windows.x, comp.answers, news.answers**

From: **steve@ecf.toronto.edu** (Steve Kotsopoulos)

Archive-name: **x-faq/Intel-UNIX-X-faq**

Summary: Explains X options for Intel-based UNIX (SYSV/386, BSD, Linux, and Mach)

Subject: WINE (WINdows Emulator) Frequently Asked Questions

Newsgroups: **comp.emulators.announce, comp.emulators.ms-windows.wine, comp.os.386bsd.announce, comp.os.linux.answers, comp.windows.x.i386unix, comp.answers, news.answers**

From: **pdg@primenet.com** (Dave Gardner)

Archive-name: **windows-emulation/wine-faq**

Summary: Lists Frequently Asked Questions (and their answers) about WINE, the WINdows Emulator project. Anyone who wants to know more about the development of this programming project, which will let users run MS Windows binary programs under certain UNIXes and UNIX clones, should read this.

Subject: LILO FAQ, version *

Newsgroup: **comp.os.linux.announce**

From: **almesber@nessie.cs.id.ethz.ch** (Werner Almesberger)

Subject: Linux FTP and BBS list #* (LONG)

Newsgroup: **comp.os.linux.announce**

From: **healyzh@Holonet.net** (Zane H. Healy)

Subject: Linux BBS list #*

Newsgroup: **comp.os.linux.announce**

From: **rasca@marie.physik.tu-berlin.de** (Matthias Gmelch)

Subject: Linux electronic mail how-to

Subject: Linux UUCP how-to

Subject: Linux News how-to

Newsgroups: **comp.os.linux.announce, comp.os.linux.admin, comp.answers, news.answers**

From: **vince@victrola.wa.com** (Vince Skahan)

Archive-name: **linux/howto/mail**

Summary: Provides information on Linux-based mail servers and clients

Subject: Linux Ethernet how-to (part */*)

Newsgroups: **comp.os.linux.announce, comp.os.linux.admin, comp.answers, news.answers**

From: **gpg109@rsphysse.anu.edu.au** (Paul Gortmaker)

Archive-name: **linux/howto/ethernet/part1**

Summary: Provides information on Ethernet hardware compatibility for Linux

Subject: Linux Printing how-to (Part */*)

Newsgroups: **comp.os.linux.announce, comp.os.linux.admin, comp.answers, news.answers**

From: **gtaylor@cs.tufts.edu** (Grant Taylor)

Archive-name: **linux/howto/printing/part1**

Summary: Gives information on printing under Linux

Subject: Linux INFO-SHEET

Newsgroups: **comp.os.linux.announce, comp.os.linux.help, comp.answers, news.answers**

From: **johnsonm@sunsite.unc.edu**

Archive-name: **linux/info-sheet**

Summary: Contains a quick summary of the Linux operating system's features and abilities. A supplement to the **comp.os.linux.announce** FAQ and META-FAQ, it should be read by anyone who wants to learn about and/or install Linux.

Subject: Linux META-FAQ

Newsgroups: **comp.os.linux.announce, comp.os.linux.help, comp.answers, news.answers**

From: johnsonm@sunsite.unc.edu

Archive-name: **linux/meta-faq**

Summary: Contains a quick summary of information available about the Linux operating system and explains where to find other information. Anyone who wants to install Linux and anyone who wants to find other information sources on Linux should read this.

Subject: Linux XFree86 how-to

Newsgroups: **comp.os.linux.announce, comp.os.linux.help, comp.os.linux.admin, comp.windows.x.i386unix, comp.answers, news.answers**

From: **geyer@polyhymnia.iwr.uni-heidelberg.de** (Helmut Geyer)

Archive-name: **linux/howto/XFree86**

Summary: Tells how to install XFree86 (X11R5) for Linux

Subject: Linux * how-to

Newsgroups: **comp.os.linux.announce, comp.os.linux.help, comp.os.linux.admin, news.answers, comp.answers**

From: **mdw@sunsite.unc.edu** (Matt Welsh)

Archive-name: **linux/howto/installation**

Summary: Tells how to obtain and install the Linux software

Subject: Linux how-to index.

Newsgroups: **comp.os.linux.announce, comp.os.linux.help, comp.os.linux.admin, news.answers, comp.answers**

From: **mdw@sunsite.unc.edu** (Matt Welsh)

Archive-name: **linux/howto/index**

Summary: Contains an index of how-to documents about Linux

Subject: Linux NET-2 how-to (part */*)

Newsgroups: **comp.os.linux.announce, comp.os.linux.help, comp.os.linux.admin, news.answers, comp.answers**

From: **terryd@extro.ucc.su.oz.au** (Terry Dawson)

Archive-name: **linux/howto/networking/part1**

Summary: Tells how to configure TCP/IP networking, SLIP, PLIP, and PPP under Linux

Subject: Welcome to the @:comp.os.linux.* hierarchy!

Newsgroups: **comp.os.linux.announce, comp.os.linux.help, comp.os.linux.development, comp.os.linux.admin, comp.os.linux.misc, news.answers, comp.answers**

From: **mdw@sunsite.unc.edu** (Matt Welsh)

Archive-name: **linux/announce/intro**

Subject: List of Linux Frequently Asked Questions and their answers (FAQ: */*)

Subject: Changes to Linux Frequently Asked Questions and their answers

Newsgroups: **comp.os.linux.answers, comp.os.linux.setup, comp.os.linux.development.apps, comp.os.linux.misc, comp.os.linux.announce, comp.os.linux.help, comp.answers, news.answers**

From: **ijackson@nyx.cs.du.edu** (Ian Jackson)

Archive-name: **linux/faq/part1**

Summary: Please read the whole FAQ before posting to **comp.os.linux.help.**

Subject: PC-clone UNIX hardware buyer's guide

Newsgroups: **comp.unix.sys5.r4, comp.unix.pc-clone.32bit, comp.sys.intel, comp.os.linux.announce, news.answers**

From: **esr@ccantares.wcupa.edu** (Eric S. Raymond)

Archive-name: **pc-unix/hardware**

Summary: Offers tips on how and where to buy hardware for your UNIX

Subject: PC-clone UNIX software buyer's guide

Newsgroups: **comp.unix.sys5.r4, comp.unix.pc-clone.32bit, comp.unix.bsd, comp.os.linux.announce, news.answers**

From: **esr@ccantares.wcupa.edu** (Eric S. Raymond)

Archive-name: **pc-unix/software**

Summary: Offers tips on how, where, and what UNIX software to buy for PC-clone hardware

CHAPTER NINE

COMPUTER PLATFORMS

This chapter describes resources for specific computing platforms, or families of platforms. It also covers any operating systems or environments that are usually considered linked to these platforms. "Generic" or "portable" operating systems and environments are covered in Chapter 8.

Here are some examples to help you understand the distinction:

➤ Although Microsoft Windows and related applications can run on Apple machines, Windows is historically associated with Intel-IBM architecture machines, so it's covered here.

➤ Because UNIX runs on many different computing platforms, it's covered in Chapter 8.

Apple Architecture

Apple supports product lines based on several architectures including Apple II, Macintosh, Newton, and PowerPC. The resource lists are, where possible, organized by platform.

The following maillists provide information on Apple platforms and related topics.

<table>
<tr><td>

**Internet
Maillists:
Apple, General**

</td><td>

Apple Internet Providers

Contact: listproc@abs.apple.com

Alternate: apple-internet-users@abs.apple.com.

Description: Discusses topics interesting to those who use Apple computers to provide services or information on the Internet.

metacard-list

Contact: listserv@grot.starconn.com

Description: Discussions of MetaCard Corporation's products, which are application development systems similar to Apple's HyperCard

MMDEVX

Contact: Mail-Server@knex.mind.org

Description: Cross-platform multimedia development tools, the Apple Media Kit (AMK), and Kaleida ScriptX

</td></tr>
<tr><td>

**Internet
Maillists:
Apple Newton**

</td><td>

wa-newt

Contact: listserv@gu.uwa.edu.au

Description: Apple Newton availability in Western Australia

</td></tr>
<tr><td>

**Internet
Maillists:
Apple
Macintosh**

</td><td>

Igor

Contact: igor-request@pica.army.mil (Tom Coradeschi)

Description: Discussion of Igor, an Apple Macintosh data plotting and analysis package

mae-users, mae-announce, mae-bugs

Contact: listproc@medraut.apple.com

</td></tr>
</table>

Description: Three lists Apple created for users of the Mac Application Environment. Lists are for user interaction, product announcements, and bug submissions.

mac-security

Contact: **mac-security-request@world.std.com** (David C. Kovar)

Description: Macintosh security

cwarrior

Contact: **listserv@netcom.com**

Description: Discussion of Metrowerks CodeWarrior Macintosh development tools. CodeWarrior includes C, C++, and Pascal compilers; a class library; and associated tools.

Info-LabVIEW

Contact: **info-labview-request@pica.army.mil**

Description: Discussions of National Instruments' LabVIEW graphical software system package for Macintosh, Windows, and SPARCstation environments

Mac-Mgrs

Contact: **Majordomo@world.std.com**

Description: Configuration and management of Macintosh systems and networks

MachTen

Contact: **MachTen-request@tenon.com** (Leonard Cuff)

Description: Discussions of MachTen, a Mach/BSD UNIX for Macintoshes

Macintosh Tcl Mailing List

Contact: listser@aic.lockheed.com

Description: Discussion of Tcl on Macintosh systems

think-c

Contact: **think-c-request@ics.uci.edu** (Mark Nagel)

Description: Use of the Think C compiler on Macintosh systems

TopSoft

Contact: **ts-request@atlas.chem.utah.edu** (Tony Jacobs)

Descripton: Macintosh programming users group developing freeware

BITNET List Server Maillists

To subscribe to a maillist, send a mail message to **listserv@bitnic.bitnet**. Leave the *Subject:* field blank. In the body of the message, write: SUBSCRIBE listname, where listname is a name in the left columns of the following sections.

BITNET Maillists: Apple General

AECP-L	Apple Education Consultants Program
ATALK-L	Campuswide AppleTalk Discussion List
INFO-APP	INFO-APP Info-Apple List

BITNET Maillists: Apple II

APPLE2-L	Apple II List
APPLE3-L	Apple III Discussion Group

BITNET Maillists: Apple Macintosh

HYPERCRD	HyperCard Discussion List

MACPB-L	Macintosh PowerBook Issues
INFINI-D	Macintosh Infini-D discussion
MAC-L	Macintosh News and Information
MAC-TEL	EARN Macintosh Users List - Extension for MacTel digests
MAC-USER	EARN Macintosh Users List
MACAPPLI	Usage tips about Macintosh applications
MACASSOC	Macintosh Association of the Capstone
MACAV-L	Macintosh Quadra 660AV and 840AV
MACCHAT	The Mac*Chat Newsletter
MACGIL-L	McGill Macintosh Users Group
MACHRDWR	Macintosh hardware and related peripherals
MACHTTP	MacHTTP Talk
MACIRC-L	Macintosh IRC Client Design List
MACLSV-L	MACLSV-L: Macintosh LISTSERV User Interface Development
MACMULTI	Macintosh Multimedia Discussion List
MACNET-L	Macintosh Networking Issues
MACPPC-L	Macintosh PowerPC List (MACPPC-L)
MACPROG	Macintosh Programming Discussion List
MACRAO	MACRAO List
MACSCRPT	Macintosh Scripting Systems
MACSYSTM	Macintosh system software
MACTURK	Turkish Macintosh Users Group
MACUO-L	University of Ottawa's Mac Users Discussion Group

BITNET Maillists: Apple Newton

```
NEWTON-L      Discussion of Apple Newton Family of
              Equipment
```

FTP and WWW Sites

Sites for Apple, General

The official Apple support sites are **ftp://ftp.info.apple.com/** and **ftp://ftp.support.apple.com/**. You can also access Apple on the WWW at **http://ftp.apple.com/**.

Sites for Apple Macintosh

Two primary sites for Mac archives of shareware, freeware, and demo software are **sumex-aim.stanford.edu** (aka "Info-Mac") and **mac.archive** at **mac.archive.umich.edu**. Both these sites are extremely busy; you might fare better accessing a mirror site such as **grind.isca.uiowa.edu//mac/info-mac** or **mirrors.aol.com//pub/mac**. You can obtain lists of mirrors from **ftp://rever.nmsu.edu//pub/macfaq/info/Mac_FTP_List.txt** or **http://rever.nmsu.edu/ pub/~elharo/faq/software.html**.

Other leading sites for Mac software, information, and tools are

seeding.apple.com

nic.switch.ch

ftp.acns.nwu.edu

ftp.qualcomm

ftp.ncsa.uiuc.edu

redback.cs.uwa.edu.au

ics.uci.edu

ftp.cc.umanitoba.ca

Sites for Apple II

apple2.archive.umich.edu

archive.orst.edu

archive.orst.educco.caltech.edu

brownvm.brown.edu

ftp.ms.uky.edu

ftp.uni-kl.de

grind.isca.uiowa.edu

plains.nodak.edu

wuarchive.wustl.edu

Internet Newsgroups

These permanent newsgroups are accessible via most network newsreader programs.

Newsgroups: Apple, General

comp.protocols.appletalk	Applebus hardware and software

Newsgroups: Apple II

comp.binaries.apple2	Binary-only postings for the Apple II computer
comp.emulators.apple2	Emulators of Apple II systems
comp.sources.apple2	Source code and discussion for the Apple II (moderated)
comp.sys.apple2	Discussion about Apple II micros
comp.sys.apple2.comm	Apple II data communications
comp.sys.apple2.gno	The Apple II GNO multitasking environment
comp.sys.apple2.marketplace	Buying, selling, and trading Apple II equipment
comp.sys.apple2.programmer	Programming on the Apple II groups
comp.sys.apple2.usergroups	All about Apple II user groups

Newsgroups: Apple, Macintosh

comp.lang.lisp.mcl
Discussing Apple's Macintosh Common LISP

comp.sources.mac
Software for the Apple Macintosh (moderated)

comp.sys.mac.digest
Apple Macintosh: info and uses, but no programs
(moderated)

comp.sys.mac.misc
General discussions about the Apple Macintosh

comp.sys.mac.programmer
Discussion by people programming the Apple Macintosh

comp.unix.aux
Version of UNIX for Apple Macintosh II computers

misc.forsale.computers.mac
Apple Macintosh related computer items

comp.binaries.mac
Encoded Macintosh programs in binary (moderated)

comp.sys.mac.advocacy
The Macintosh computer family compared to others

comp.sys.mac.announce
Important notices for Macintosh users (moderated)

comp.sys.mac.apps
Discussions of Macintosh applications

comp.sys.mac.comm
Discussion of Macintosh communications

comp.sys.mac.databases
Database systems for the Apple Macintosh

comp.sys.mac.games
Discussions of games on the Macintosh

`comp.sys.mac.graphics`
Discussions of Macintosh graphics: paint, draw, 3D, CAD, animation

`comp.sys.mac.hardware`
Macintosh hardware issues and discussions

`comp.sys.mac.hypercard`
Macintosh Hypercard: information and uses

`comp.sys.mac.portables`
Discussion particular to laptop Macintoshes

`comp.sys.mac.programmer.help`
Help with Macintosh programming

`comp.sys.mac.programmer.misc`
Other issues of Macintosh programming

`comp.sys.mac.programmer.tools`
Macintosh programming tools

`comp.sys.mac.scitech`
Using the Macintosh in scientific and technological work

`comp.sys.mac.system`
Discussions of Macintosh system software

`comp.sys.mac.programmer.codewarrior`
Macintosh programming using CodeWarrior

`misc.forsale.computers.mac-specific.cards.misc`
Macintosh expansion cards

`misc.forsale.computers.mac-specific.cards.video`
Macintosh video cards

`misc.forsale.computers.mac-specific.misc`
Other Macintosh equipment

`misc.forsale.computers.mac-specific.portables`
Portable Macintosh systems

misc.forsale.computers.mac-specific.software
Macintosh software

misc.forsale.computers.mac-specific.systems
Complete Macintosh systems

Newsgroups: Apple Newton

comp.binaries.newton	Apple Newton binaries, sources, books, and so forth (moderated)
comp.sys.newton.announce	Newton information postings (moderated)
comp.sys.newton.misc	Miscellaneous discussion about Newton systems
comp.sys.newton.programmer	Discussion of Newton software development

Newsgroups: Apple PowerPC

comp.sys.powerpc	General PowerPC Discussion

Online Data Services

Commercial online data services provide much support for Apple products.

CompuServe: Apple, General

Apple Feedback(FREE)	APLFBK
Apple News Clips($)	APPLENEWS
Apple Support Forum	APLSUP
Apple Tech Info Library	APLTIL
Apple What's New Library	APLNEW

CompuServe: Apple II

Apple II Prog. Forum	APPROG

Apple II Users Forum   APPUSER

Apple II Vendor Forum   APIIVEN

CompuServe: Macintosh

Mac A Vendor Forum   MACAVEN

Mac Applications Forum   MACAP

Mac B Vendor Forum   MACBVEN

Mac C Vendor Forum   MACCVEN

Mac Communications Forum MACCOMM

Mac Community/Club Forum MACCLUB

Mac D Vendor Forum   MACDVEN

Mac Developers Forum   MACDEV

Mac Entertainment Forum MACFUN

Mac Hypertext Forum   MACHYPER

Mac New Users Help Forum MACNEW

Macintosh File Finder   MACFF

Macintosh Forums   MACINTOSH

Macintosh O/S Forum   MACSYS

MacUser Forum   MACUSER

MacWAREHOUSE(FREE)   MW

QuickTime 2.0 Download Ar QTIME

Symantec CPS WinMac Forum SYMCPWIN

ZIFFNET/Mac   ZMAC

CompuServe: Newton

Apple Support Forum   APLSP

Apple Tech Info Library APLTIL

Macintosh File Finder   MACFF

Macintosh Hardware Forum MACHW

```
Macintosh O/S Forum          MACSYS

MacWEEK Forum                MACWEEK

Newton Developers Forum      NEWTDEV

Newton/PIE Forum             NEWTON

Newton Vendor Forum          NEWTVEN

Palmtop Forum                PALMTOP

ZIFFNET/Mac Download Forum   DOWNTECH
```

America Online Forums

America Online's computing area has several Apple-related forums.

The Apple Computing Forums have material on both Apple II and Macintosh development. A forum devoted exclusively to personal digital assistants in general has a subarea about Newtons.

The development area also has material on program development for PDAs and Newtons in particular. This area includes the Programmer's University of online courses. Both areas include message boards, software libraries, and vendor support areas.

BIX Conferences

The BIX programming area supports Apple topics in the conferences:

```
o apple      Apple II family conference

o mac.apple  The word from Cupertino
```

Periodic Postings and FAQs

FAQs whose archive-name is listed are available on the anonymous FTP server **rtfm.mit.edu**.

FAQs: Apple, General

Subject: CAP FAQ

Newsgroups: **comp.protocols.appletalk, comp.sys.mac.comm**

From: **djh@cs.mu.OZ.AU (David Hornsby)**

Comment: The latest version of this posting is available via anonymous FTP from **munnari.OZ.AU//mac/cap.patches/CAP.faq.**

Subject: Apple A/UX FAQ List (*/*)

Newsgroups: **comp.unix.aux, news.answers, comp.answers**

From: **jim@jagubox.gsfc.nasa.gov** (Jim Jagielski)

Archive-name: **aux-faq/part1**

Summary: Latest posting of FAQs for A/UX

FAQs: Apple II

Subject: COMP.EMULATORS.apple2: Mini-FAQ v* (*/*)

Newsgroups: **comp.emulators.apple2, comp.emulators.announce, comp.answers, news.answers**

From: **amaddiso@extro.ucc.su.OZ.AU** (Alex Maddison)

Archive-name: **apple2/emulators-faq/part1**

Subject: **comp.sys.apple2**—Frequently Asked Questions (and answers) part * of *

Newsgroups: **comp.sys.apple2, news.answers, comp.answers**

From: **dmag@caen.engin.umich.edu** (Dan DeMaggio)

Archive-name: **apple2/part1**

Summary: What you need to know about the **comp.sys.apple2** news-groups

Subject: Apple II anti-viral archive sites last changed * * *

Newsgroup: **comp.virus**

From: **jwright@cfht.hawaii.edu** (Jim Wright)

FAQs: Apple Macintosh

Subject: FAQ: Apple DOS Compatibility Card (Houdini) v* */*

Newsgroup: **comp.sys.mac.hardware**

From: **prastowo@vms2.macc.wisc.edu** (Anton Prastowo)

Subject: **alt.sources.mac** FAQ

Newsgroups: **alt.sources.mac, alt.answers, news.answers**

From: **f8dy@netaxs.com** (Mark Pilgrim)

Archive-name: **macintosh/alt-sources-mac**

Summary: Please read this before posting anything to **alt.sources.mac**.

Subject: Macintosh image processing information sources (FAQ)

Newsgroups: **sci.image.processing, comp.sys.mac.scitech@sci.answers, news.answers**

From: **huff@mcclb0.med.nyu.edu** (Edward J. Huff)

Archive-name: **image-processing/Macintosh**

Summary: Macintosh image processing information available via GOPHER, FTP, USENET, e-mail, telephone, and snail mail

Subject: Macintosh application software Frequently Asked Questions (FAQ)

Newsgroups: comp.sys.mac.apps, comp.answers, news.answers

From: **elharo@shock.njit.edu** (Elliott Rusty Harold)

Archive-name: **macintosh/apps-faq**

Summary: Answers many of the most Frequently Asked Questions about Macintosh application software on USENET. To avoid wasting bandwidth and as a courtesy, please be familiar with this document BEFORE posting.

Subject: Macintosh screensaver Frequently Asked Questions (FAQ)

Newsgroups: **comp.sys.mac.apps, comp.sys.mac.misc, comp.sys.mac.system, comp.answers, news.answers**

From: **L.H.Wood@student.lut.ac.uk**

Archive-name: **macintosh/screensaver-faq**

Summary: Lists Frequently Asked Questions on Macintosh screensavers with answers. Before asking a question about screensavers in these newsgroups, please read this document.

Subject: Introductory Macintosh Frequently Asked Questions (FAQ)

Newsgroups: **comp.sys.mac.apps, comp.sys.mac.misc, comp.sys.mac.system, comp.sys.mac.wanted, comp.sys.mac.hardware, comp.answers, news.answers**

From: **elharo@shock.njit.edu** (Elliott Rusty Harold)

Archive-name: **macintosh/general-faq**

Summary: Answers a number of the most Frequently Asked Questions on USENET about Macintosh computers. To avoid wasting bandwidth and as a courtesy, please be familiar with this document BEFORE posting.

Subject: **comp.sys.mac.comm** Frequently Asked Questions [*/*]

Newsgroups: **comp.sys.mac.comm, news.answers, comp.answers**

From: **davido@Princeton.EDU** (David L. Oppenheimer)

Archive-name: **macintosh/comm-faq/part1**

Summary: Intends to provide information specific to Macintosh computer communications, including modems, networks, and the like. You are encouraged to read this FAQ before posting to the newsgroup.

Subject: **comp.sys.mac.games** FAQ

Newsgroups: **comp.sys.mac.games, comp.answers, news.answers**

From: **schulman+@pitt.edu** (Christina Schulman)

Archive-name: **macintosh/games-faq**

Summary: Answers Frequently Asked Questions about Mac computer games

Subject: Macintosh hardware Frequently Asked Questions (FAQ)

Newsgroups: **comp.sys.mac.hardware, comp.answers, news.answers**

From: **elharo@shock.njit.edu** (Elliott Rusty Harold)

Archive-name: **macintosh/hardware-faq**

Summary: Answers several most Frequently Asked Questions about Macintosh hardware on USENET. To avoid wasting bandwidth and as a courtesy, please be familiar with this document BEFORE posting.

Subject: Macintosh PowerPC FAQ

Newsgroups: **comp.sys.mac.hardware, comp.sys.mac.misc, comp.sys.powerpc, comp.answers, news.answers**

From: **mac_ppc_faq@postbox.acs.ohio-state.edu**

Archive-name: **macintosh/PowerPC-FAQ**

Summary: Lists questions and (often speculative) answers about PowerPC in relation to the Macintosh

Subject: Miscellaneous Macintosh Frequently Asked Questions (FAQ)

Newsgroups: **comp.sys.mac.misc, comp.answers, news.answers**

From: **elharo@shock.njit.edu** (Elliott Rusty Harold)

Archive-name: **macintosh/misc-faq**

Summary: Answers many most Frequently Asked Questions about Macintoshes on USENET. To avoid wasting bandwidth and as a courtesy, please be familiar with this document BEFORE posting.

Subject: Comp.Sys.Mac.Programmer FAQ Part */* (*/*/*)

Newsgroups: **comp.sys.mac.programmer, news.answers**

From: **Daryl_Spitzer@mindlink.bc.ca** (Daryl Spitzer)

Archive-name: **macintosh/programmer-faq/part1**

Summary: Lists Frequently Asked Questions about **comp.sys.mac.programmer**

Subject: Mac Programming FAQ answer sheet. [READ ME!]

Newsgroups: **comp.sys.mac.programmer.misc, comp.answers, news.answers**

From: **h+@metrowerks.com**

Archive-name: **macintosh/programming-faq**

Subject: Macintosh system software Frequently Asked Questions (FAQ)

Newsgroups: **comp.sys.mac.system, comp.answers, news.answers**

From: **elharo@shock.njit.edu** (Elliott Rusty Harold)

Archive-name: **macintosh/system-faq**

Summary: Answers many most Frequently Asked Questions about Macintoshes on USENET. To avoid wasting bandwidth and as a courtesy, please be familiar with this document BEFORE posting.

Subject: Macintosh for sale Frequently Asked Questions (FAQ)

Newsgroups: **comp.sys.mac.wanted, misc.forsale.computers.mac, comp.answers, misc.answers, news.answers**

From: **elharo@shock.njit.edu** (Elliott Rusty Harold)

Archive-name: **macintosh/wanted-faq**

Summary: Answers many most Frequently Asked Questions about Macintoshes on USENET. To avoid wasting bandwidth and as a courtesy, please be familiar with this document BEFORE posting.

Subject: Macintosh anti-viral archive sites last changed * * *

Newsgroup: comp.virus

From: jwright@cfht.hawaii.edu (Jim Wright)

FAQs: Apple Newton

Subject: Nwt MPs Facts and FAQs v*.*, */*

Newsgroup: comp.sys.newton.misc

From: ashley@amug.org (Ashley Barnard)

Subject: Newton MPs Facts and FAQs, Part */*

Newsgroups: comp.sys.newton.misc, comp.answers, news.answers

From: JC@easynet.co.uk (J.C. Bousson)

Subject: Canonical List of Newton Q and A * part *

Newsgroup: comp.sys.pen

From: potts@oit.itd.umich.edu (Paul Potts)

FAQs: Apple PowerPC

Subject: Mac and IBM Info-Version * Pt *

Newsgroups: comp.sys.ibm.pc.misc, comp.sys.ibm.pc.hardware, comp.os.ms-windows.advocacy, comp.os.os2.advocacy, comp.sys.intel, comp.sys.mac.advocacy, comp.sys.powerpc

From: bgrubb@scf.nmsu.edu (Bruce Grubb)

Subject: comp.sys.m68k Frequently Asked Questions (FAQ)

Newsgroups: comp.sys.m68k, comp.answers, news.answers

From: boys@fis.utoronto.ca

Archive-name: **motorola/68k-chips-faq**

Summary: Lists Frequently Asked Questions (and answers) about the Motorola 32-bit microprocessors, MC680x0, MC63x0, and their peripheral parts. Provides some information on the VMEbus, HC11, HC16, and PowerPC parts. Lists resources Motorola provides to its customers.

Subject: Macintosh PowerPC FAQ

Newsgroups: **comp.sys.mac.hardware, comp.sys.mac.misc, comp.sys.powerpc, comp.answers, news.answers**

From: **mac_ppc_faq@postbox.acs.ohio-state.edu**

Archive-name: **macintosh/PowerPC-FAQ**

Summary: Lists questions and (often speculative) answers about PowerPC in relation to the Macintosh

Subject: PowerPC Frequently Asked Questions (FAQ)

Newsgroups: **comp.sys.powerpc, comp.answers, news.answers**

From: **derekn@ece.cmu.edu** (Derek B. Noonburg)

Archive-name: **powerpc-faq**

Summary: Lists Frequently Asked Questions about the PowerPC architecture and PowerPC-based computers

IBM-Intel PC

This section covers both hardware platforms and the most common operating systems—MS-DOS, MS Windows, and MS Windows NT.

The next sections describe maillists that provide information on Intel-IBM architecture equipment and related topics.

Hardware

att-pc+

Contact: **bill@ssbn.wlk.com** (Bill Kennedy)

Description: AT&T PC 63xx series of systems

BITNET List Server Maillists

To subscribe to a maillist, send a mail message to **listserv@bitnic.bitnet**. Leave the *Subject:* field blank. In the body of the message, write: **SUBSCRIBE listname**, where listname is a name in the left column in the sections that follow.

MS-DOS

```
ILDOS-L        ILDOS-L Israeli anonymous FTP update
               information for DOS

PCTECH-L       MS-DOS Compatibles Support Group
```

MS Windows

```
WFW-L          Microsoft Windows for Workgroups

WINDOWS        WINDOWS: A forum for Q&A, rumors, and
               insights about Microsoft

WINHLP-L       Windows Help Compiler (WINHELP) Discussion
               List

WIN3-L         Microsoft Windows Version 3 Forum
```

MS Windows NT

```
LANMAN-L       MS Windows NT Adv Server and LAN Man
               Discussion List
```

FTP Sites

DOS and Windows applications, source code, and information files must be the most heavily archived files on earth! Because it is simply impractical to categorize or even list here all relevant archive sites, I list only the primary archive sites—sites whose main purpose appears to be to serve as a library.

Three sites that I see most commonly referenced as DOS and Windows archives are **oak.oakland.edu**, the SimTel site at the University of Oakland in Rochester, Michigan, **garbo.uwasa.fi**; and the "garbo" site at the University of Vaasa in Finland, run by Mr. Timo Salmi, and **wuarchive.wustl.edu**.

All these sites are very heavily "mirrored" around the world. Although there is some file overlap at these sites, each also has unique files.

In the Internet tradition of creating lists of lists, here are three methods for locating more sites or scanning multiple sites:

➤ The files **/pc/pd2/moder35.zip** at Garbo and **/pub/msdos/info/moder35.zip** at SimTel contain a directory of download sites.

➤ The Virtual Shareware Library (VSL) at the AUDREY server provides a mechanism to search for a file across the three sites and at least six others. You can access this library via the WWW at **http://www.fagg.uni-lj.si/** or via anonymous FTP at **audrey.fagg.uni-lj.si**.

➤ The Web site **www.yahoo.com** provides a mechanism to search WWW sites and also link to the AUDREY server.

Internet Newsgroups

You can access the permanent newsgroups listed in the next sections via most network newsreader programs.

MS-DOS

comp.archives.msdos.announce
Announcements about MS-DOS archives (moderated)

comp.archives.msdos.d
Discussion of materials available in MS-DOS archives

comp.os.msdos.apps
Discussion of applications that run under MS-DOS

comp.os.msdos.desqview
Quarterdeck's DESQview and related products

comp.os.msdos.mail-news
Administering mail and network news systems under MS-DOS

```
comp.os.msdos.misc
```
Miscellaneous topics about MS-DOS machines

```
comp.os.msdos.pcgeos
```
GeoWorks PC/GEOs and PC/GEO-based packages

```
comp.os.msdos.programmer
```
Programming MS-DOS machines

```
comp.os.msdos.programmer.turbovision
```
Borland's text application libraries

MS Windows

```
comp.binaries.ms-windows
```
Binary programs for Microsoft Windows (moderated)

```
comp.emulators.ms-windows.wine
```
A free MS Windows emulator under X

```
comp.os.ms-windows.advocacy
```
Speculation and debate about Microsoft Windows

```
comp.os.ms-windows.announce
```
Announcements relating to Windows (moderated)

```
comp.os.ms-windows.apps.comm
```
MS Windows communication applications

```
comp.os.ms-windows.apps.financial
```
MS Windows financial and tax software

```
comp.os.ms-windows.apps.misc
```
MS Windows applications

```
comp.os.ms-windows.apps.utilities
```
MS Windows utilities

```
comp.os.ms-windows.apps.word-proc
```
MS Windows word processing applications

```
comp.os.ms-windows.misc
```
General discussions about Windows issues

```
comp.os.ms-windows.networking.misc
```
Windows and other networks

comp.os.ms-windows.networking.tcp-ip
Windows and TCP/IP networking

comp.os.ms-windows.networking.windows
Windows' built-in networking

comp.os.ms-windows.programmer.controls
Controls, dialogues, and VBXs

comp.os.ms-windows.programmer.drivers
Drivers and VxDs—no driver requests!

comp.os.ms-windows.programmer.graphics
GDI, graphics, and printing

comp.os.ms-windows.programmer.memory
Memory management issues

comp.os.ms-windows.programmer.misc
Programming Microsoft Windows

comp.os.ms-windows.programmer.multimedia
Multimedia programming

comp.os.ms-windows.programmer.networks
Network programming

comp.os.ms-windows.programmer.ole
OLE2, COM, and DDE programming

comp.os.ms-windows.programmer.tools
Development tools in Windows

comp.os.ms-windows.programmer.win32
32-bit Windows programming interfaces

comp.os.ms-windows.programmer.winhelp
WinHelp/Multimedia Viewer development

comp.os.ms-windows.setup
Installing and configuring Microsoft Windows

comp.os.ms-windows.video
Video adapters and drivers for Windows

MS Windows NT

comp.os.ms-windows.nt.misc	General discussion about Windows NT
comp.os.ms-windows.nt.setup	Configuring Windows NT systems

Online Data Services

DOS and Windows tools, information, applications, and source code are widespread on the commercial online data services. The next sections list several key forums for each.

CompuServe

MS-DOS

LDOS/TRSDOS6 Users Forum	LDOS
MS-DOS Forum	MSDOS
MS-DOS 6.2 DLOAD (Microsoft)	MSDOS62
MS-DOS 6.2 DOWNLOAD (PCWORLD)	PCWDOS62
MS-DOS 6.2 STEPUP (GERMAN)	DMSDOS
Symantec CPS DOS Forum	SYMCPDOS

MS Windows

Microsoft Windows Intl. D	WINTLDEV
MS Windows Extensions Forum	WINEXT
MS Windows Forum	MSWIN
MS Windows News Forum	WINNEWS
MS Windows Objects Forum	WINOBJECTS
MS Windows SDK Forum	WINSDK
MS Windows Shareware Forum	WINSHARE
MS Windows Workgroups Forum	MSWFWG
Windows Networking A Forum	WINETA
Windows Sources Forum	WINSOURCES
Windows Utility Forum	WINUTIL

America Online

Like CompuServe, America Online abounds with information on DOS and Windows. The primary sources are the DOS and Windows (surprised?) forums in the computing area.

BIX

BIX's numerous conferences on DOS and Windows topics include those listed in the next sections.

MS-DOS	o `ibm.dos`	PC-DOS and MS-DOS operating systems
	o `other.dos`	Operating systems without their own conference

MS Windows	o `windows`	Windows listings area; join from any wix conference
	o `windows.apps`	End-user applications, questions, and wish lists
	o `windows.hw`	Hardware questions on such subjects as CD-ROM, printers, and video
	o `windows.net`	Windows and networking
	o `windows.novice`	Help for new Windows users
	o `windows.supp`	The Windows Vendor Support Conference
	o `windows.tech`	Technical discussions for Windows developers
	o `winmag`	*Windows Magazine*

MS Windows NT	o `windows.nt`	Microsoft's New Technology (NT) Operating System

Periodic Postings and FAQs	FAQs with an archive-name listed are available on the anonymous FTP server **rtfm.mit.edu**.

Software: General

Subject: **comp.archives.msdos.{announced} FAQ** (Frequently Asked Questions)

Newsgroups: **comp.archives.msdos.announce, comp.archives.msdos.d, comp.answers, news.answers**

From: **ts@chyde.uwasa.fi** (Timo Salmi)

Archive-name: **msdos-archives/faq**

Summary: Usually posted every Saturday or every four weeks to the answers groups

Subject: Useful MS-DOS programs at SimTel, Garbo, and Cica (Part * of *)

Newsgroups: **comp.archives.msdos.d, comp.binaries.ibm.pc.wanted, comp.os.msdos.apps, comp.os.msdos.misc, comp.sys.ibm.pc.misc, comp.os.ms-windows.misc, comp.answers, news.answers**

From: **sko@helix.net** (Samuel Ko)

Archive-name: **msdos-archives/part1**

Summary: Lists recommended DOS/WIN programs available from major FTP sites

Subject: DESQview/QEMM Frequently Asked Questions: READ BEFORE POSTING

Newsgroups: **comp.os.msdos.desqview, news.answers, comp.answers**

From: **aml@world.std.com** (Andrew Langmead)

Archive-name: **desqview-faq**

Summary: Lists FAQs for the MS-DOS multitasker DESQview and memory manager QEMM

Subject: Message Passing Interface (MPI) FAQ

Newsgroups: **comp.parallel.mpi, comp.answers, news.answers**

From: **doss@ERC.MsState.Edu** (Nathan Doss)

Archive-name: **mpi-faq**

Summary: List of common questions (and their answers) about the Message Passing Interface (MPI)standard

Hardware

Subject: PC-clone hardware newsgroup pointer

Newsgroups: **comp.os.msdos.misc, comp.sys.ibm.pc.hardware.misc, comp.os.ms-windows.misc, comp.sys.ibm.pc.misc, alt.cd-rom, alt.sys.pc-clone.gateway2000, alt.sys.pc-clone.micron, alt.sys.pc-clone.zeos, alt.sys.pc-clone.dell, comp.binaries.ibm.pc.d, comp.binaries.ibm.pc.wanted, comp.answers, news.answers**

From: **grohol@alpha.acast.nova.edu** (John M. Grohol)

Archive-name: **finding-groups/pc-hardware**

Summary: Newsgroup subject pointer for PC-clone hardware

Subject: Overclocking FAQ *.*.* (**Comp.sys.ibm.pc.hardware.chips**)

Newsgroup: **comp.sys.ibm.pc.hardware.chips**

From: **hpapaleo@magnus.acs.ohio-state.edu** (H. B. Papaleonardos)

MS-DOS

Subject: **comp.os.msdos.programmer** FAQ

Subject: **comp.os.msdos.programmer** FAQ diffs

Newsgroups: **comp.os.msdos.programmer, comp.answers, news.answers**

From: **jeffrey.carlyle@bgamug.com** (Jeffrey Carlyle)

Archive-name: **msdos-programmer-faq/faq**

Comp-OS-MS-DOS-programmer-archive-name: **dos-faq**

Summary: Frequently Asked Questions by DOS programmers with tested answers. Please read this before posting.

MS Windows

Subject: INFO: A guide to the Windows newsgroups

Newsgroups: **comp.os.ms-windows.advocacy, comp.os.ms-windows.apps, comp.os.ms-windows.setup, comp.os.ms-windows.misc, comp.os.ms-windows.nt.setup, comp.os.ms-windows.nt.misc, comp.os.ms-windows.programmer.tools, comp.os.ms-windows.programmer.win32, comp.os.ms-windows.programmer.misc, bit.listserv.win3-l**

From: **tomh@metrics.com** (Tom Haapanen)

Archive-name: **ms-windows/newsgrp.guide**

Subject: WINE (WINdows Emulator) Frequently Asked Questions

Newsgroups: **comp.emulators.announce, comp.emulators.ms-windows.wine, comp.os.386bsd.announce, comp.os.linux.answers, comp.windows.x.i386unix, comp.answers, news.answers**

From: **dave@milonet.la.ca.us** (Dave Gardner)

From: **pdg@primenet.com** (Dave Gardner)

Subject: MS Windows COM and Ns16550A UART FAQ

Newsgroups: **comp.dcom.modems, comp.sys.ibm.pc.hardware.comm, comp.answers, news.answers**

From: **rjn@fc.hp.com** (Bob Niland)

Archive-name: **windows-com-faq**

Summary: Gives tips for improving Windows 3.x COM performance and reliability

Subject: Windows FAQ: How to get it

Newsgroups: **comp.os.ms-windows.apps, comp.os.ms-windows.misc, comp.os.ms-windows.setup, comp.os.ms-windows.nt.misc, comp.os.ms-windows.nt.setup, bit.listserv.win3-l**

From: **tomh@metrics.com** (Tom Haapanen)

Archive-name: **ms-windows/faqwin.how-to**

Subject: **comp.os.ms-windows.programmer.drivers Frequently Asked Questions (FAQ)**

Newsgroups: **comp.os.ms-windows.programmer.drivers, comp.answers, news.answers**

From: **Berlin@vireo.com**

Archive-name: **windows/programming/device-drivers**

Summary: Contains Frequently Asked Questions (with answers) for the **comp.os.ms-windows.programmer.drivers** newsgroup. This newsgroup addresses issues raised by people writing device drivers for Microsoft Windows. Please do not post requests for device drivers to this group. Direct requests to **comp.os.ms-windows.setup.**

Subject: Windows programmer FAQ: How to get it

Newsgroups: **comp.os.ms-windows.programmer.misc, comp.os.ms-windows.programmer.tools, comp.os.ms-windows.programmer.win32, bit.listserv.win3-l**

From: **tomh@metrics.com** (Tom Haapanen)

Archive-name: **ms-windows/faqprg.how-to**

MS Windows NT

Subject: Windows NT Internet FAQ, Part */*

Newsgroups: **comp.os.ms-windows.nt.misc, comp.os.ms-windows.nt.setup, comp.answers, news.answers**

From: **sscoggin@enet.net** (Steve Scoggins)

Archive-name: **windows-nt/internet-faq/part1**

Summary: Lists Frequently Asked Questions and answers about how to set up Windows NT for Internet access and about various Internet resources specific to Windows NT. Anyone who uses the built-in Windows NT RAS for SLIP or PPP connections to an Internet provider should read this.

Sun/SPARC

The next sections provide information on the Sun family of computers and operating systems.

Internet Maillists

The maillists listed next provide information on Sun systems and related topics.

Sun-386i

Contact: **sun-386i-request@ssg.com** (Rick Emerson)

Description: 386i-based Sun systems

Sun-managers

Contact: **sun-managers-request@eecs.nwu.edu**

Description: For managers of sites with Sun workstations and/or servers

Sun-nets

Contact: **sun-nets-request@umiacs.umd.edu**

Description: Networks using Sun hardware and/or software

Sunflash

Contact: **sunflash-request@Sun.com.** or **info-sunflash@Sun.com**

Description: Press releases, newsletters, announcements, and so forth, from Sun

---

**BITNET
List Server
Maillists**

To subscribe to a maillist, send a mail message to **listserv@bitnic.bitnet.** Leave the *Subject:* field blank. In the body of the message, write: **SUBSCRIBE listname**, where listname is the name in the left column below.

```
TECSUN-L      SUN Computer Technical Users List
```

**Internet
Newsgroups**

You can access these permanent newsgroups via most network news-reader programs.

```
comp.org.sug          Talk about/for the Sun User's
                      Group

comp.sources.sun      Software for Sun workstations
                      (moderated)

comp.sys.sun.admin    Sun system administration issues
                      and questions

comp.sys.sun.announce Sun announcements and Sunergy
                      mailings (moderated)

comp.sys.sun.apps     Software applications for Sun
                      computer systems

comp.sys.sun.hardware Sun Microsystems hardware

comp.sys.sun.misc     Miscellaneous discussions about
                      Sun products

comp.sys.sun.wanted   People looking for Sun products
                      and support

comp.windows.news     Sun Microsystems' News window
                      system
```

FTP and WWW Sites

The sites described in the next sections contain support information and binaries or source code to run on Sun machines. Sun itself runs several of these.

FTP Sites

ftp.x.org

camus.quintus.com:/pub/GNU

ftp.uu.net

opcom.sun.ca

prep.ai.mit.edu

ftp.fwi.uva.nl

WWW Sites

http://www.sun.com - Sun Computer home page

http://sunsite.unc.edu/newhome.html

http://sunsite.sut.ac.jp/homepage.html

http://src.doc.ic.ac.uk/public

http://sunsite.cs.msu.su/

http://sunsite.nus.sg/

http://sunsite.wits.ac.za/

Online Data Services

Support information for Sun and SPARC products are available from CompuServe and BIX Forums.

CompuServe

Primary Sun information is at

SunSoft Forum   SUNSOFT

BIX Forums

Two BIX conferences relate to Sun computers in the programming area.

```
o sun      Sun workstations, SPARC

o tops     Sitka (formerly TOPS), a Sun Microsystems
           company
```

Periodic Postings and FAQs

FAQs with an archive-name listed are available on the anonymous FTP server **rtfm.mit.edu.**

Subject: OpenLook GUI FAQ */*: *

Newsgroups: **comp.windows.open-look, alt.toolkits.xview, comp.windows.news, alt.sys.sun, alt.toolkits.intrinsics, comp.answers, alt.answers, news.answers**

From: **lee@sq.sq.com** (Liam Quin)

Archive-name: **open-look/01-general**

Summary: Overview of OpenLook graphical user interface

Subject: v*INF3: Location and format of FTP archive site

Newsgroup: **comp.sources.sun**

From: **mcgrew@dartagnan.rutgers.edu** (Charles McGrew)

Subject: Monthly Intro Message

Newsgroup: **comp.sys.sun**

From: **rgreene@ricecsvm.rice.edu** (Bob Greene)

Subject: Master Sun format.dat

Newsgroup: **comp.sys.sun.admin**

From: **jdd@cdf.toronto.edu** (John DiMarco)

Subject: FAQ: Sun Computer Administration Frequently Asked Questions

Newsgroups: **comp.sys.sun.admin, comp.sys.sun.misc, comp.unix.solaris, comp.answers, news.answers**

From: **montjoy@thor.ece.uc.edu** (Rob Montjoy)

Archive-name: **comp-sys-sun-faq**

Summary: Answers questions that appear in **comp.sys.sun***

Subject: **Comp.Sys.Sun.Announce** Moderation Policies [last modified: *]

Newsgroup: **comp.sys.sun.announce**

From: **zorch@ftp.UU.NET** (Scott Hazen Mueller)

Subject: Sun hardware reference part */*

Newsgroup: **comp.sys.sun.hardware**

From: **jwbirdsa@picarefy.picarefy.com** (James W. Birdsall)

Subject: **comp.sys.sun.hardware** FAQ

Newsgroup: **comp.sys.sun.hardware**

From: **mueller@cs.unc.edu** (Carl Mueller)

Subject: FAQ: CD-ROM drives on Sun hardware

Newsgroups: **comp.sys.sun.hardware, alt.cdrom**

From: **Kyle.F.Downey@williams.edu** (Kyle Downey)

Archive-name: **sun-cdrom-faq**

Subject: Solaris 2 Frequently Asked Questions (FAQ) *

Newsgroups: **comp.unix.solaris, comp.sys.sun.admin, comp.answers, news.answers.nl**

From: **casper@fwi.uva.nl** (Casper H.S. Dik)

Archive-name: **Solaris2/FAQ**

Summary: Lists general Frequently Asked Questions (and answers) about Sun Microsystem's Solaris 2.x system. Also see the FAQs archived as Solaris2/Porting and Solaris2/x86.

Digital Equipment Corp

The next sections cover the VAX and Alpha computing platforms and the VMS, OSF, Ultrix, AVMS, and AOSF operating systems.

Internet Maillists

The maillists described in the next sections provide information on DEC platforms and related topics.

alpha-osf-managers

Contact: **alpha-osf-managers-request@ornl.gov**

Contact: **majordomo@ornl.gov**

Description: Troubleshooting tool for DEC Alpha AXP systems running OSF/1

BITNET List Server Maillists

To subscribe to a maillist, send a mail message to **listserv@bitnic.bitnet**. Leave the *Subject:* field blank. In the body of the message, write: **SUBSCRIBE listname**, where listname is a name in the left column below.

INFO-VAX	Info VAX
MS-STORE	VMS Store administrators
NADVMS-D	German Node Administrators (NAD) VMS
OPGRP-L	Virginia Tech VAX Operations Group/LUG
VAXVMS	VMS discussion
VMS-L	VMS give-and-take forum

Internet Newsgroups

You can access permanent Internet newsgroups via most network news-reader programs.

`comp.os.vms`	`DEC's VAX* line of computers and VMS`
`comp.unix.osf.misc`	`Various aspects of Open Software Foundation products`
`comp.unix.osf.osf1`	`The Open Software Foundation's OSF/1`
`comp.unix.ultrix`	`Discussions about DEC's Ultrix`
`news.software.anu-news`	`VMS B news software from Australian National Univ.`

Archive Sites

You can access a copy of Digital's OpenVMS manuals for read-only (they're copyrighted!) via TELNET to **vtbook@condist.acornsw.com**.

Digital has prepared and distributed CDs of OpenVMS freeware. You can obtain them by anonymous FTP or WWW connection to

ftp://ftp.montagar.com/

http://www.montagar.com/dfwlug/

ftp://degh.fps.mcw.edu/

ftp://flash.acornsw.com/

gopher://gopher.acornsw.com/

http://www.acornsw.com/

ftp://ftp.dct.ac.uk/

The **montagar.com** server also provides many white papers, articles, and other information about VMS.

Digital has a WWW home page at **http://www.digital.com** with lots of freeware and utilities in path **/info/vms-freeware.html**.

Other WWW and FTP sites for VAX/VMS or related information are at

http://www.wku.edu/www/fileserv/fileserv.html

http://www.hhs.dk/vms/

ftp://ftp.decus.org/ (the DEC User's Society site)

http://www.decus.org/ (the DEC User's Society site, again)

ftp://axp.psl.ku.dk/decwindows

ftp://ftp2.cnam.fr/decwindows

ftp://ftp.et.tudelft.nl/decwindows

ftp://ftp.ctrl-c.liu.se/decwindows

http://axp616.gsi.de:8080/wwwar/cena/decwindows/cena.html

Online Data Services

A primary site of VAX information on CompuServe is the forum

VAX Forum   VAXFORUM

Periodic Postings and FAQs

FAQs with an archive-name list are available on the anonymous FTP server rtfm.mit.edu.

Subject: Monthly information posting: VMSnet on BITNET

Newsgroups: **vmsnet.announce.newusers, comp.os.vms**

From: **tp@mccall.com**

Subject: Monthly information posting: What Is VMSnet?

Newsgroups: **vmsnet.announce.newusers, comp.os.vms, comp.org.decus, comp.sys.dec**

From: **tp@mccall.com**

Subject: Monthly checkgroups posting for VMSnet

Newsgroup: **vmsnet.groups**

From: **tp@mccall.com**

Subject: Info-VAX: *

Newsgroups: **vmsnet.misc, comp.os.vms, news.answers, comp.answers**

From: **munroe@dmc.com**

Archive-name: **info-vax/part01**

Comment: These articles are currently posted (archive-names, in parentheses, are in the **info-vax** archive directory): "Introduction to Info-VAX," (part01); "Basic Common Questions" (part02); "Advanced Common Questions" (part03); "How to Find VAX/VMS Software (part04).

Subject: Monthly information posting: **vmsnet.sources** archive sites

Newsgroups: **vmsnet.sources.d, comp.os.vms**

From: **tp@mccall.com**

Subject: DECUS Questions Answered (last modified *)

Newsgroups: **comp.org.decus, comp.os.vms, comp.sys.dec**

From: **ctp@cs.utexas.edu** (Clyde T. Poole)

Subject: OpenVMS Frequently Asked Questions (FAQ)

Newsgroups: **comp.os.vms, comp.sys.dec, vmsnet.alpha, vmsnet.misc, comp.answers, news.answers**

From: **lionel@quark.enet.dec.com** (Steve Lionel)

Archive-name: **dec-faq/vms**

Summary: Contains answers to Frequently Asked Questions about the OpenVMS operating system from Digital Equipment Corporation and the computer systems on which it runs.

Subject: DEC OSF/1 AXP Frequently Asked Questions

Newsgroups: **comp.unix.ultrix, comp.unix.osf.osf1, comp.sys.dec, vmsnet.alpha, comp.answers, news.answers**

From: **lionel@quark.enet.dec.com** (Steve Lionel)

Archive-name: **dec-faq**/osf1

Summary: Lists Frequently Asked Questions (and their answers) about the DEC OSF/1 AXP operating system from Digital Equipment Corporation.

Amiga

This section covers the Amiga computer platform.

Internet Maillists

The maillists described in the next sections provide information on the Amiga platform and related topics.

Amiga CD-ROM

Contact: **cdrom-list-request@ben.com**

Description: Use of CD-ROMs on Amiga systems

AMOS

Contact: **amos-request@access.digex.net** (Michael Cox)

Description: Discusses programming in the AMOS family: AMOS Creator, AMOS Pro, and Easy AMOS. Used on the Amiga computer.

CSAA

Contact: **announce-request@cs.ucdavis.edu** (Carlos Amezaga)

Description: **Comp.Sys.Amiga.Announce** mailing list

Dice C

Contact: **emailurl@flevel.demon.co.uk**

Description: Dice C programming techniques for Amiga computers

hyperami

Contact: **listserv@archive.oit.unc.edu**

Description: Informal product regarding AmigaVision, CanDo, DeluxeVideo III, and related products.

BITNET ListServer Maillists

To subscribe to a maillist, send a mail message to **listserv@bitnic.bitnet**. Leave the *Subject:* field blank. In the body of the message, write: **SUBSCRIBE listname**, where listname is a name in the left column below.

```
AMIGAHAR      AMIGAGHAR COMP.SYS.AMIGA.HARDWARE redist.

CSAMIGA       CSAMIGA COMP.SYS.AMIGA.TECH redist.

I-AMIGA       Info-Amiga List
```

Internet Newsgroups

Several newsgroups provide information on Amiga hardware, software, and programming.

```
comp.binaries.amiga          Encoded public domain pro-
                             grams in binary (moderated)

comp.sources.amiga           Source code-only postings
                             for the Amiga (moderated)

comp.sys.amiga.advocacy      Why an Amiga is better than
                             XYZ

comp.sys.amiga.announce      Announcements about the
                             Amiga (moderated)

comp.sys.amiga.applications  Miscellaneous applications
```

comp.sys.amiga.audio	Music, MIDI, speech synthesis, and other sounds
comp.sys.amiga.cd32	Technical and computing talk for Commodore Amiga CD32
comp.sys.amiga.datacomm	Methods of getting bytes in and out
comp.sys.amiga.emulations	Various hardware and software emulators
comp.sys.amiga.games	Discussion of games for the Commodore Amiga
comp.sys.amiga.graphics	Charts, graphs, pictures, and so forth
comp.sys.amiga.hardware	Amiga computer hardware, Q&A, reviews, and so forth
comp.sys.amiga.introduction	Group for Amiga newcomers
comp.sys.amiga.marketplace	Where to find it, prices, and so forth
comp.sys.amiga.misc	Discussions not falling in Amiga group
comp.sys.amiga.multimedia	Animations, video, and multimedia
comp.sys.amiga.networking	Amiga networking software and hardware
comp.sys.amiga.programmer	Developers and hobbyists discuss code
comp.sys.amiga.reviews	Reviews of Amiga software and hardware (moderated)
comp.sys.amiga.uucp	Amiga UUCP packages
comp.unix.amiga	Minix, SYSV4, and other *nix on an Amiga
rec.games.video.cd32	Gaming talk, information, and help for the Amiga CD32

FTP Sites

AMINET, a collection of sites that mirror each others' Amiga files, is a subdirectory on sites that also archive a lot of software in addition to Amiga. Some primary AMINET sites are

ftp.wustl.edu

ftp.luth.se

ftp.eunet.ch

ftp.uni-paderborn.de

ftp.doc.ic.ac.uk

ftp.cica.indiana.edu

Most, if not all, AMINET sites have a subdirectory **/pub/amiga** or **/pub/aminet**. The file AmigaSciSchool lists Amiga software and location and is periodically posted to newsgroups such as **comp.sys.amiga.applications**, **comp.unix.amiga**, and **news.answers**.

The Fish Collection is a set of more than 1000 cataloged discs of Amiga software. You will often see files referred to by their Fish Disc number. (I am reminded of the way J. S. Bach's music is cataloged.)

The Fish Collection is larger than most AMINET sites offer. However, these following sites do contain the whole Fish Collection:

ftp.isca.uiowa.edu

ftp.hawaii.edu

ftp.funet.fi

An index file of the Fish Collection is maintained on AMINET sites at 'fish/doc/fishcon-???.lzh'.

Online Data Services

Information on the Amiga computer can be found on the commercial online data services.

CompuServe Forums

Amiga Arts Forum	AMIGAARTS
Amiga File Finder	AMIGAFF

```
Amiga Tech Forum        AMIGATECH
Amiga User's Forum      AMIGAUSER
Amiga Vendor Forum      AMIGAVENDOR
```

BIX Conferences

BIX's programming area has numerous Amiga-related conferences:

o `amiga.exchange`   Amiga Exchange: Everything for Amiga users

o `amiga`   Historical digs. Lots of old information.

o `amiga.user`   Exchange ideas, solve problems, compare notes

o `amiga.sw`   Amiga programming and developer issues

o `amiga.hw`   Amiga hardware design, use, and hookup

o `amiga.arts`   Artistry using the Amiga

o `amiga.special`   Special guests and events

o `amiga.unix`   UNIX on the Amiga

o `amiga.vendors`   Support from various Amiga vendors

o `amiga.games`   Games on the Amiga

o `amiga.dev`   Commodore's conference for developers

o `amiga.com`   For commercial developers. See `amiga.dev/instructions` #2.

o `amiga.cert`   For certified developers. See `amiga.dev/instructions` #3.

o `amiga.world`   *Amiga World magazine*

o `commodore`   Commodore computers other than the Amiga

o `amiga.dev`   Amiga developers support

o `amiga.com`   Commercial developers conference; e-mail `jwiede` for entry.

o `amiga.cert`   Certified developers conference; e-mail `jwiede` for entry.

Periodic Postings and FAQs

FAQs with an archive-name listed are available on the anonymous FTP server **rtfm.mit.edu.**

Subject: Amiga Mosaic and WWW Frequently Asked Questions (FAQ)

Newsgroup: **comp.sys.amiga.networking, comp.sys.amiga.datacomm, comp.sys.amiga.applications, comp.answers, news.answers**

From: **mwm@contessa.phone.net** (Mike Meyer)

Subject: ZyXEL U1496 series modems resellers FAQ (bimonthly)

Newsgroups: **comp.dcom.modems, comp.sys.amiga.datacomm, comp.sys.ibm.pc.hardware, comp.sys.mac.comm, comp.sys.apple2.comm, comp.answers, news.answers**

From: **kgoodwin@icaen.uiowa.edu** (Kirk Wilson Goodwin)

Summary: Lists ZyXEL series U1496 modem resalers and the modem's features

Subject: [**comp.sys.amiga.applications**] Science, School, and UNIX software

Newsgroups: **comp.sys.amiga.applications, comp.unix.amiga, comp.answers, news.answers**

From: **dak@uts.cc.utexas.edu** (Donald A. Kassebaum)

Archive-name: **amiga/science-faq**

Summary: Where to find Amiga software for science, school, and UNIX

Subject: FAQ: comp.sys.amiga.cd32

Newsgroup: comp.sys.amiga.cd32

From: eb15+@andrew.cmu.edu (Edward D. Berger)

Subject: comp.sys.amiga.cd32, rec.games.video.cd32 FAQ (Frequently Asked Questions)

Newsgroups: comp.sys.amiga.cd32, rec.games.video.cd32, comp.answers, rec.answers, news.answers

From: dan@blender.demon.co.uk (Dan Cannon)

Reply To: Dan—CD32-FAQ Mailbox <cd32-faq@blender.demon.co.uk>

Archive-name: amiga/CD32-FAQ

Summary: Frequently Asked Questions about the Amiga CD32, including how to expand the CD32 to a computer and how to use the CD32 as an external CD-ROM drive for other computers

Subject: Amiga Point Manager Frequently Asked Questions (FAQ)

Newsgroups: comp.sys.amiga.datacomm, comp.answers, news.answers

From: pm_faq@quasar.xs4all.nl (Eric Krieger)

Archive-name: amiga/point-manager-faq

Summary: Lists Frequently Asked Questions (and answers) about Point Manager, a FidoNet-compatible Scanner/Tosser/Reader/Editor for the Amiga

Subject: [comp.sys.amiga.datacomm]: AmigaNOS Frequently Asked Questions

Newsgroups: comp.sys.amiga.datacomm, news.answers, comp.answers

From: mcr@sandelman.ocunix.on.ca

Archive-name: amiga/AmigaNOS-faq

Subject: Amiga FAQ (Frequently Asked Questions) (Part * of *)

Newsgroups: **comp.sys.amiga.introduction, comp.sys.amiga.misc, comp.sys.amiga.programmer, comp.answers, news.answers**

From: **kellerer@informatik.tu-muenchen.de** (Ignaz Kellerer)

Archive-name: **amiga/introduction/part1**

Summary: Frequently Asked Questions on the Amiga. New users should read this!

Subject: Amiga-FAQ (biweekly posting)

Newsgroup: **comp.sys.amiga.misc**

From: **uf341ea@sun4.LRZ-Muenchen.DE** (Kajetan Hinner)

Summary: Frequently Asked Questions concerning the Amiga

Subject: Amiga Related Books FAQ

Newsgroups: **comp.sys.amiga.misc, comp.sys.amiga.introduction, comp.sys.amiga.programmer, comp.answers, news.answers**

From: **atkin@cs.umass.edu** (Marc Atkin)

Archive-name: **amiga/books**

Summary: Lists books relating to the Amiga Personal Computer. Gives information about each book, including comments from people in the **comp.sys.amiga.*** newsgroups.

Atari

This section is about the Atari computing platforms.

Internet Maillists

The maillists in the next sections provide information on Atari and related topics.

cubase-users

Contact: **Majordomo@mcc.ac.uk**

Description: Discussion of Cubase, a MIDI sequencer for Atari, PC, and Mac platforms

Lexicor Graphics Support List

Contact: **lexicor-list-request@lexicor.com**

Description: Discusses Atari computer graphics, hardware, software, and programming techniques

STOS

Contact: **ae-a@minster.york.ac.uk**

Description: Discusses STOS BASIC for the Atari ST computer family

BITNET List Server Maillists

To subscribe to a maillist, send a mail message to **listserv@bitnic.bitnet**. Leave the *Subject:* field blank. In the body of the message, write: **SUBSCRIBE listname**, where listname is a name in the left column below.

```
INFO-ATARI8        INFO-ATARI Discussion
INFO-ATARI16       INFO-ATARI16 Discussion
```

Internet Newsgroups

These newsgroups provide information on Atari hardware, software, and programming.

```
comp.binaries.atari.st    Binary-only postings for the
                          Atari ST (moderated)

comp.sources.atari.st     Source code-only postings for
                          the Atari ST (moderated)

comp.sys.atari.8bit       Discussion about 8-bit Atari
                          Micros
```

comp.sys.atari.advocacy   Attacking and defending Atari computers

comp.sys.atari.announce   Atari-related hardware and software announcements (moderated)

comp.sys.atari.programmer   Programming on the Atari computer

comp.sys.atari.st   Discussion about 16-bit Atari micros

comp.sys.atari.st.tech   Technical discussions about Atari ST hardware and software

FTP Sites

Two major Atari archive sites are

atari.archive.umich.edu/atari/8bit
Atari archives at Merit University of Michigan Software Archives

cs-ftp.bu.edu/PC/ATARI
Boston Archive

Some lesser known or smaller archive sites are

nova.pvv.unit.no/pub/Atari/8bit
University of Trondheim, Norway

ftp.clark.net/pub/atari
ClarkNet Archive

ftp.cs.vu.nl/pub/ipoorten/atari.8bit
Gatekeeper's Archive

closer.brisnet.org.au/pub/archive1/8_bit
Closer To Home Archive

ftp.xmission.com/pub/users/j/jeking/8bit
James King Archive

SIGs/BBSs

Several BBSs with Atari sections are accessible via TELNET.

freenet-in-c.cwru.edu   Cleveland Free-Net. Type
                         "GO ATARI."

Note: The Cleveland Free-Net Atari SIG publishes the *Central Atari Information Network (CAIN)* newsletter. You get on the mailing list by enrolling in the Atari SIG.

visitor@yfn.ysu.edu   Youngstown Free-Net. Type
                         "GO ATARI."

guest@freenet.carleton.ca   National Capital Free-Net.
                             Type "GO ATARI."

guest@closer.brisnet.org.au Closer to Home BBS
                             (Australia)

Also, You can obtain an 8-bit Atari users group listing by sending mail to *jeking7@delphi.com*.

Emulators Available Online

Two emulators for Atari systems are available as freeware:

➤ PC Xformer, a freeware 8-bit Atari emulator for DOS/Windows/OS/2 (**atari.archive.umich.edu/atari/8bit, Xf2/xf2.zip and Xf2/xf25.zip**). A commercial version is also available.

➤ ST Xformer 2.55, a freeware 8-bit Atari emulator for the Atari ST (**atari.archive.umich.edu/atari/8bit//Emulators/stxf255.lzh**)

Online Data Services

The commercial online data services offer support and information for Atari products.

CompuServe Forums

Atari File Finder   ATARIFF
Atari GAMING Forum   ATARIGAMING
Atari ST Prod. Forum   ATARIPRO
Atari Users Network   ATARINET
Atari Vendor Forum   ATARIVEN

BIX Conferences

In the programming area go into

```
o atari.st     Atari ST machines
```

Periodic Postings and FAQs

FAQs with an archive-name listed are available on the anonymous FTP server **rtfm.mit.edu**.

Subject: v*INF*: Introduction to **comp.sources.atari.st**

Newsgroups: **comp.sources.atari.st, comp.sys.atari.st**

From: **avg@cwi.nl** (Annius Groenink)

Archive-name: **intro**

Subject: Atari 8-bit computers: Frequently Asked Questions

Subject: Atari 8-bit computers: vendors and developers

Newsgroups: **comp.sys.atari.8bit, comp.answers, news.answers**

From: **MCURRENT@carleton.edu** (Michael Current)

Archive-name: **atari-8-bit/faq**

Summary: Lists Frequently Asked Questions (and their answers) about Atari 8-bit computers. Anyone who wishes to post to the **comp.sys.atari.8bit** newsgroup should read this.

Subject: Welcome to **comp.sys.atari.st!**

Newsgroups: **comp.sys.atari.st, news.answers, comp.answers**

From: **sourada@iastate.edu** (Steven D. Ourada)

Archive-name: **csas-faq/part1**

Summary: Lists some frequently asked questions and answers about Atari 16/32 bit computers. Please read this before asking a question on **comp.sys.atari.st**.

Subject: Welcome to **comp.sys.atari.st!** (hardware)

Newsgroups: **comp.sys.atari.st, news.answers, comp.answers**

From: **sourada@iastate.edu** (Steven D. Ourada)

Archive-name: **csas-faq/part3**

Summary: Lists some frequently asked questions and answers about Atari 16/32-bit computers. Please read this before asking a question on **comp.sys.atari.st.**

Subject: Welcome to **comp.sys.atari.st!** (software)

Newsgroups: **comp.sys.atari.st, news.answers, comp.answers**

From: **sourada@iastate.edu** (Steven D. Ourada)

Archive-name: **csas-faq/part2**

Summary: Lists some frequently asked questions and answers about Atari 16/32-bit computers. Please read this before asking a question on **comp.sys.atari.st.**

CHAPTER TEN

GRAPHICS

The term "graphics" covers a wide range of applications—the electronic post-processing of photographs, developing 3D graphics and backdrops or "worlds" for games and virtual reality, astrophysics imaging, and medical imaging are just a few. Typically the resources for graphics and imaging are not narrowly focused but serve many applications. This chapter is consequently something of a hodgepodge of a large number of resources that cover many different aspects of graphics and imaging.

It begins with two top-level pieces of information.

Two Key FAQs

Two FAQs in particular give a good overview of some key graphics/imaging topics.

> ➤ The **comp.graphics** FAQ includes a reference list, a description of online resources, detailed explanations of some very specific yet common graphics programming techniques, and pointers to standard documents and online software.

> ➤ The Medical Image Volume Visualization Software FAQ provides detailed reviews of a great many commercial image-processing software packages and a list of key repositories of medical imaging information, software, and example files.

SIGGRAPH

SIGGRAPH is the Special Interest Group for Graphics of the Association for Computing Machinery. The leading professional organization in the computer graphics world, it provides many online resources including

> ➤ An online information site at **ftp://siggraph.org** or http://www.siggraph.org.

> ➤ The Online Bibliography Project, a database of over 15,000 computer graphics and computational geometry references. It is available in BibTeX format on the **siggraph.org** site.

Graphics Software Online

The sections that follows describe some key tools available online for graphic/image file manipulation. A location is given for each, but many can also be found at numerous archive sites.

xv by John Bradley

This X-based image display, manipulation, and format conversion package displays many image formats and permits editing of GIF files, among others. The latest version, 3.00a, may be found at John's site, **ftp.cis.upenn.edu/pub/xv/xv-3.00a.tar.Z**.

PBMPLUS by Jef Poskanzer

A comprehensive format conversion and image manipulation package available at **ftp.ee.lbl.gov/pbmplus10dec91.tar.Z** and at **wuarchive.wustl.edu/graphics/graphics/packages/pbmplus/pbmplus10dec91.tar.Z**.

NETPBM

This USENET community–supported version of the PBMPLUS toolkit includes many new and updated converters. It is available at **wuarchive.wustl.edu/graphics/graphics/packages/NetPBM/netpbm-1mar1994.tar.gz**. A maillist list exists as well.

IM Raster Toolkit by Alan Paeth

(**awpaeth@watcgl.uwaterloo.ca**) This portable and efficiently formatted toolkit supports pixels of arbitrary channels, components, and bit precisions while allowing compression and machine byte-order independence. The kit contains more than 50 tools with extensive support of image manipulation, digital halftoning, and format conversion. Previously distributed on tape from the University of Waterloo, an FTP version will appear someday.

Utah RLE Toolkit

A conversion and manipulation package similar to PBMPLUS is available via FTP as **cs.utah.edu:pub/urt-***, **princeton.edu:pub/Graphics/urt-***, and **freebie.engin.umich.edu:pub/urt-***.

Fuzzy Pixmap Manipulation by Michael Mauldin

Also similar to PBMPLUS, Version 1.0 of this conversion and manipulation package is available via FTP at **network.ucsd.edu/graphics/fbm.tar.Z**.

Xim (X Image Manipulator) by Philip R. Thompson

Capable of essential interactive image manipulations, Xim uses x11r4 and the OSF/Motif toolkit for the interface. It supports images in 1-, 8-, 24-, and 32-bit formats, and reads and writes and converts to and from GIF, xwd, xbm, tiff, rle, xim, and other formats. It also writes level 2 PostScript. Other utilities and an image application library are included, but this is not a paint package. Available at **gis.mit.edu/pub/xim3i.tar.Z**.

xloadimage by Jim Frost

xloadimage reads in images in various formats and displays them on an X11 screen. It's available via FTP in your nearest **comp.sources.x archive**.

xli by Graeme Gill

This updated xloadimage with numerous improvements in both speed and number of formats supported is available at **ftp.x.org/contrib/applications/xli.1.16.tar.gz**.

TIFF Software by Sam Leffler

This nice portable library for reading and writing TIFF files also offers a few tools for manipulating the files and reading other formats. It's available via FTP as **sgi.com:graphics/tiff/*.tar.Z**.

xtiff

This X11 tool for viewing TIFF files was written to handle as many different kinds of TIFF files as possible while remaining simple, portable, and efficient. xtiff illustrates some common problems with building pixmaps and using different visual classes. It is distributed as part of Sam Leffler's libtiff package and is also available on **ftp.uu.net** and **comp.sources.x**. Announced in April 1991, xtiff 2.0 includes Xlib and XT versions.

ALV

Version 2.0.6 of this Sun-specific image toolkit was posted to **comp.sources.sun** on December 11, 1989. It's also available via e-mail to **alv-users-request@cs.bris.ac.uk**.

popi

Version 2.1 of this image manipulation language was posted to **comp.sources.misc** on December 12, 1989.

ImageMagick

An X11 package for display and interactive manipulation of images, this includes tools for image conversion, annotation, compositing, animation, and creating montages. ImageMagick can read and write many more popular image formats. It's available from **ftp.x.org/contrib/applications/ImageMagick/ImageMagick-3.3.tar.gz**.

Khoros

This huge (more than 100 Mbyte) graphical development environment is based on X11R4. Khoros components include a visual programming language, code generators for extending the visual language and adding new application packages to the system, an interactive user interface editor, an interactive image display package, an extensive library of image and signal processing routines, and 2D/3D plotting packages. It's available at **ftp.eece.unm.edu/pub/khoros/***. A newsgroup, **comp.soft-sys.khoros**, exists for the discussion of Khoros and Khoros-related topics.

LaboImage

This SunView-based image processing and analysis package includes more than 200 image manipulation, processing, and measurement routines, and online help, plus tools such as an image editor, a color table editor, and several biomedical utilities. Available via anonymous FTP on **nic.funet.fi/pub/graphics/packages**.

San Diego Supercomputer Center Image Tools

These software tools read, write, and manipulate raster images. Binaries for some machines are available at **sdsc.edu/pub/sdsc/graphics/imtools/***.

Independent JPEG Group's Free JPEG Software

The Independent JPEG Group has written a package for reading and writing JPEG files. To find them, FTP to **ftp.uu.net:graphics/jpeg/jpegsrc.v?.tar.gz**.

bit (Bitmap Image Touchup) by T. C. Zhao

This full-color viewer/editor offers a variety of features (SGI only). You can obtain it via FTP at **monte.svec.uh.edu/pub/bit**.

Libreria de Utilidades Graficas or Graphic Utilities Library

This library of subroutines for image manipulation has routines for loading, viewing, and manipulating a variety of formats. You can obtain it at **ftpuniovi.es /uniovi/mathdept/src/liblug.tar.gz**.

Doré (Dynamic Object Rendering Environment)

Doré, a powerful 3D graphics subroutine library, provides a comprehensive set of tools for creating graphics applications. It is also easy to use, portable, and extendable. This version has interfaces/drivers to X11, PEX, IrisGL, OpenGL, PostScript, and more. It runs on NetBSD 1.0, Linux, FreeBSD, Solaris 2.3, and OSF/1. It has also been ported to Windows NT 3.5. The official distribution site is **sunsite.unc.edu/pub/packages/ development/graphics/Dore** as **pdore-6.0.tar.Z**.

XMegaWave

XMegaWave is a graphics Windows environment oriented to image processing and based on collaboration between researchers from the University of Balear Islands (U.I.B.), the University of Las Palmas (U.L.P.G.C.), and the University of Paris IX Dauphine (UPD). XMW is oriented to UNIX workstations that work with X11R4 and Motif 1.1 libraries (this XMW version). Currently, it is available for HP-Apollo and SGI workstations. Full source is not available yet, but the authors say they will cooperate to build other versions. XMW may be obtained at **ftp.dis.ulpgc.es/investigacion/ami/XMegaWave**.

Internet Maillists

The following sections describe maillists that provide information on graphics and related topics.

GLEList

Contact: **listproc@tbone.biol.scarolina.edu**

Description: Supports users of the GLE graphics package for scientists. Supported on several platforms (PCs, VAXes, and UNIX). To enroll, send message **sub glelist your name** to **tproc@tbone.biol.scarolina.edu**.

Lexicor Graphics Support List

Contact: lexicor-list-request@lexicor.com

Description: Discusses Atari computer graphics, hardware, software, and programming techniques.

PERQ-fanatics

Contact: PERQ-fanatics-request@hicom.org

Description: Discusses the PERQ graphics workstations.

BITNET List Server Maillists

Contact: listproc@tbone.biol.scarolina.edu

Description: Discusses quantitative morphology.

rend386

Contact: rend386-request@sunee.uwaterloo.ca

Description: Discusses the REND386 software package to develop fast polygon-based graphics on 386 and 486 systems.

S-news

Contact: S-news-request@stat.wisc.edu (Douglas Bates)

Description: Discusses S language for data analysis and graphics.

Imagine

Contact: imagine-request@email.sp.paramax.com (Dave Wickard)

Description: Discusses Imagine, a 3D computer rendering package for Amiga and MS-DOS systems.

info-ei

Contact: info-ei-request@spie.org

Description: Electronic imaging discussion list.

iti151

Contact: iti151-request@oce.orst.edu (John Stanley)

Description: Discusses Imaging Technology's series 150 and 151 image processing systems and ITEX151 software.

PhotoForum

Contact: listserv@listserver.isc.rit.edu

Description: An educational network for photo educators and others.

DCTV Maillist

Contact: DCTV-request@nova.cc.purdue.edu

Description: Discussion forum for the Amiga graphics module DCTV from Digital Creations. To enroll, send a message to **DCTV-request@nova.cc.purdue.edu** with *Subject:* = **subscribe**.

Rayshade-L

Contact: rayshade-request@cs.princeton.edu

Description: For users of Rayshade, a public domain raytracer. To enroll, send a message to **rayshade-request@cs.princeton.edu** with *Subject:* = **subscribe**.

Lightwave-L

Contact: **to lightwave-request@bobsbox.rent.com**

Description: Discussion list for Lightwave 3D Rendering and Animation package from Newtek.

Toaster-L (Video Toaster Maillist)

Contact: **toaster-request@bobsbox.rent.com**

Description: For users of Netwerks Video Toaster, an Amiga board that includes lightwave and video functionality.

Maillist for Massive Parallel Rendering

Contact: mp-render-request@icase.edu

Description: Discusses massive parallel rendering on UNIX systems. To enroll, send a message to **mp-render-request@icase.edu** with *Subject:* = **subscribe**.

POV-Ray Maillist

Contact:

Description: Discusses POV-Ray , a public domain raytrace for UNIX, Amiga, Mac, and PC platforms. To enroll, send a message to **listserv@vm3090.ege.edu.tr** with *Subject:* = **subscribe dkb-1**.

Raydream-L

Contact: listserv@cornell.edu

Description: Discusses the Ray Dream Rendering and Animation package for Macintosh.

Photoshop Maillist

Contact: **photshop@bgu.edu**

Description: Discusses the Photoshop image conversion and manipulation package from Adobe for Windows, Macintosh, and SGI platforms.

3Dstudio

Contact: **majordomo@autodesk.com**

Description: Discussion of the 3D Studio modeling and rendering package from Autodesk for PCs.

Kpt-List

Contact: listserv@netcom.com

Description: Discusses Kai's Power Tools, a set of cool texture plug-ins for Adobe Photoshop and other packages such as Windows and the Mac.

PhotoCD

Contact: listserv@info.kodak.com

Description: Discusses Kodak's PhotoCD format and related topics.

Caligari TrueSpace Maillist

Contact: **truespace-request@cs.uregina.ca**

Description: Discusses the Caligari TrueSpace Rendering and Animation package from Caligari.

BITNET List Server Maillists

To subscribe to a maillist, send a mail message to **listserv@bitnic.bitnet**. Leave the *Subject:* field blank. In the body of the message, write: **SUBSCRIBE listname**, where listname is a name in the left column of the following list.

AMIA-L	Association for Moving Image Archivists
CGE	Computer Graphics Education Newsletter
GIF-L	GIF Graphics and Applications List
GIK2-L	Graphics Interface Kit/2 Discussion
GRAPH-L	Mathematical Aspects of Computer Graphics, Caos, Fractal
GRAPH-UG	KFUPM Graphics Users Group
GRAPHICS	Graphic Design Discussion
IMAGRS-L	Digital Image Processing of Remotely Sensed Data
INGRAFX	Information Graphics
L3GRAF-L	L3 Graphics/Interactivity Group
MEDIMAGE	Medical Imaging Discussion List

Internet Newsgroups

These permanent newsgroups are accessible via most network newsreader programs

comp.graphics
Computer graphics, art, animation, image processing

comp.graphics.algorithms
Algorithms used in producing computer graphics

comp.graphics.animation
Technical aspects of computer animation

comp.graphics.avs
Application Visualization System

comp.graphics.data-explorer
IBM's Visualization Data Explorer, aka DX

comp.graphics.explorer
Explorer Modular Visualization Environment (MVE)

comp.graphics.gnuplot
GNUPLOT interactive function plotter

comp.graphics.opengl
OpenGL 3D application programming interface

comp.graphics.packages.alias
3D graphics software from Alias Research

comp.graphics.packages.lightwave
NewTek's Lightwave 3D and related topics

comp.graphics.raytracing
Ray tracing software, tools, and methods

comp.graphics.research
Highly technical computer graphics discussion (moderated)

comp.graphics.visualization
Info on scientific visualization

comp.os.ms-windows.programmer.graphics
GDI, graphics, and printing

comp.sys.amiga.graphics
Charts, graphs, pictures, and so forth

comp.protocols.dicom
Digital Imaging and Communications in Medicine

comp.soft-sys.khoros
Khoros X11 Visualization System

comp.sys.mac.graphics
Macintosh graphics: paint, draw, 3D, CAD, animation

comp.sys.mentor
Mentor Graphics products and the Silicon Compiler System

comp.sys.sgi.admin
System administration on Silicon Graphics' Irises

comp.sys.sgi.graphics
Graphics packages and issues on SGI machines

```
comp.sys.sgi.misc
```
General discussion about Silicon Graphics' machines

```
sci.astro.fits
```
Issues related to the Flexible Image Transport System

```
sci.image.processing
```
Scientific image processing and analysis

```
sci.techniques.mag-resonance
```
Magnetic resonance imaging and spectroscopy

Commercial Online Services

The next sections cover graphics resources offered by commercial online data services.

CompuServe

Many CompuServe forums support graphics. However, be careful when you are scanning them: Most are not so much about graphics programming as they are about accessing and downloading graphics files from the service.

A quick scan using the Find Services function turns up over a hundred forums, but the ones specifically related to graphics programming are

➤ The Borland C and C++ Forums (GO BCPPDOS)

➤ The Macintosh Development Learn Programming Forum (GO MACDEV)

➤ The Zenith Graphics forum (GO ZENITH)

➤ The Microsoft BASIC Programming Issues Forum (GO MSBASIC)

America Online

AOL's Graphics and Animation Forum in its computing area focuses more on computer art and, like CompuServe, tools for accessing picture files than on computer graphics programming.

A Resource Center contains areas of special interest, such as 3D rendering, CAD, Corel, DTP, digital imaging, and electronic publishing. Also, the 3D rendering resource contains the POV Ray Tracing program with a lot of support information. AOL also offers an informative message board and a graphics-oriented software library.

**BIX
Conferences**

These conferences on in the programming area of BIX support graphics topics:

o hubb   Hagen Graphics Users Group

o graphic.pgms   Programming and graphics

o ti.graphics   TI graphics chip conference

Periodic Postings and FAQs

Because the number of FAQs available for graphics and related topics is so large, a brief listing is given here to help you locate specific topics:

Welcome to **alt.graphics.pixutils**—automated posting

Medical Image Volume Visualization Software FAQ

FAQ: 3D Information for the Programmer

Computer Graphics Resource Listing: BIWEEKLY [part */*]

comp.graphics Frequently Asked Questions (FAQ)

Graphics File Formats FAQ: General Graphics Format Questions (Part * of *)

Graphics File Formats FAQ: Image Conversion and Display Programs (Part * of *)

Graphics File Formats FAQ: Where to Get File Format Specifications (Part * of *)

Graphics File Formats FAQ: Tips and Tricks of the Trade (Part * of *)

MPEG-FAQ: multimedia compression [*/6]

SuperVGA/VESA programmer's notes

Color space FAQ

comp.graphics.algorithms Frequently Asked Questions (FAQ)

comp.graphics.animation FAQ v* (* *)

comp.graphics.gnuplot FAQ (Frequent Answered Questions)

comp.graphics.opengl Frequently Asked Questions (FAQ) [*/*]

comp.graphics.rendering.renderman FAQ

PostScript monthly FAQ v* *-*-* [* of *]

Medical Image Format FAQ, Part */*

FAQ: Astronomical Image Processing System (AIPS)

Fractal Frequently Asked Questions and Answers

Macintosh Image Processing Information Sources (FAQ)

JPEG image compression FAQ, part */2

Khoros FAQ: *

Subject: (*) Welcome to **alt.graphics.pixutils**—automated posting

Newsgroups: **alt.graphics.pixutils, alt.answers**

From: **jef@netcom.com** (Jef Poskanzer)

Archive-name: **pixutils-faq**

Subject: Medical Image Volume Visualization Software FAQ

Newsgroups: **alt.image.medical, alt.sci.nmr, comp.graphics.visualization, comp.sys.mac.scitech, sci.image.processing, sci.med.radiology, sci.techniques.mag-resonance, alt.answers, comp.answers, sci.answers, news.answers**

From: **mhaveri@cc.oulu.fi** (Matti Haveri)

Archive-name: **medical-image-faq/volume-visualization**

Summary: List of software packages, user's notes, references, and other information relating to medical volume visualization and imaging.

Subject: FAQ: 3D Information for the Programmer

Newsgroups: **rec.games.programmer, comp.graphics, rec.answers, comp.answers, news.answers**

From: **pat@mail.csh.rit.edu**

Archive-name: **3d-programmer-info**

Summary Still in progress, fill-in-the-blanks

Subject: SuperVGA/VESA programmer's notes

Newsgroups: **comp.graphics, comp.lang.pascal, comp.answers, news.answers**

From: **myles@giaec.cc.monash.edu.au**

Subject: **comp.graphics.rendering.renderman** FAQ

Newsgroups: **comp.graphics.rendering.renderman, comp.answers, news.answers**

From: **gritz@seas.gwu.edu** (Larry Gritz)

Subject: (*) Computer Graphics Resource Listing: BIWEEKLY [part */*]

Newsgroups: **comp.graphics, comp.answers, news.answers**

From: **nfotis@theseas.ntua.gr** (Nick C. Fotis)

Archive-name: **graphics/resources-list/part1**

Subject: (*) **comp.graphics** Frequently Asked Questions (FAQ)

Newsgroups: **comp.graphics, comp.answers, news.answers**

From: **grieggs@netcom.com** (John T. Grieggs)

Archive-name: **graphics/faq**

Summary: Answers many most Frequently Asked Questions about graphics on USENET. To avoid wasting bandwidth and as a courtesy, please look for the answer to your question in this document BEFORE posting to **comp.graphics.**

Subject: Graphics File Formats FAQ: General Graphics Format Questions (Part * of *)

Subject: Graphics File Formats FAQ: Image Conversion and Display Programs (Part * of *)

Subject: Graphics File Formats FAQ: Where to Get File Format Specifications (Part * of *)

Subject: Graphics File Formats FAQ: Tips and Tricks of the Trade (Part * of *)

Newsgroups: **comp.graphics, comp.answers, news.answers**

From: **jdm@netcom.com**

Archive-name: **graphics/fileformats-faq/part1**

Summary: Answers many most Frequently Asked Questions about graphics file formats on USENET.

Subject: MPEG-FAQ: multimedia compression [*/6]

Newsgroups: **comp.graphics, comp.graphics.animation, comp.compression, comp.multimedia, alt.binaries.multimedia, alt.binaries.pictures.utilities, alt.binaries.pictures, alt.binaries.pictures.d, alt.answers, comp.answers, news.answers**

From: **phade@cs.tu-berlin.de** (Frank Gadegast)

Archive-name: **mpeg-faq**/part0

Summary: Summarizes the ISO-Videoformats MPEG 1 and MPEG 2

Subject: SuperVGA/VESA programmer's notes

Newsgroups: comp.graphics, comp.lang.pascal, comp.answers, news.answers

From: myles@giaec.cc.monash.edu.au

Subject: Color space FAQ

*Newsgroups:*comp.graphics, sci.image.processing, comp.answers, sci.answers, news.answers

From: ajoec1@westminster.ac.uk (Adrian Ford)

Archive-name: graphics/colorspace-faq

Summary: Lists Frequently Asked Questions (and their answers) about colors and color spaces. It provides an extension to the short 4 and 5 items of **comp.graphics** FAQ. Read item 1 for more details. A copy of this document is available by anonymous FTP in **rtfm.mit.edu/pub/usenet/news.answers/graphics/colorspace-faq** or **turing.imag.fr: /pub/compression/colorspace-faq.**

Subject: **comp.graphics.algorithms** Frequently Asked Questions (FAQ)

Newsgroups: **comp.graphics.algorithms, comp.answers, news.answers**

From: **jdstone@destin.dazixco.ingr.com** (Jon Stone)

Archive-name: **graphics/algorithms-faq**

Summary: Lists Frequently Asked Questions (and their answers) about computer graphics algorithms. Anyone who wishes to post to the **comp.graphics.algorithms** newsgroup should read this.

Subject: **comp.graphics.animation** FAQ v* (* *)

Newsgroups: **comp.graphics.animation, comp.answers, news.answers**

From: **angus@cgl.citri.edu.au** (Angus Y. Montgomery)

Archive-name: **graphics/animation-faq**

Summary: Currently passes for a **comp.graphics.animation** FAQ. It has information on computer animation for end users, hobbyists, career animators, and programmers. Please read this FAQ before posting to **comp.graphics.animation.**

Subject: **comp.graphics.gnuplot** FAQ (Frequently Asked Questions)

Newsgroups: **comp.graphics.gnuplot, comp.answers, news.answers**

From: **ig25@fg70.rz.uni-karlsruhe.de** (Thomas Koenig)

Archive-name: **graphics/gnuplot-faq**

Summary: Lists FAQ (Frequently Asked Questions) of the **comp.graphics.gnuplot** newsgroup, which discusses the gnuplot program for plotting 2D and 3D graphs

Subject: **comp.graphics.opengl** Frequently Asked Questions (FAQ) [*/*]

Newsgroups: **comp.graphics.opengl, comp.answers, news.answers**

From: **woo@kicksave.asd.sgi.com** (Mason Woo)

Archive-name: **graphics/opengl-faq**

Summary: Lists Frequently Asked Questions about OpenGL®

Subject: **comp.graphics.rendering.renderman** FAQ

Newsgroups: **comp.graphics.rendering.renderman, comp.answers, news.answers**

From: **gritz@seas.gwu.edu** (Larry Gritz)

Subject: PostScript monthly FAQ v* *-*-* [* of *]

Newsgroups: **comp.lang.postscript, comp.answers, news.answers**

From: **postscript-request@cs.brown.edu** (Jonathan Monsarrat)

Archive-name: **postscript/faq/part1-4**

Summary: Useful facts about the PostScript graphics programming language

Subject: Medical Image Format FAQ, Part */*

Newsgroups: **alt.image.medical, comp.protocols.dicom, sci.data.formats, alt.answers, comp.answers, sci.answers, news.answers**

From: **dclunie@flash.us.com** (David A. Clunie)

Archive-name: **medical-image-faq/part1**

Summary: Contains answers to the most Frequently Asked Questions on **alt.image.medical**—how do I convert from image format X from vendor Y to something I can use? In addition, it contains information about various standard formats.

Subject: FAQ: Astronomical Image Processing System (AIPS)

Newsgroups: **alt.sci.astro.aips, alt.answers, news.answers**

From: **pmurphy@nrao.edu** (Patrick P. Murphy)

Archive-name: **astronomy/aips-faq**

Summary: Briefly introduces AIPS, the Astronomical Image Processing System, and answers a few basic questions about AIPS. This is a package for reduction and analysis of Radio Astronomy Data. Please read this before posting anything to **alt.sci.astro.aips.**

Subject: Fractal Frequently Asked Questions and Answers

Newsgroups: **sci.fractals, sci.answers, news.answers**

From: **STEPP@MUVMS6.MU.WVNET.EDU** (Ermel Stepp)

Reply To: **stepp@marshall.edu**

Archive-name: **fractal-faq**

Summary: Contains fractal images, software, algorithms, definitions, and references

Subject: Macintosh Image Processing Information Sources (FAQ)

Newsgroups: **sci.image.processing, comp.sys.mac.scitech, sci.answers, news.answers**

From: **huff@mcclb0.med.nyu.edu** (Edward J. Huff)

Archive-name: **image-processing/Macintosh**

Sci-image-processing-archive-name: **MacImageProc**

Comp-sys-mac-scitech-archive-name: **MacImageProc**

Summary: Macintosh image processing information available via GOPHER, FTP, USENET, e-mail, telephone, and snail mail

Subject: JPEG image compression FAQ, part */2

Newsgroups: **comp.graphics, alt.graphics.pixutils, alt.binaries.pictures.utilities, alt.binaries.pictures.d, alt.binaries.pictures.erotica.d, comp.answers, alt.answers, news.answers**

From: **tgl@netcom.com** (Tom Lane)

Archive-name: **jpeg-faq/part1**

Summary: Contains general questions and answers about JPEG

Subject: Color space FAQ

Newsgroups: **comp.graphics, sci.image.processing, comp.answers, sci.answers, news.answers**

From: **ajoec1@westminster.ac.uk** (Adrian Ford)

Archive-name: **graphics/colorspace-faq**

Summary: Lists Frequently Asked Questions (and their answers) about colors and color spaces. It's an extension to the short 4 and 5 items of **comp.graphics** FAQ. Read item 1 for more details. A copy of this document is available by anonymous FTP in **rtfm.mit.edu/pub/usenet/news.answers/graphics/colorspace-faq** or **turing.imag.fr:/pub/compression/colorspace-faq.**

Subject: Khoros FAQ: *

Newsgroups: **comp.soft-sys.khoros**

From: **khoros-faq@khoros.unm.edu** (the Khoros FAQs)

Comment: The following articles are currently being posted: general issues related to Khoros, compiling Khoros, image processing with Khoros, the Meta-FAQ.

CHAPTER ELEVEN

MULTIMEDIA

The material in this chapter relates somewhat to that of Chapter 10, "Graphics," and Chapter 13, "Games." Games increasingly depend upon multiple media, and graphics are part of the visual media.

However, multimedia also have other applications of wider interest. Some are related to either electronic publishing or hypertext.

In general, many programs, even those not specifically games oriented, are hopping on the multimedia buzzword bandwagon and either incorporating some mixed audio/visual interfaces, or are at least being distributed on CD-ROM.

So, depending upon your particular area of interest, you might want to investigate the resources this chapter and Chapters 10 and 13 identify.

Internet Maillists

The next sections describe the maillists that provide information on multimedia, CD-ROM, and related topics.

hyperami

Contact: listserv@archive.oit.unc.ed

Description: Informal regarding AmigaVision, CanDo, DeluxeVideo III, and related products.

MMDEVX

Contact: Mail-Server@knex.mind.org

Description: Cross-platform multimedia development tools, the Apple Media Kit (AMK), and Kaleida ScriptX

**Amiga
CD-ROM**

Contact: cdrom-list-request@ben.com

Description: Use of CD-ROMs on Amiga Systems

CDPub

Contact: Mail-Server@knex.mind.org

Description: CD-ROM publishing in general, desktop CD-ROM recorders, and publishing systems

BITNET List Server Maillists

To subscribe to a maillist, send a mail message to **listserv@bitnic.bitnet**. Leave the *Subject:* field blank. In the body of the message, write: **SUBSCRIBE listname**, where listname is a name in the left column below.

CD-ROM-L	CD-ROM
CD-ROMLAN	USE OF CD-ROM PRODUCTS IN LAN ENVIRONMENTS
IMAMEDIA	Compatibility of Multimedia Applications
MACMULTI	Macintosh Multimedia Discussion List
MAX	Discussion of Interactive Music/Multimedia Standard Environment
MMEDIA-L	Multimedia Discussion List

```
MULTI        Multimedia Talk Group to Discuss Current
             Multimedia Issues

OHIOMM       Ohio Multimedia Development
```

Internet Newsgroups

These permanent newsgroups are accessible via most network newsreader programs:

```
comp.multimedia
Interactive multimedia technologies of all kinds

comp.os.ms-windows.programmer.multimedia
Multimedia programming

comp.os.ms-windows.programmer.winhelp
WinHelp/multimedia VR development

comp.os.os2.multimedia
Multimedia on OS/2 systems

comp.publish.cdrom.multimedia
Software for multimedia authoring and publishing

comp.sys.amiga.multimedia
Animations, video, and multimedia

misc.education.multimedia
Multimedia for education (moderated)

comp.publish.cdrom.hardware
Hardware used in publishing with CD-ROM

comp.publish.cdrom.software
Software used in publishing with CD-ROM

comp.sys.ibm.pc.hardware.cd-rom
CD-ROM drives and interfaces for the PC
```

Commercial Online Data Services

Several CompuServe forums are related to multimedia topics and CD-ROM use or publishing. This area changes frequently, so it's a good idea to use the Search For Services function to determine the most current offerings. Some existing forums are

```
MS Win Multimedia Forum      WINMM

Macintosh Multimedia Forum   MACMULTI

Multimedia A Vendor Forum    MULTIVEN

Multimedia B Vendor Forum    MULTIBVEN

Multimedia C Vendor Forum    MULTICVEN

Multimedia Forum             MULTIMEDIA

CD-ROM A Vendor Forum        CDVEN

CD-ROM B Vendor Forum        CDVENB

CD-ROM Forum                 CD-ROM
```

America Online's Multimedia Forum in its computing forums area is geared towards end-user applications and output files, or how-to hardware and software tips. However, two topics cover the publisher's side:

➤ The Multimedia Reference Guide has several topics, in particular, a legal guide for multimedia publishers.

➤ The Epub Resource Center has a lot of information on authoring tools and techniques including several resources on hypertext development.

Periodic Postings and FAQs

FAQs with an archive-name listed are available on the anonymous FTP server **rtfm.mit.ed**.

Subject: **alt.cd-rom** FAQ

Newsgroups: **alt.cd-rom, comp.multimedia, comp.publish.cdrom.multimedia, comp.publish.cdrom.hardware, comp.publish.cdrom.software, alt.answers, comp.answers, news.answers**

From: **rab@cdrom.com**

Archive-name: **cdrom-faq**

Summary: Frequently Asked Questions about CD-ROMs

Subject: MPEG-FAQ: multimedia compression [*/6]

Newsgroups: **comp.graphics, comp.graphics.animation, comp.compression, comp.multimedia, alt.binaries.multimedia, alt.binaries.pictures.utilities, alt.binaries.pictures, alt.binaries.pictures.d, alt.answers, comp.answers, news.answers**

From: **phade@cs.tu-berlin.de** (Frank Gadegast)

Archive-name: **mpeg-faq/part0**

Summary: Summarizes the ISO-Videoformats MPEG 1 and MPEG 2

Subject: **comp.sys.amiga.cd32, rec.games.video.cd32** FAQ (Frequently Asked Questions)

Newsgroups: **comp.sys.amiga.cd32, rec.games.video.cd32, comp.answers, rec.answers, news.answers**

From: **dan@blender.demon.co.uk** (Dan Cannon)

Reply To: Dan—CD32-FAQ Mailbox **cd32faq@blender.demon.co.uk**

Archive-name: **amiga/CD32-FAQ**

Summary: Frequently Asked Questions about the Amiga CD32; includes how to expand the CD32 to a computer and how to use the CD32 as an external CD-ROM drive for other computers

CHAPTER TWELVE

VIRTUAL REALITY/WORLDS

Virtual reality has been a hot topic over the past year or two as the press and other media have embraced the cyberworld. Actually, VR activities range from the recreational (games) to the business/practical/scientific (training simulators). Also, while you might first think of it as 3D vision (with or without helmets and sensory systems), VR also encompasses non-graphic topics: Some virtual worlds are developed in text-only environments where the accent is on content rather than display.

One of the best ways to locate and identify material on VR is to use some form of Web browser or search engine. For example, accessing YAHOO (**http://www.yahoo.com**) and using its search function to look for virtual reality turns up a number of commercial, amateur, recreational, and scientific sites or sources of information.

Some links you can find this way include pointers to

➤ A number of companies engaged in developing VR tools and applications

➤ Several magazines such as *VR World* and *Wired*

➤ Colleges engaged in VR research

➤ Numerous game sites including MUDs, MOOs, call it M**, and so forth

An important aspect of virtual reality development is that there is a (draft) standard language called the Virtual Reality Modeling Language. The draft standard is available via anonymous FTP to **ftp.u.washington.edu**, the Human Interface Technology Lab (HITLab) archive site. There is also a maillist (described later on) called the www-vrml maillist. You can join by mailing a request to **majordomo@wired.com**.

Key Sites and Organizations

This list is by no means a complete list, but it does include some names that pop up frequently in browsing around the Net.

➤ HITLab (the Human Interface Technology Lab mentioned above) maintains the primary Internet newslist on virtual reality. Their archive site is **ftp.u.washington.edu**. You can also reach them via the Web at **http://www.hitl.washington.edu**.

➤ VRASP (Virtual Reality Alliance of Students and Professionals) maintains a Web site with information on VR tools, development, news, and so on. Their URL is **http://www.vrasp.org**.

➤ EVE (Encyclopedia of Virtual Environments) is available at the University of Maryland FTP site **gimble.cs.umd.edu**.

➤ STB (Virtual Reality Lab at Johnson Space Center) focuses on developing VR for practical purposes such as training simulators. The URL is **http://www.jsc.nasa.gov**.

➤ NCSA is a site focused on using VR to provide new ways to examine large amounts of scientific data and information. Their home page is **http://www.ncsa.uiuc.edu**. (FTP site **ftp.ncsa.uiuc.edu**)

Internet Newsgroups

Two Internet maillists focus specifically on virtual reality:

`sci.virtual-worlds`	Virtual reality technology and culture (moderated)
`sci.virtual-worlds.apps`	Current and future uses of virtual-world's technology (moderated)

A number of other newsgroups deal with topics closely allied to virtual reality.

`comp.graphics`	Computer graphics, art, animation, image processing
`comp.human-factors`	Issues related to human-computer interaction (HCI)
`comp.multimedia`	Interactive multimedia technologies of all kinds
`comp.realtime`	Issues related to real-time computing
`comp.robotics`	All aspects of robots and their applications
`comp.simulation`	Simulation methods, problems, uses (moderated)
`comp.sys.sgi.graphics`	Graphics packages and issues on SGI machines
`comp.theory.dynamic-sys`	Theory of dynamic systems
`sci.cognitive`	Perception, memory, judgment, and reasoning
`sci.med.telemedicine`	Clinical consulting through computer networks

sci.optics	Discussion relating to the science of optics
sci.research	Research methods, funding, ethics, and whatever

Internet Maillists

The maillists described in the next sections provide information on virtual reality and related topics.

rend386

Contact: rend386request@sunee.uwaterloo.ca

Description: REND386 software package for developing fast polygon-based graphics on 386 and 486 systems

Homebrew-VR

Contact: homebrew-vr-request@acm.uiuc.edu

Description: Discusses homemade virtual-reality devices and applications

**RW-LIST
RenderWare**

Contact: listproc@canon.co.uk

Description: Contains information about RenderWare

VIGIS-L

Contact: listserv@uwavm.bitnet

Description: Contains information about the use of VR interfaces in Geographic Information Systems (GIS)

vworlds-list

Contact: send mail to **vworlds-list-request@netcom.com** for instructions

Description: Provides information on aesthetic and artistic aspects of virtual worlds

BITNET List Server Maillists

To subscribe to a maillist, send a mail message to **listserv@bitnic.bitnet**. Leave the *Subject:* field blank. In the body of the message, write: **SUBSCRIBE listname**, where listname is a name in the left column below.

EJVC-L   *Electronic Journal on Virtual Culture*

JVRE-ALL   *Journal of Virtual Reality in Education*
            (complete journal)

JVRE-TOC   *Journal of Virtual Reality in Education*
            Table of Contents

VIRTU-L   VR / sci.virtual-worlds

VRAPP-L   VR Apps / sci.virtual-worlds.apps

VRINST-L   Virtual Reality—Implications for Instruction

VRSCHOOL   Distributed Virtual R for K-12 Education

VRSURGER   Virtual Reality Surgical Simulator Group

FTP Sites

Some key FTP sites related to virtual reality programming and resources are listed next. Also, several lists of hot VR FTP sites are available.

ftp.apple.com//pub/VR
Information on Macintosh VR applications; lists FTP sites
in the file vr_sites

ftp.u.washington.edu
HITLab archive site and also the sci.virtual-worlds
archive

ftp.ncsa.uiuc.edu//VR
Contains utilities and papers for VR use and development;
oriented towards scientific visualization

```
sunee.uwaterloo.ca/pub/vr, pub/rend386, pub/glove
Numerous demo files and some tools
```

```
sunsite.unc.edu//pub/academic/computer-science/virtual-reality
Archive of a great many VR informational files
```

```
avalon.chinalake.navy.mil
3D object repository
```

Other sites with incidental VR-related material are

wuarchive.wustl.edu

src.doc.ic.ac.uk

parcftp.xerox.com

Also, by using Archie and searching for VR or virtual reality, you can identify many sites that have some VR-related material.

Online Data Services

Several CompuServe forums offer material related to virtual reality. Two primary forums are at GO COMART and GO GRAPHDEV. You can access others using the service's search tool:

```
AI EXPERT Forum              AIEXPERT
Autodesk Multimedia Forum    ASOFT
Cyber Forum                  CYBERFORUM
Gamers Forum                 GAMERS
Graphics Vendor Forum        GRAPHVEN
```

In its computing area America Online maintains a Virtual Reality Resource Center (keyword = Virtual Reality). This center has a large amount of information on a variety of topics:

➤ VR Utilities—applications and utilities

➤ VR Presentations—executable programs

➤ VR Text—documents on VR hardware and software

➤ REND386—information on REND386 and VR-386.

➤ Vendor Contacts

➤ A message board and a file upload area

BIX

BIX has one conference, the **virtual.world** conference, that covers a variety of VR-related topics.

Periodic Postings and FAQs

As mentioned earlier there are two primary Internet newsgroups on virtual reality; both have FAQs available:

Subject: EPUB: Sci.Virtual-Worlds Monthly Meta-FAQ

Newsgroups: **sci.virtual-worlds, sci.answers, news.answers**

From: **pulkka@cs.washington.edu** (Aaron Kaleva Pulkka)

Archive-name: **virtual-worlds/meta-faq**

Summary: This is the Frequently Asked Questions post for **sci.virtual-worlds**, which contains information on the newsgroup's purpose, moderating group, submission guidelines, suggested readings, terminology, and archives.

Subject: **sci.virtual-worlds.apps** Introductory FAQ Posting

Newsgroups: **sci.virtual-worlds.apps**

From: **deloura@cs.unc.edu** (Mark A. DeLoura)

Archive-name: **scivwa-faq**

Subject: Homebrew-VR FAQ

Summary : FAQ for the Homebrew-VR mailist, which promotes the development of homebrew virtual-reality devices and applications. Available at URL=**http://www.acm.uiuc.edu/homebrew/faq.html**.

CHAPTER THIRTEEN

GAMES DEVELOPMENT

GAMES DEVELOPMENT

This chapter is about the development of games software, not actual games. Perhaps no single type of software is as widely available or takes up as much disc space worldwide as games software. As a result, a significant amount of information and resources has grown up around games development.

Online Game Development Resource Centers

Many games are available on commercial online data services, as well as information on games development.

CompuServe   CompuServe's Games Development Forum (GO GAMEDEV) provides one of the most comprehensive locations where games developers can access tools and information, and share experiences and problem-solving techniques. Titles of the forum libraries give a good indication of the scope of material covered:

Game Developers Forum

1 General/Help

2 General Programming

3 DOS Games

4 Windows Games

5 Other Platforms

6 Video Games

7 Coin-op/VR Games

8 Online/Modem Games

9 *HOT* Topics

10 Design Theory

11 Hardware Issues

12 Writing

13 Art/Graphics

14 Music/Sound

15 Business/Marketing

16 Legal Issues

17 Jobs Network

18 Industry News

19 Conferences

20 CGDA

21 The Lounge

Other places of interest on CompuServe are

GAMERS	What people are playing and what they like
VBPJ and MSBASIC	Useful for VB programmers
WINMM	Microsoft forum for multimedia and games development under Windows

America Online

Although not as comprehensive as the CompuServe collection, America Online has a very useful section dedicated to games development. In the computing area, the Development Forums include a separate Games Designers Forum with a message board system and a significant library of tools, utilities, and information files.

Internet Newsgroups

Several Internet newsgroups are related to games. Also, the maintainers of the **rec.games.programmer** newsgroup mentioned below have generated an encyclopedia of games development information.

rec.games.programmer

rec.games.announce

rec.games.design

rec.games.video.programmer

rec.games.video.sega

rec.games.frp.misc

comp.sys.ibm.pc.games.misc

Internet Maillists

This section describes Internet maillists relevant to games development.

crossfire

Contact: **crossfire-request@ifi.uio.no**

Description: Discusses the development of the Crossfire, a multiplayer game for the X Windows environment

pd-games

Contact: **pd-games-request@math.uio.no**

Description: A maillist for game theory, especially those similar to Prisoner's Dilemma

tinymush-programmers

Contact: **tinymush-programmers-request@cygnus.com**

Description: Discusses the programming language integral to the TinyMUSH subfamily of mud servers

Turbo

Contact: **turbo-list-request@cpac.washington.edu**

Description: Information for users of Turbo Duo and Turbografx-16 home video game systems

Tutorials on Game Development

Three major FAQs or tutorials are available on games development. The next sections briefly describe each and provide information on how to obtain them.

The Getting Started Guide to Game Development FAQ

Available on the CompuServe Games Developers Forum (filename gdevfaq.txt), this is an excellent tutorial for newcomers to games development. It also has reference material that will be of interest to mid- and senior-level developers. It covers such topics as

➤ The life cycle of games development

➤ Overview of the different game families (3D, RPG, Edutainment, and so on)

➤ Descriptions of various language options and compilers

➤ A list of related commercial and shareware tools useful for games development (sound editors, paint tools, and so on)

➤ Good game design and coding techniques

➤ List of useful books, magazines, organizations, trade shows, and conferences

➤ List of online resources

➤ Business topics including marketing techniques, copyright protection, and so on

This reference material is mixed with a lot of real-life tips, among them: "If you seriously want to develop games programs, be prepared for a hard life."

PC Games Developers Encyclopedia

This collection of text files, coupled together with a reader, covers many topics relevant to games development. The people who run the **rec.games.programmer** newsgroup created this encyclopedia. It is available in two formats: a Windows Help file and a DOS-based reader program.

The files, WCPGE.ZIP (Windows Help file format) and PCPGE.ZIP (DOS version), are available in the CompuServe GAMEDEV Forum. (The DOS filename is reported differently in different sources; sometimes it's called "PCPGE," and other times it's called "PCGPE.") In compressed format, each file is more than 700 Kbytes, so prepare to spend time downloading. The files are also available via anonymous FTP from **teeri.oulu.fi/pub/msdos/programming/gpe**.

The encyclopedia is somewhat hardware focused, covering topics like how to program sound or video cards, but it is in continual development. More content on software will be added. Also, it presently focuses on PC-architecture machines. Its creators plan to cover Mac and other systems and to include cross-platform development tools.

Some of the main topics covered are

➤ An assembly language tutorial

➤ A VGA programming primer

➤ Information on graphics file formats

➤ Sound programming, from PC speakers through the major sound cards

➤ Memory considerations

➤ I/O device programming (keyboards, joysticks, mice, gamepads)

The 3D Development FAQ

Three-dimensional programming has become very important in many aspects of overall games development. This fairly technical FAQ details 3D programming. It covers such topics as vector math, matrix math, shadings, perspective, and so on.

Besides detailed technical design information, the FAQ covers general topics such as good books and several FTP archives of 3D-related files and information.

It is available from the anonymous FTP site **rtfm.mit.edu**. The path (subject to change) is **/pub/usenet-by-group/rec.games.programmer/3d-programmer-info**.

Tools

Several tools related to games development are available for download.

FASTGRAPH

This library includes graphics routines and software used in screen Mode_X and other game-oriented tools. You can obtain a shareware version, FastGraph Lite, from CompuServe's GAMEDEV Forum.

Windows API Extensions

These extensions and revisions to the Windows API are available on CompuServe in the WINMM Forum and via anonymous FTP to **ftp.microsoft.com**:

➤ WAVEMIX, an API to manipulate .WAV files in real time

➤ WING.DLL, a new version of the Windows API with specific hooks helpful to games development

➤ WINTOON, a useful collection of animation-intensive applications

GoldWave

This sound editor is available in the WINFUN Forum and other places on CompuServe.

WinJammerPro

This MIDI editing program is also available in the CompuServe WIN-FUN Forum.

Archive Sites

The Game Programmer's Encyclopedia, described previously, includes an entire section on FTP sites relevant to games development. It lists sites and specific files for such topics as

➤ Development libraries or systems

➤ Painting, Sprite designers

➤ Sound development

➤ Source code

In addition to the list in the encyclopedia, some key archive sites and paths you might want to browse are

nic.funet.fi /pub/msdos/games/programming

garbo.uwasa.fi /pc/turbopas

ftp.wustl.edu /mirrors/garbo.uwasa.fi/pc/turbopas

ftp.netcom.com /pub/profile/game-dev/tools

ftp.uwp.edu /pub/msdos/games/game-dev/tools

x2ftp.oula.fi

ftp.uml.edu

A WWW site worth checking is

http://www.coriolis.com/coriolis

The Coriolis Group, the book publisher, runs this site. In addition to being a sales site for their books, it is also becoming a site for posting overall games resources for developers.

CHAPTER FOURTEEN

SECURITY, ENCRYPTION, AND (ANTI-) VIRUS

The umbrella subject of security has evolved to cover a variety of topics including the use of

➤ Firewalls and other mechanisms to limit the flow of networked traffic into or out of computer systems.

➤ Encryption techniques to prevent unauthorized access to information. This can mean keeping stored information safe or, more commonly, to preventing "snooping" on communications, especially e-mail and file transfers.

➤ Anti-virus mechanisms.

A large number of Internet resources cover some or all of these topics. Because of legal considerations, access to some information is more complicated than usual. FTP sites may not accept anonymous FTP and may require instead some sort of validated access. Maillists may not have automatic enrollment—some form of questionnaire may have to be answered first. In particular, many resources are only available to U.S.-based users. In any event, a few hotkeys for resources and information are

➤ The multiplatform e-mail security mechanism PGP (Pretty Good Privacy) is available as a freeware tool. TELNET to **net-dist.mit.edu** and log in as **getpgp** for instructions.

➤ The Computer Incident Advisory Capability (CIAC), part of the Department of Energy (DoE), maintains an anonymous FTP site at **ciac.llnl.gov**, which includes a large amount of information on numerous aspects of security.

➤ The Internet newsgroup **alt.security** covers many security topics and provides several FAQs. The Computer-security/Vendor-contacts FAQ provides contact points (mostly via the Internet) at numerous major computer vendors to obtain system security information or to report problems. The FAQ is archived at **rtfm.mit.edu/pub/usenet/alt.security**.

➤ The Computer Virus Catalog, a highly technical description of computer viruses on several platforms, is published by the Virus Test Center in Hamburg, Germany. It is available via anonymous FTP at **ftp.informatik.uni-hamburg.de** (IP=134.100.4.42), **//pub/virus/texts/catalog**, and at **cert.org/pub/virus-l/docs/vtc**.

This chapter contains listings of many resource sites.

Internet Maillists

The next sections describe the maillists that provide information on security and related topics.

Info-PGP

Contact: **info-pgp-request@lucpul.it.luc.edu**

Description: The Pretty Good Privacy (PGP) public key encryption program for MS-DOS, UNIX, SPARC, VMS, Atari, Amiga, and other platforms

mac-security

Contact: **mac-security-request@world.std.com** (David C. Kovar)

Description: Security for Macintosh systems and networks

FIREWALLS

Contact: **majordomo@GREATCIRCLE.COM**

Description: Internet security firewall systems

security

Contact: **uunet!zardoz!security-request** (Neil Gorsuch)

Contact: **security-request@cpd.com**

Description: Notification of UNIX security flaws and related security topics. Restricted membership. Enrollment requests must be mailed from a system administration account and must include the full name of the recipient and the address to send the list to.

ST Viruses

Contact: **r.c.karsmakers@stud.let.ruu.nl**

Description: Provides information on computer viruses affecting the Atari ST/TT/Falcon only—that is, it is not for MS-DOS or compatibles. This maillist also serves the electronic help line for registered users of the Ultimate Virus Killer program.

CWS

Contact: **security-alert@Sun.COM**

Description: Sun security bulletins

BITNET Maillists

To subscribe to a maillist, send a mail message to **listserv@bitnic.bitnet**. Leave the *Subject:* field blank. In the body of the message, write: **SUBSCRIBE listname**, where listname is a name in the left column below.

CRYPTO-L	Forum on Cryptology and Related Mathematics
DEFSEC	Defense and Security Network
ETHICRND	CAUSE—Electronic Roundtable Discussion on Ethics and Security

FI455	FI455-SECURITY ANALYSIS
ISSC	Information Systems Security Committee
ISSTFL	Information System Security Task Force Leaders
KNS	Kent Network Security
OSCE	Organization for Security and Cooperation in Europe (OSCE)
OSTF	Operations Security Task Force
SECURITY	*Security Digest*
UNINFSEC	University Administrative Information Security List
VIRUS-L	Open Discussion List about PC Viruses

FTP Sites

Key FTP sites that have information about security are listed next.

Site: **archive.afit.af.mil**

Files: virus research

Site: **corsa.ucr.edu**

Files: anti-virus tools; Linux; papers; Virus-L (mirror of **ftp.cert.org**)

Site: **beach.gal.utexas.edu**

Files: anti-virus utilities

Site: ciac.llnl.gov

Files: CIAC: bulletins, documents, notes, patches (Ultrix), security-related documents from other response teams (ASSIST, CERT, CONFER, DDN, NASA, NIST, Virus-L), security tools (Mac, PC), utils (crypto, Mac, PC); NID; SPI

Site: **coast.cs.purdue.edu**

Files: alert (CERT, CIAC, DEC, HP, Mac, NIST, NeXT, SERT, SGI, Solbourne, Sun); doc (documents relating to computer security and security tools); mirrors (numerous sites with security information are mirrored here)

Site: **csrc.ncsl.nist.gov**

Files: computer-security related alerts, articles, and other information; FIRST; NISTbulletin; NISTgen; NISTir; NISTnews; NISTpubs; POSIX; privacy; risk forum; secalert; secnews; secpolicy; secpubs; training; vir-info; virreviews; virus-l; warning

Site: **mcafee.com**

Files: McAfee anti-virus utilities; Patricia Hoffmann's VSUM

Site: **tasman.cc.utas.edu.au**

Files: anti-virus utilities

Site: **ftp.mb3.tu-chemnitz.de**

Files: IBM PC anti-virus programs (mirrored from **risc.ua.edu**); McAfee anti-virus programs (mirrored from **ftp.mcafee.com**); NetWare; NeXT (mirrored from **ftp.informatik.uni-muenchen.de**); Perl (mirrored from **ftp.informatik.uni-hamburg.de**)

Site: **ftp.symantec.com**

Files: anti-virus (CPAV, NAV); apps; devtools; utils

Site: **first.org**

Files: FIRST/CERT advisories; security-related material

Site: **ftp.delmarva.com**

Files: archive for security documents in PostScript form; some Banyan VINES software and documents; Help Desk Management System (HDMS); radio; RAIDdocuments; documents and maillists regarding the products that provide firewall systems, from the vendor Raptor Systems; SCO; security documents; Sun; wellfleet-mibs

Site: **ftp.win.tue.nl**

Files: security tools (TCP wrapper)

Site: **net.tamu.edu**

Files: dsn; network; TAMU Linux and security archives; UNIX

Site: **pyrite.rutgers.edu**

Files: security maillist archives

Site: **rogue.llnl.gov**

Files: DECnet security tools; VMS PostScript

Site: **sparkyfs.erg.sri.com**

Files: improving the security of your UNIX system

Site: **thor.ece.uc.edu**

Files: dinesh; Mtl; pdl; Sun-FAQ (docs, FAQs, OpenWin, Sendmail, Solaris, SunOS, SunSecurityBulletins, Utils); synthesis benchmarks; Vhdl

Site: **wzv.win.tue.nl**

Files: security-related files

Site: **ftp.tis.com**

Files: 386 users mailinglist archive; crypto; firewall; PCIP; SNMPr2; TMACH

Site: **ftp.cs.uwm.edu**

Files: **comp.privacy** (CPD archives Vols. 1-4, Privacy Library); crypto94

Site: **ftp.eff.org**

Files: EFF-related materials (newsletters, press releases, legislative analyses, etc.); legal and government information (crypto/privacy, case law, bill and government, report texts, action alerts, censorship and free speech, NII/GII/III)

Site: **ftp.fwi.uva.nl**

Files: cryptanalyse

Site: **ftp.twi.tudelft.nl**

Files: anti-virus (MS-DOS: TBAV); FTP software; GNU; Linux (slackware: daily mirror from **ftp.cdrom.com**); Novell encryption; UNIX; WWW; X11; ZyXEL firmware

Site: **niord.shsu.edu**

Files: ZCrypt

Site: **vesta.sunquest.com**

Files: VMS cryptodisk and virtual disk driver; VMS software

Newsgroups

These permanent newsgroups are accessible via most network newsreader programs.

`comp.security.misc`	Security issues of computers and networks
`comp.security.unix`	Discussion of UNIX security
`comp.virus`	Computer viruses and security (moderated)
`sci.crypt`	Different methods of data encryption and decryption
`sci.crypt.research`	Cryptography, cryptanalysis, and related issues (moderated)
`talk.politics.crypto`	The relationship between cryptography and government

Online Data Services

The next sections describe information related to security that may be obtained on commercial online data services.

CompuServe Forums

NCSA InfoSecurity Forum	NCSAFORUM
Nat. Computer Security Assoc.	NCSA
Securities Screening($E)	SCREEN
KAOS AntiVirus	ANTIVIRUS
McAfee Virus Forum	NCSAVIRUS
Symantec AntiVirus Production Forum	SYMVIRUS

**BIX
Conferences**

o programmers   Programmers Exchange / 17

o security   Computer security issues

Periodic Postings and FAQs

FAQs with an archive-name listed are available on the anonymous FTP server **rtfm.mit.edu.**

Subject: Computer security/compromise FAQ

Subject: Computer security/anonymous-FTP FAQ

Subject: Computer security/vendor contacts FAQ

Subject: Computer security/security patches FAQ

Newsgroups: **alt.security, comp.security.misc, comp.security.unix, comp.unix.admin, comp.answers, alt.answers, news.answers**

From: **cklaus@anshar.shadow.net** (Christopher Klaus)

Archive-name: **computer security/compromise-faq**

Subject: FAQ: Computer security Frequently Asked Questions

Newsgroups: **alt.security, comp.security.misc, comp.security.unix, news.answers**

From: **Alec.Muffett@UK.Sun.COM**

Archive-name: **security-faq**

Summary: Answers to questions that appear in **comp.security.misc**

Subject: PGP Frequently Asked Questions with answers, Part */*

Newsgroups: **alt.security.pgp, alt.answers, news.answers**

From: jalicqui@prairienet.org

Archive-name: **pgp-faq/part1**

Summary: Seeks to answer the most commonly asked questions about the Pretty Good Privacy (PGP) encryption program

Subject: Where to get the latest PGP (Pretty Good Privacy) FAQ

Newsgroups: **alt.security.pgp, alt.answers, news.answers**

From: **mpj@netcom.com** (Michael Paul Johnson)

Archive-name: **pgp-faq/where-is-PGP**

Summary: Where to get the latest version of Pretty Good Privacy (PGP) electronic mail privacy program for your platform and country

Subject: RSA Cryptography Today FAQ (*/*)

Newsgroups: **sci.crypt, talk.politics.crypto, alt.security.ripem, sci.answers, talk.answers, alt.answers, news.answers**

From: **faq-editor@rsa.com**

Archive-name: **cryptography-faq/rsa/part1**

Subject: Call security, public key voice cryptography FAQ

Newsgroups: **sci.crypt, talk.politics.crypto, talk.politics.drugs, comp.sys.ibm.pc.soundcard, alt.wired, comp.sys.ibm.pc.soundcard.misc, comp.security.announce, alt.security, alt.hemp, sci.answers, talk.answers, comp.answers, alt.answers, news.answers**

From: **njj@jericho.mc.com** (Neil Johnson)

Subject: alt.security.pgp FAQ (Part */5)

Subject: PGP Frequently Asked Questions with Answers, Part */*

Newsgroups: **alt.security.pgp, alt.answers, news.answers**

From: **gbe@netcom.com** (Gary Edstrom)

From: **jalicqui@prairienet.org**

Subject: Anti-viral contacts listing

Newsgroups: **comp.virus, comp.security.misc**

From: **roberts@decus.ca,rslade@sfu.ca** (Robert Slade)

Subject: Quick reference anti-viral review chart

Newsgroups: **comp.virus, comp.security.misc**

From: **roberts@decus.ca** (Rob Slade)

Subject: Firewalls FAQ (Rev *, updated *)

Newsgroups: **comp.security.unix, comp.security.misc, comp.answers, news.answers**

From: **fwalls-faq@tis.com** (Internet firewalls FAQ maintainer)

Archive-name: **firewalls-faq**

Summary: Lists Frequently Asked Questions about Internet firewalls and gives answers

Subject: UNIX security archive sites last changed * * *

Newsgroups: **comp.virus**

From: **<jwright@cfht.hawaii.edu>** (Jim Wright)

Subject: Anti-viral BBS listing

Newsgroups: **comp.virus, comp.security.misc**

From: **roberts@decus.ca,rslade@sfu.ca** (Robert Slade)

Subject: Cryptography FAQ (*/*: *)

Newsgroups: **sci.crypt, talk.politics.crypto, sci.answers, news.answers, talk.answers**

From: **crypt-comments@math.ncsu.edu**

Comment: These articles are currently being posted (their archive-names are in parentheses, and they're located in the **cryptography-faq** archive directory): Overview (part01); Net Etiquette (part02); Basic Cryptology (part03); Mathematical Cryptology (part04); Product Ciphers (part05); Public Key Cryptography (part06); Digital Signatures (part07); Technical Miscellany (part08); Other Miscellany (part09); References (part10).

Archive-name: **cryptography-faq/part01**

Summary: Part 1 of 10 of the **sci.crypt** FAQ, Overview—table of contents, contributors, feedback, archives, administrivia, changes

Subject: Call security, public key voice cryptography FAQ

Newsgroups: **sci.crypt, talk.politics.crypto, talk.politics.drugs, comp.sys.ibm.pc.soundcard, alt.wired, comp.sys.ibm.pc.soundcard.misc, comp.security.announce, alt.security, alt.hemp, sci.answers, talk.answers, comp.answers, alt.answers, news.answers**

From: **njj@jericho.mc.com** (Neil Johnson)

Subject: **sci.crypt.research** FAQ

Newsgroups: **sci.crypt.research, sci.answers, news.answers**

From: **mpj@netcom.com** (Michael Paul Johnson)

Archive-name: **cryptography-faq/research**

Summary: Frequently Asked Questions in **sci.crypt.research** answered

Subject: Amiga anti-viral archive sites last changed * * *

Newsgroups: **comp.virus**

From: **jwright@cfht.hawaii.edu** (Jim Wright)

Subject: Anti-viral documentation archive sites last changed * * *

Newsgroups: **comp.virus**

From: **jwright@cfht.hawaii.edu** (Jim Wright)

Subject: Apple II anti-viral archive sites last changed * * *

Newsgroups: **comp.virus**

From: **jwright@cfht.hawaii.edu** (Jim Wright)

Subject: Archive access without anonymous FTP last changed * * *

Newsgroups: **comp.virus**

From: **jwright@cfht.hawaii.edu** (Jim Wright)

Subject: Atari ST anti-viral archive sites last changed * * *

Newsgroups: **comp.virus**

From: **jwright@cfht.hawaii.edu** (Jim Wright)

Subject: Brief guide to file formats last changed * * *

Newsgroups: **comp.virus**

From: **jwright@cfht.hawaii.edu** (Jim Wright)

Subject: IBM PC anti-viral archive sites last changed * * *

Newsgroups: **comp.virus**

From: **jwright@cfht.hawaii.edu** (Jim Wright)

Subject: Introduction to the anti-viral archives listing

Newsgroups: **comp.virus**

From: **jwright@cfht.hawaii.edu** (Jim Wright)

Subject: Macintosh anti-viral archive sites last changed * * *

Newsgroups: **comp.virus**

From: **jwright@cfht.hawaii.edu** (Jim Wright)

Subject: VIRUS-L/comp.virus Frequently Asked Questions (FAQ)

Newsgroups: **comp.virus, comp.answers, news.answers**

From: **krvw@cert.org** (Kenneth R. van Wyk)

Archive-name: **computer-virus-faq**

Summary: Lists Frequently Asked Questions about computer viruses and their answers. Anyone who wants to post to VIRUS-L/comp.virus should read this.

CHAPTER FIFTEEN

NETWORKING AND TELECOMMUNICATIONS

It's not surprising that a lot of information on the Internet is about networking and related topics. To bring some order to the information in this chapter, the resources are divided into these groups:

➤ Network operating systems, principally from Novell and Banyan

➤ Other vendor-specific information about Cisco, IBM, and others

➤ Protocols such as TCP/IP and NFS

➤ Platform-specific networking for DECnet, Mac-Networking, and others

➤ Telecommunications in general

➤ Other

I do want to discuss one microdetail up front. One of the most useful things, for many people at least, is to have information on standards. A FAQ on this is posted periodically to the newsgroups **comp.std.internet**, **comp.std.misc**, **comp.protocols.iso**, **comp.answers**, and **news.answers**.

It is archived at the anonymous FTP server **rtfm.mit.edu/pub/usenet-by-group/news.answers/ standards-faq**.

NOS Vendors Maillist

These resources relate to suppliers of network operating systems (NOSs).

Internet Maillists

The next sections describe the maillists that provide information on NOS products.

appware-info

Contact: **appware-info@parallel.com**

Description: Information on Novell Inc.'s AppWare. To subscribe, send a message in the form **SUBSCRIBE appware-info** by e-mail to **majordomo@parallel.com**.

List owner: **weidl@parallel.com**

NWP (NetWare Programming)

Contact: **listproc@uel.ac.uk**

Description: Discussion of programming for Novell NetWare and related topics

List owner: **M.Dewell@uel.ac.uk**

Univel

Contact: **univel-request@telly.on.ca**

Description: Discusses the products of Univel, a Novell subsidiary producing UNIX system software for PC-architecture systems.

BITNET List Server Maillists

To subscribe to a maillist, send a mail message to **listserv@bitnic.bitnet**. Leave the *Subject:* field blank. In the body of the message, write: **SUBSCRIBE listname**, where listname is a name in the left column below.

BANYAN	Banyan Networks Discussion List
NOVELL	Novell LAN Interest Group

NOVOPS	Novell Technology Operations List
NOVTTP	Novell Technology Transfer Partners List
NOVUSRGP	West Virginia University Novell User Group
VTNOVELL	Virginia Tech NOVELL Users

Internet Newsgroups

These permanent newsgroups are accessible via most network newsreader programs:

comp.sys.novell	Discussion of Novell NetWare products
comp.unix.unixware	Discussion of Novell's UNIXWare products

Commercial Online Services

Over 20 CompuServe forums cover topics associated with the Novell product line. A good starting point is GO NOVELL. Some other forums are

Novell Client Forum	NOVCLIENT
Novell Connectivity Forum	NCONNECT
Novell Dev. Info. Forum	NDEVINFO
Novell Dev. Support Forum	NDEVSUPPORT
Novell Files Database	NOVFILES
Novell Hardware Forum	NOVHW
Novell Information Forum	NGENERAL
Novell Library Forum	NOVLIB
Novell Net. Management Forum	NOVMAN
Novell NetWare 2.X Forum	NETW2X
Novell NetWare 3.X Forum	NETW3X
Novell NetWare 4X Forum	NETW4X
Novell NetWire	NOVELL
Novell OS/2 Forum	NOVOS2
Novell Tech Bullet. Dbase	NTB
Novell User Library	NOVUSER

Periodic Postings and FAQs

FAQs with an archive-name listed are available on the anonymous FTP server **rtfm.mit.edu.**

Subject: Banyan networking Frequently Asked Questions (FAQ)

Newsgroups: **bit.listservbanyan-l, news.answers**

From: **gary@wheel.tiac.net** (Gary D. Duzan)

Archive-name: **LANs/NOS/banyan-faq**

Summary: Networking with Banyan

Subject: **comp.unix.unixware** Frequently Asked Questions (FAQ) list

Newsgroups: **comp.unix.unixware, comp.unix.sys5.r4, news.answers, comp.answers**

From: **vlcek@byteware.com** (James Vlcek)

Archive-name: **unix-faq/unixware/general**

Summary: Answers to questions frequently asked about Novell's UNIXWare product

Other Vendor-specific Information

Most of the following information concerns vendors other than NOS-specific vendors.

Internet Maillists

The next sections give instructions for joining the maillists.

cisco

Contact: **cisco-request@spot.colorado.edu** (David Wood)

Description: Discusses network products from Cisco Systems, Inc.

BITNET List Server Maillists

To subscribe to a maillist, send a mail message to **listserv@bitnic.bitnet**. Leave the *Subject:* field blank. In the body of the message, write: SUBSCRIBE listname, where listname is a name in the left column of the following list.

3COM-L	3Com Discussion List
IBM-NETS	IBM Networking
CISCO-L	CISCO-L Redistribution List
CISCO-NEWS	CISCO News
RICUG-L	Rhode Island Cisco Users Group List

Internet Newsgroups

These permanent newsgroups are accessible via most network newsreader programs:

comp.dcom.sys.cisco	Information on Cisco routers and bridges
comp.dcom.sys.wellfleet	Wellfleet bridge and router systems hardware and software

FTP and WWW Sites

Most major companies related to networking maintain some form of Internet presence, typically an anonymous FTP site or a Web site. You can usually deduce the FTP or WWW name as follows:
Web URL = http://www.company_name.com
FTP address = ftp.company_name.com.

A few major companies provide FTP sites:

ftp.novell.com	Novell
ftp.banyan.com	Banyan
ftp.ub.com	UB Networks (formerly Ungermann-Bass Networks)
ftp.cisco.com	Cisco
ftp.synoptics.com	Synoptics, now merged into Bay Networks
ftp.wellfleet.com	Wellfleet Communications, now merged into Bay Networks
ftp.3com.com	3Com

Periodic Postings and FAQs

FAQs with an archive-name listed are available on the anonymous FTP server **rtfm.mit.edu**.

Subject: **comp.dcom.sys.cisco** Frequently Asked Questions (FAQ)

Newsgroups: **comp.dcom.syscisco, comp.protocols.tcp-ip, comp.dcom.servers, comp.answers, news.answers**

From: **jhawk@panix.com** (John Hawkinson)

Archive-name: **cisco-networking-faq**

Summary: Consists of Frequently Asked Questions about routers manufactured by Cisco Systems, Inc. Also provides additional information on IP routing that may be useful in other Cisco environments.

Protocols: TCP/IP, AppleTalk, and Others

The next sections contain information on many types of protocols used in various aspects of computer networking.

Internet Maillists

Each section below gives instructions for joining the maillists.

mtxinu-users

Contact: **dunike!mtxinu-users-request**

Contact: **mtxinu-users-request@nike.cair.du.edu**

Description: Discussion of the 4.3+NFS release from Mt. Xinu

commune

Contact: **commune-request@stealth.acf.nyu.edu** (Dan Bernstein)

Description: Discusses the COMMUNE protocol, a TELNET replacement

fsp-discussion

Contact: listmaster@Germany.EU.net

Description: Discusses the FSP protocol. FSP is a set of programs to implement a public-access archive similar to an anonymous FTP archive.

IXO

Contact: **majordomo@plts.org**

Description: Discusses pagers and software that implement the IXO protocol

ntp

Contact: **ntp-request@trantor.umd.edu**

Description: Discusses the Network Time Protocol

operlist

Contact: **operlist-request@eff.org** (Helen Trillian Rose)

Description: Discussion list for anything having to do with IRC

POP

Contact: **pop-request@jhunix.hcf.jhu.edu** (Andy S. Poling)

Description: List to discuss the Post Office Protocol (POP2 and POP3) as described in RFCs 918, 937, 1081, and 1082

**BITNET
List Server
Maillists**

To subscribe to a maillist, send a mail message to **listserv@bitnic.bitnet**. Leave the *Subject:* field blank. In the body of the message, write: SUBSCRIBE **listname**, where listname is a name in the left column of the following list.

IBM7171	Protocol Converter List
ISODE	ISO/OSI Protocol Development Environment Discussion Group
MPG-L	Yale MultiProtocol Gateway Discussion Group
MSP-L	Msg Send Protocol (RFC1312) Discussion
NNRP-L	Network Newsreader Protocol List
PCIP	TCP/IP Protocol Implementations for PC Discussion Group
PROTOCOL	Computer Protocol Discussion
TCP-IP	Comp.Protocols.TCP/IP Redistribution
TCPIP-L	TCP/IP Information Distribution List
TN3270-L	TN3270 Protocol Discussion List
X25-L	X-25 Protocol Discussion List
X400-L	X.400 Protocol List

Internet Newsgroups

These permanent newsgroups are accessible via most network newsreader programs.

comp.os.ms-windows.networking.tcp-ip
Windows and TCP/IP networking

comp.os.os2.networking.tcp-ip
TCP/IP under OS/2

comp.protocols.ibm
Networking with IBM mainframes

comp.protocols.nfs
Discussion about the Network File System protocol

comp.protocols.tcp-ip
TCP and IP network protocols

comp.protocols.appletalk
Applebus hardware and software

```
comp.protocols.dicom
```
Digital Imaging and Communications in Medicine

```
comp.protocols.iso
```
The ISO protocol stack

```
comp.protocols.kerberos
```
The Kerberos authentication server

```
comp.protocols.kermit.annouce
```
Kermit announcements (moderated)

```
comp.protocols.kermit.misc
```
Kermit protocol and software

```
comp.protocols.misc
```
Various forms and types of protocol

```
comp.protocols.ppp
```
Discussion of the Internet Point-to-Point Protocol

```
comp.protocols.smb
```
SMB file sharing protocol and Samba SMB client/server

```
comp.protocols.tcp-ip.ibmpc
```
TCP/IP for IBM(-like) personal computers

```
comp.sys.xerox
```
Xerox 1100 workstations and protocols

```
comp.dcom.fax
```
Fax hardware, software, and protocols

```
comp.dcom.lans.ethernet
```
Discussions of the Ethernet/IEEE 802.3 protocols

```
comp.dcom.lans.fddi
```
Discussions of the FDDI protocol suite

Periodic Postings and FAQs

FAQs with an archive-name listed are available on the anonymous FTP server **rtfm.mit.edu**.

Subject: DEC TCP/IP Services for OpenVMS (UCX) FAQ

Newsgroups: **vmsnet.networks.tcp-ip.ucx, news.answers**

From: tillman@swdev.si.com (Brian Tillman)

Archive-name: dec-faq/ucx

Subject: comp.protocols.tcp-ip.ibmpc Frequently Asked Questions (FAQ), part * of *

Newsgroups: comp.protocols.tcp-ip.ibmpc, comp.protocols.tcp-ip, alt.winsock, comp.os.ms-windows.networking.tcp-ip, alt.answers, comp.answers, news.answers

From: aboba@netcom.com (Bernard Aboba)

Archive-name: ibmpc-tcp-ip-faq/part1

Summary: Frequently Asked Questions (and answers) about TCP/IP on PC-Compatible Computers

Subject: AmiTCP/IP Frequently Asked Questions (FAQ)

Newsgroups: comp.sys.amiga.networking, comp.sys.amiga.datacomm, comp.sys.amiga.applications, comp.answers, news.answers

From: amitcp@contessa.phone.net

Archive-name: amiga/AmiTCP-faq

Summary: Lists Frequently Asked Questions (and their answers) about AmiTCP/IP. Anyone who wishes to post about or use AmiTCP/IP should read this.

Subject: File Service Protocol (FSP) Frequently Asked Questions [Part */*]

Newsgroups: alt.comp.fsp, alt.answers, news.answers

From: A.J.Doherty@reading.ac.uk (A. J. Doherty)

Archive-name: fsp-faq/part1

Summary: Lists Frequently Asked Questions (and their answers) about the FSP protocol. Please read this before you post to **alt.comp.fsp**.

Subject: **comp.dcom.syscisco** Frequently Asked Questions (FAQ)

Newsgroups: **comp.dcom.syscisco, comp.protocols.tcp-ip, comp.dcom.servers, comp.answers, news.answers**

From: **jhawk@panix.com** (John Hawkinson)

Archive-name: **cisco-networking-faq**

Summary: Answers Frequently Asked Questions about routers manufactured by Cisco Systems, Inc. Provides additional information on IP routing that may be useful in non-Cisco environments.

Subject: GOPHER (**comp.infosystems.gopher**) Frequently Asked Questions (FAQ)

Newsgroups: **comp.infosystems.gopher, news.answers, comp.answers**

From: **gopher@boombox.micro.umn.edu** (University of Minnesota GOPHER Team)

Archive-name: **gopher-faq**

Summary: Common questions and answers about the Internet GOPHER, a client/server protocol for making a worldwide information service, with many implementations.

Subject: Client/server mail protocols FAQ

Newsgroups: **comp.mail.misc, comp.answers, news.answers**

From: **pauls@CIC.Net**

Archive-name: **mail/mailclient-faq**

Subject: LAN Mail Protocols Summary

Newsgroups: **comp.mail.misc, comp.answers, news.answers**

From: **jmwobus@mailbox.syr.edu** (John Wobus)

Archive-name: **LANs/mail-protocols**

Subject: CAP FAQ

Newsgroups: comp.protocols.appletalk, comp.sys.mac.comm

From: djh@cs.mu.OZ.AU (David Hornsby)

Comment: The latest version of this posting is available via anonymous FTP from **munnari.OZ.AU** in **mac/cap.patches/CAP.faq.**

Subject: **comp.protocols.iso** FAQ

Newsgroups: comp.protocols.iso, comp.answers, news.answers

From: **unrza3@cd4680fs.rrze.uni-erlangen.de** (Markus Kuhn)

Archive-name: **osi-protocols**

Summary: Introduces OSI, a family of internationally standardized computer communication protocols and services

Subject: Kerberos Users' Frequently Asked Questions *

Newsgroups: comp.protocols.kerberos, comp.answers, news.answers

From: bjaspan@cam.ov.com (Barry Jaspan)

Archive-name: **kerberos-faq/user**

Summary: Answers Frequently Asked Questions about the Kerberos authentication system. Read this before you post a question to **comp.protocols.kerberos** or **kerberos@athena.mit.edu.**

Subject: **comp.protocols.ppp** part* of * of frequently wanted information

Newsgroups: comp.protocols.ppp, news.answers, comp.answers

From: **ignatios@cs.uni-bonn.de** (Ignatios Souvatzis)

Archive-name: **ppp-faq/part1**

Summary: This document contains information about the Internet Point-to-Point Protocol, including a bibliography, a list of public domain and commercial software and hardware implementations, a section on configuration hints and a list of Frequently Asked Questions and answers. It should be read by anyone interested in connecting to Internet via serial lines and by anyone wanting to post to **comp.protocols.ppp** (before he/she does it!).

Subject: **comp.protocols.snmp** [SNMP] Frequently Asked Questions (FAQ)

Newsgroups: **comp.protocols.snmp, comp.answers, news.answers**

From: **splinter@seltd.jvnc.net** (Panther Digital)

Reply To: **panther@seltd.newnet.com**

Archive-name: **snmp-faq**

Summary: Introduces SNMP and **comp.protocols.snmp** newsgroup

Subject: TCP/IP FAQ for *

Newsgroup: **comp.protocols.tcp-ip.**

From: **gnn@netcom.com** (George Neville-Neil)

Archive-name: **tcp-ip/FAQ**

Subject: **comp.protocols.tcp-ip.ibmpc** Frequently Asked Questions (FAQ), part * of *

Newsgroups: **comp.protocols.tcp-ip.ibmpc, comp.protocols.tcp-ip, alt.winsock, comp.os.ms-windows.networking.tcp-ip, alt.answers, comp.answers, news.answers**

From: **aboba@netcom.com** (Bernard Aboba)

Archive-name: **ibmpc-tcp-ip-faq/part1**

Summary: Answers Frequently Asked Questions about TCP/IP on PC-compatible computers

Subject: Standards FAQ

Newsgroups: **comp.std.internat, comp.std.misc, comp.protocols.iso, comp.answers, news.answers**

From: **unrza3@cd4680fs.rrze.uni-erlangen.de** (Markus Kuhn)

Archive-name: **standards-faq**

Summary: Answers questions such as: What are ISO standards? Where can I get standards? What are ISO/ITU/ANSI/ and so forth? What standards are relevant to computing? A periodic posting in **comp.protocols.iso**, **comp.std.misc**, and **comp.std.internat**.

Platform-specific Networking

Internet Maillists

The next sections give instructions for maillists.

Mac-Mgrs

Contact: **majordomo @world.std.com** (Juan A. Pons)

Description: Discussions of interest to Macintosh system managers

ParNET

Contact: **parnet-list-request@ben.com** (Ben Jackson)

Description: Discusses ParNET, an Amiga-to-Amiga networking program

sun-nets

Contact: **sun-nets-request@umiacs.umd.edu**

Description: Discusses networks using Sun hardware and/or software

**BITNET
List Server
Maillists**

To subscribe to a maillist, send a mail message to **listserv@bitnic.bitnet**. Leave the *Subject:* field blank. In the body of the message, write: **SUBSCRIBE listname**, where listname is a name in the left column below.

HEP-CLNS	HEP DECnet Phase V Group
MACNET-L	Macintosh networking issues
PILOT5-L	DECnet Phase V Pilot Group
UKPILOT5	Discussion on UK HEP/SPAN DECnet Phase V Pilot Project

**Internet
Newsgroups**

These permanent newsgroups are accessible via most network newsreader programs.

comp.os.linux.networking
Networking and communications under Linux

comp.os.msdos.mail-news
Administrative mail/network news systems under MS-DOS

comp.os.ms-windows.networking.misc
Windows and other networks

comp.os.ms-windows.networking.windows
Windows' built-in networking

comp.os.ms-windows.programmer.networks
Network programming

comp.os.os2.networking.misc
Miscellaneous OS/2 networking issues

comp.sys.amiga.networking
Amiga networking software and hardware

comp.sys.ibm.pc.hardware.networking
Network hardware and equipment for the PC

**Periodic
Postings and
FAQs**

FAQs with an archive-name listed are available on the anonymous FTP server **rtfm.mit.edu**.

Subject: Amiga Mosaic and WWW Frequently Asked Questions (FAQ)

Newsgroups: **comp.sys.amiga.networking, comp.sys.amiga.datacomm, comp.sys.amiga.applications, comp.answers, news.answers**

From: **mwm@contessa.phone.net** (Mike Meyer)

Subject: Linux NET-2 HOWTO (part */*)

Newsgroups: **comp.os.linux.annouce, comp.os.linux.help, comp.os.linux.admin, news.answers, comp.answers**

From: **terryd@extro.ucc.su.oz.au** (Terry Dawson)

Archive-name: **linux/howto/networking/part1**

Summary: How to configure TCP/IP networking, SLIP, PLIP, and PPP under Linux

Subject: Amiga networking Frequently Asked Questions (FAQ) Part */*

Newsgroups: **comp.sys.amiga.datacomm, comp.sys.amiga.hardware, comp.answers, news.answers**

From: **norman@afas.msfc.nasa.gov** (Richard Norman)

Archive-name: **amiga/networking-faq/part1**

Summary: Answers both generic and Amiga-specific networking questions. Covers both hardware and software questions. Anyone who has a network-related question should read this before posting it to the **comp.sys.amiga.datacomm** or **comp.sys.amiga.hardware** newsgroups.

Subject: Amiga Mosaic and WWW Frequently Asked Questions (FAQ)

Newsgroups: **comp.sys.amiga.networking, comp.sys.amiga.datacomm, comp.sys.amiga.applications, comp.answers, news.answers**

From: **mwm@contessa.phone.net** (Mike Meyer)

Subject: **comp.sys.mac.com** Frequently Asked Questions [*/*]

Newsgroups: **comp.sys.mac.comm, news.answers, comp.answers**

From: **davido@Princeton.EDU** (David L. Oppenheimer)

Archive-name: **macintosh/comm-faq/part1**

Summary: The **comp.sys.mac.comm** Frequently Asked Questions list is intended to provide information specific to Macintosh computer communications, including modems, networks, and the like. You are encouraged to read this FAQ before posting to the newsgroup.

Telecommunications in General

Internet Maillists

The next sections give instructions for joining the maillists.

telecomdocs

Contact: **listserver@relay.adp.wisc.edu**

Description: Distribution of telecommunications rules, regulations, and other official communications

List owner: **owner-telecomdocs@relay.adp.wisc.edu**

telecomreg

Contact: **listserver@relay.adp.wisc.edu**

Description: Discussion of regulation of telecommunications including cable television and telephony

Telecom-Tech

Contact: **TeleTech-Request@zygot.ati.com**

Description: Discussion of technical aspects of modern and historical telecommunications

**BITNET
List Server
Maillists**

To subscribe to a maillist, send a mail message to **listserv@bitnic.bitnet**. Leave the *Subject:* field blank. In the body of the message, write: **SUBSCRIBE listname,** where listname is a name in the left column below.

ASAT-STC   AG-SAT satellite telecommunications coordinators

EUEARN-L   Discussion of Eastern Europe telecommunications

SIGTEL-L   SIG/Tel (special interest group/telecommunications) of ISTE

TPR-NE   Telecomm policy roundtable—Northeast

**Internet
Newsgroups**

These permanent newsgroups are accessible via most network newsreader programs.

comp.dcom.telecom   *Telecommunications Digest* (moderated)

comp.dcom.telecom.tech   Discussion of technical aspects of telephony

**Periodic
Postings and
FAQs**

FAQs with an archive-name listed are available on the anonymous FTP server **rtfm.mit.edu**.

Subject: **uk.telecom** FAQ, Part 1/*—questions and contacts

Subject: **uk.telecom** FAQ, Part 2/*—telephone services

Subject: **uk.telecom** FAQ, Part 3/*—technical matters

Newsgroups: **uk.telecom, news.answers**

From: **jrg@blodwen.demon.co.uk** (James R. Grinter)

Archive-name: **uk-telecom/part1**

Summary: **uk.telecom** Frequently Asked Questions and answers. Lists answers to Frequently Asked Questions for the newsgroup **uk.telecom,** including U.K. contact and resource information, U.K. telephone service information (part 2), and technical information (part 3).

Subject: Telecom Frequently Asked Questions—revised *

Newsgroups: **comp.dcom.telecom**

From: **telecom@eecs.nwu.edu** (Telecom moderator)

Other

Internet Maillists

The next sections give instructions for joining maillists.

info-MOON

Contact: **moon-request @one.it** (Giovanni Boniardi)

Description: Discusses MOON (Managing Objects On Network). Also provides information about MOON and UNIX system management in general.

KISKEYA

Contact: **listserv@conicit.ve**

Description: Discusses the development of an efficient telecommunications network in the Dominican Republic and the rest of the Caribbean.

BITNET List Server Maillists

To subscribe to a maillist, send a mail message to **listserv@bitnic.bitnet.** Leave the *Subject:* field blank. In the body of the message, write: **SUBSCRIBE listname**, where listname is the name in the left column below.

```
CNEDUC-L    Computer Networking Education Discussion List
```

Internet Newsgroups

These permanent newsgroups are accessible via most network newsreader programs:

```
comp.dcom.frame-relay        Technology and issues regard-
                             ing frame relay networks
```

comp.dcom.isdn	Integrated Services Digital Network (ISDN)
comp.dcom.lans.misc	Local area network hardware and software
comp.dcom.lans.token-ring	Installing and using Token-Ring networks

Commercial Online Services

Several CompuServe forums address networking-related topics. A general search for services under "network" turns up many. Some key forums are

Bay Networks Forum	BAYNETWORKS
Client/Server Computing Forum	MSNETWORKS
IBM COS Network Solution Forum	IBMCOS
MS Networks Forum	MSNETWORKS
Windows Networking A Forum	WINETA
Telecommunications Forum	TELECOM
Ask3Com	THREECOM
Ask3Com Forum	ASKFORUM
Cabletron Systems, Inc.	CTRON
Cabletron Systems Forum	CTRONFORUM

In its Computing Forums area, America Online has a Telecommunications and Networking Forum, which provides message boards and a software library. There are also separate subforums on such topics as

- ➤ LANs and networking
- ➤ Novell NetWare utilities
- ➤ OS/2 networking
- ➤ Protocols
- ➤ Security telecommunications

Several BIX conferences relate to networking in the Professionals—Professional and User Groups Exchange.

`lans`	The conference on local area networks (LANs)
`networks`	Information networks
`packet.net`s	Packet-switching networks
`windows.net`	Windows and networking
`international`	Telecommunications and the global computer village
`telecomm.tech`	Telecommunications technology
`telecomm`	Listings for `telecomm.tech`
`telecomm.pgms`	Telecommunications programs

Periodic Postings and FAQs

FAQs with an archive-name listed are available on the anonymous FTP server **rtfm.mit.edu**.

Subject: **comp.dcom.lans.ethernet** FAQ (Frequently Asked Questions)

Newsgroups: **comp.dcom.lans.ethernet, comp.answers, news.answers**

From: **mrunkel@steph.admin.umass.edu** (Marc A. Runkel)

Archive-name: **LANs/ethernet-faq**

Summary: Lists Frequently Asked Questions (and their answers) about Ethernet and 802.3 networking. A good source of information on lower-layer Ethernet standards and issues.

CHAPTER SIXTEEN

DATABASES

Since their introduction, database products have steadily grown, and many may be customized so that they either appear to be languages themselves or incorporate other programming languages (such as Visual BASIC) to create their extensions.

Many resources included in this chapter represent various forms of support offered by database vendors. These range in complexity from how to use the basic functions of the product as is to detailed instructions on utilizing the product's programming features.

Internet Maillists

Several maillists provide information on databases and related topics.

informix-list
Contact: **informix-list-request@rmy.emory.edu** (Walt Hultgren)

Description: Informix software and related subjects

informix_sig_nca *Contact:* **informix_sig_nca-request@adaclabs.com**

Description: Informix Users Group of Northern California

linux-postgres *Contact:* **linux-postgres-request@native-ed.bc.ca**

Description: For the Linux port of the Postgres database system

UUG-dist *Contact:* **uug-dist-request@dsi.com** (Syd Weinstein)

Description: Discusses Unify Corporation's database products including Unify, Accell/IDS, Accell/SQl, and Accell.

MS-Access *Contact:* **MS-ACCESS-REQUEST@EUNET.CO.AT** (Martin Hilger)

Description: Microsoft's Access database product

BIG-DB *Contact:* Send mail to moderator at **big-DB@midway.uchicago.edu** for enrollment information.

Description: Discusses databases with over 1 million records

BITNET List Server Maillists

To subscribe to a maillist, send a mail message to **listserv@bitnic.bitnet**. Leave the *Subject:* field blank. In the body of the message, write: **SUBSCRIBE listname**, where listname is a name in the left column below.

ACCESS-L	Microsoft Access Database Discussion List
ADR-L	ADR Database Products Discussion List
ORACLE-L	ORACLE Database Maillist
ORALIST	Texas A&M ORACLE Users List
RDBMS-L	Relational Database Management System Research Committee (RDBMS+)

FOXPRO-L	KU FoxPro List
VBDATA-L	Discussion for Microsoft Visual BASIC Data Access
CLIPPER	List for Clipper and DBMS systems for IBM PC
DECRDB-L	ORACLE RDB (formerly DEC RDB) Maillist
PARADOX	List for Borland Paradox users

Internet Newsgroups

These permanent newsgroups are accessible via most network newsreader programs:

comp.databases	Database and data management issues and theory
comp.databases.informix	Informix database management software discussions
comp.databases.ingres	Issues relating to Ingres products
comp.databases.ms-access	MS Windows' relational database system, Access
comp.databases.object	Object-oriented paradigms in database systems
comp.databases.olap	Analytical processing, multidimensional DBMS, EIS, DSS
comp.databases.oracle	ORACLE Corporations's SQL database products
comp.databases.paradox	Borland's database for DOS and MS Windows

comp.databases.pick	Pick-like, post-relational database systems
comp.databases.rdb	DEC's relational database engine RDB
comp.databases.sybase	Implementations of SQL server
comp.databases.theory	Discussing advances in database technology
comp.databases.xbase.fox	Fox Software's xBase system and compatibles
comp.databases.xbase.misc	Discussion of xBase (dBASE-like) products
comp.lang.basic.visual.database	Database aspects of Visual BASIC
comp.soft-sys.powerbuilder	Application development tools from Powersoft
comp.sys.mac.databases	Database systems for the Apple Macintosh

Commercial Online Data Services

Several CompuServe forums focus on supporting major database programs. (Be sure to use the "Search for Services" feature to locate others.)

MS Access Forum	MSACCESS
Clipper Forum	CLIPPER
Borland dBASE For Windows	DBASEWIN
Borland dBASE Forum	DBASEDOS
ORACLE Forum	ORAUSER

Periodic Postings and FAQs

FAQs with an archive-name listed are available on the anonymous FTP server **rtfm.mit.edu.**

Subject: Catalog of free database systems

Newsgroups: **comp.databases, comp.answers, news.answers**

From: **muir@idiom.com** (David Muir Sharnoff)

Archive-name: **databases/free-databases**

Note: This article is occasionally cross-posted to other relevant news-groups, in addition to the ones listed above, possibly including: **comp.sources.d, comp.archives.admin, comp.os.linux.announce, gnu.misc.discuss, comp.lang.perl, comp.lang.tcl, comp.object, comp.lang.c++, comp.unix.programmer.**

Subject: **comp.databases.paradox** FAQ

Newsgroups: **comp.databases, comp.databases.paradox, comp.answers, news.answers**

From: **ryee@dsigroup.com** (Roger L. Yee)

Archive-name: **paradox-faq**

Subject: **comp.databases.sybase** Frequently Asked Questions (FAQ)

Newsgroups: **comp.databases.sybase, comp.databases, comp.answers, news.answers**

From: **davidp@meaddata.com** (David Pledger)

Archive-name: **sybase-faq**

Summary: This monthly posting lists Frequently Asked Questions about the Sybase Relational Database Management System (RDBMS).

Subject: FoxPro Databases FAQ #0: Welcome to the Machine

Subject: FoxPro Databases FAQ #1: You Say You Want a Revolution?

Subject: FoxPro Databases FAQ #2: See Fox. See Fox Run. Run, Fox, Run.

Subject: FoxPro Databases FAQ #3: Things Your Mamma Never Told You

Subject: FoxPro Databases FAQ #5: WHERE resource = onthenet

Newsgroups: **comp.databases.xbase.fox, comp.answers, news.answers**

From: **kcochran@nyx10.cs.du.edu** (Keith "Justified and Ancient" Cochran)

Archive-name: **databases/foxpro/general**

Summary: General information about Fox* database products posted monthly to **comp.databases.xbase.fox, comp.answers,** and **news.answers**

Subject: Comp.Object FAQ Version * (*) Announcement

Newsgroups: **comp.lang.c, comp.lang.eiffel, comp.lang.smalltalk, comp.lang.clos, comp.lang.ada, comp.databases.object, comp.lang.sather, comp.lang.misc, comp.software-eng, comp.sw.components, comp.lang.modula3, comp.lang.objective-c, comp.sys.next.programmer, comp.lang.oberon, comp.object.logic, comp.lang.scheme, comp.answers, news.answers**

From: **rjh@geodesic.com** (Bob Hathaway)

Archive-name: **object-faq/announce**

Summary: Frequently Asked Questions (FAQ) list and available systems for object-oriented technology

TOP SITES

This is a completely arbitrary and unordered list of sites found to be useful when searching online for information or help about programming-related topics. Chapter 3 describes several of these sites in more detail.

http://www.yahoo.com

Actually an index of other WWW sites, this WWW site provides a search engine for titles and contents, and links to over 30,000 WWW home pages.

rtfm.mit.edu

This anonymous FTP site, a massive archive of information about newsgroups, stores, in particular, all FAQ lists for newsgroups.

http://www.microsoft.com

This commercial site is the home page for Microsoft. It's included here because it is the home of the Microsoft Knowledge Base (MSKB), a collection of about 40,000 articles and technical updates on programming with Microsoft language products. MSKB is also available on the commercial online data services, but this is the home site, and it is also free. You can access it via anonymous FTP.

oak.oakland.edu

One of the largest and best known anonymous FTP archive sites, this is actually one of several mirrors of an archive system generally referred to as SimTel. Mostly oriented towards MS-DOS and Windows material, it archives applications, programming utilities, source code, and informational files on several hundred topics.

CompuServe MS-Languages

Typing GO MSLANG on CompuServe opens support areas for all Microsoft language products. There are a large number of software libraries, message boards (where MS staff may answer questions), and third-party support areas.

CompuServe MAUG

On CompuServe, GO MAUG connects you to the Micronetworked Apple Users Group. This users group, completely independent of Apple, is a great site for information about using Apple systems and programming.

IMPORTANT INTERNET LISTS

The files in this must-have list give information about either getting onto the Internet or locating things once you are connected. Obtaining these files can save you countless hours of searching.

About the Sources

One or more sources are given for each file. With experience you will find that many files are replicated at numerous Internet locations. If you need something that doesn't appear to be covered here, an excellent place to look is the anonymous FTP server **rtfm.mit.edu**. Also, many similar files are periodically reposted in the newsgroups **news.lists**, **news.answers**, and **news.announce.newusers**.

Name: **pdial.txt**

Description: Lists dial-in Internet access providers. Describes about 100 providers. Arranged alphabetically and by area code. Provides phone numbers, how to contact sysops, and rate information where available.

Size: 68 Kbytes, non-compressed

Location: Anonymous FTP server **nic.merit.edu./internet/providers/pdial**; also at **rtfm.mit.edu/pub/usenet-by-group/news.answers**

Filename: pdial

Name: **Publicly_Accessible_Mailing_Lists**

Description: Lists maillists on the Internet, as well as contact procedures. Briefly describes the subjects of 1000 maillists available on the Internet.

Size: 660 Kbytes, non-compressed

Location: Anonymous FTP server **rtfm.mit.edu/pub/usenet-by-group/news.lists**. Also reposted periodically in newsgroup **news.announce.newusers**.

Filename: publicly_accessible_mailing_lists (14 or more parts)

Name: **listserv.txt**

Description: Lists BITNET discussion groups on the Internet/BITNET. Briefly describes the subjects of more than 500 maillists available on BITNET, a network related to the Internet. This differs from maillist.txt.

Size: 600 Kbytes, non-compressed

Location: Send a mail message to **listserv@.bitnet**. In the body of the message, include the single entry **list global**. Leave the *Subject:* field blank.

Name: **refcard.txt**

Description: Instructions for using BITNET list servers

Size: 18 Kbytes, non-compressed

Location: Send a mail message to **listserv@bitnic.bitnet**. In the body of the message, include the single entry **info refcard**.

Name: **List_of_Active_Newsgroups**

Description: Lists the names and gives one-line descriptions of all active newsgroups

Size: Approximately 96 Kbytes, non-compressed

Location: Anonymous FTP server **rtfm.mit.edu/pub/usenet-by-group/news.lists**

Filename: List_of_Active_Newsgroups (2 parts)

Name: **ftp-sitelist.txt**

Description: Comprehensive list of all known FTP servers worldwide.

Size: 1 Mbyte, non-compressed

Location: Anonymous FTP server **rtfm.mit.edu/pub/usenet/new.answers/ftp-list/sitelist/part**** (now 17 parts and growing)

Name: **moder.lst**

Description: Anonymous FTP sites (and moderators) specializing in DOS/Windows files. Lists approximately 60 sites around the world. Arranged geographically. Gives net addresses and describes key directories, as well as the moderator's net address and name.

Size: 18 Kbytes, compressed

Location: Anonymous FTP server **oak.oakland.edu/simtel/msdos/info/moder**.zip** (** = periodically changing revision number)

Name: **usbbs***.lst**

Description: Lists dial-in numbers for about 3000 BBSs in the United States. Arranged by area code. Gives dial-in number, charges, and BBS software type.

Size: Approximately 120 Kbytes, compressed

Location: Anonymous FTP server
oak.oakland.edu/Simtel/msdos/bbslist/usbbs***.zip
(*** = periodically changing revision number)

Name: **SBI-LIST**

Description: Lists BBSs that can be logged onto via the Internet. Gives net addresses, descriptions of contents, log-on procedures

Size: 220 Kbytes non-compressed

Location: Download from **dkunix.dkeep.com in /pub/sbi** or via the WWW at **http://dkeep.com/sbi.htm**

Name: **inet.services.txt** "The Yanoff List"

Description: Miscellaneous useful SIGs, resources on Internet via FTP, mail

Size: 80 Kbytes, non-compressed

Location: Anonymous FTP server **ftp.csd.uwm.edu/pub/inet.services.txt**

INDEX